OWNERSHIP, AUTHORITY, AND SELF-DETERMINATION

OWNERSHIP, AUTHORITY, AND SELF-DETERMINATION

BURKE A. HENDRIX

THE PENNSYLVANIA STATE UNIVERSITY PRESS   UNIVERSITY PARK, PENNSYLVANIA

LIBRARY OF CONGRESS CATALOGING-IN-PUBLICATION DATA

Hendrix, Burke A.
Ownership, authority, and self-determination / Burke A. Hendrix.
p.   cm.
Summary: "Considers the contributions of philosophical theories of property rights, political obligation, and self-determination to our moral understanding of political control over geographical space. Focuses on American Indian and other indigenous claims to a separate political status, including potentially to full legal independence"—Provided by publisher.
Includes bibliographical references and index.
ISBN 978-0-271-03399-0 (pbk : alk. paper)
1. Indians of North America—Government relations.
2. Aboriginal Australians—Government relations.
3. Indians of North America—Land tenure.
4. Aboriginal Australians—Land tenure.
5. Self-determination, National—North America.
6. Self-determination, National—Australia.
7. United States—Ethnic relations.
8. Canada—Ethnic relations.
9. Australia—Ethnic relations.
I. Title.

E91.H46 2008
323.1197—DC22
2008007785

Copyright © 2008 The Pennsylvania State University
All rights reserved
Printed in the United States of America
Published by The Pennsylvania State University Press,
University Park, PA 16802-1003

The Pennsylvania State University Press is a member of the
Association of American University Presses.

It is the policy of The Pennsylvania State University Press to
use acid-free paper. This book is printed on
stock that meets the
minimum requirements of American National Standard
for Information Sciences—Permanence of Paper for
Printed Library Material, ANSI Z39.48–1992.

TO MY MOTHER,

who can now see what I've been doing all this time.

CONTENTS

Acknowledgments   IX

1
Thinking About Authority   1

2
International Law   15

3
The Limits of Ownership   35

4
Ownership and Social Contract   61

5
Duties to Aid   83

6
Authority Without Consent   99

7
Deliberation and Self-Determination   125

8
Culture and Moral Disagreement   153

9
Ending Colonialism   181

Notes   191

Works Cited   205

Index   213

ACKNOWLEDGMENTS

Any project of this sort is inevitably a collective one in many ways, and the present book is no exception. It owes a great deal to the many individuals who discussed its ideas or read its chapters in both formal and informal venues, some of whom have doubtless been unfairly forgotten here.

Robert Munoz deserves first mention, for persuading me (in the most informal of circumstances) that indigenous issues raised far more complex moral questions than I had previously recognized. Simone Chambers, Horst Mewes, Roland Paris, and Jim Nickel helped to shape this project in its beginning stages, while Marcello Kohen, Alec Murphy, and Neve Gordon provided invaluable feedback through an early exchange in the journal *Geopolitics*. Others who read or discussed chapters at various stages of development include Jeremy Rabkin, Allen Carlson, Lida Maxwell, Alison McQueen, Ryan Canning, Richard Miller, Arthur Ripstein, Richard Bensel, Nir Eyal, Michel Seymour, Fred Chernoff, Britt Cartrite, Kathleen O'Neil, Rob Preuss, Walter Mebane, Atilla Ataner, Andy Stock, Julian Ouellet, Mark Bonica, Lesleigh Force, Kaolin Fire, and Michele Smith.

Other debts are more diffuse, to those who have endured discussions of these issues in less formal ways. Michele Moody-Adams, Henry Shue, and Tom Berry have been excellent and supportive colleagues in Cornell's Program on Ethics and Public Life. Susan Buck-Morss, Anna Marie Smith, Isaac Kramnick, Jason Frank, Karuna Mantena, and Diane Rubenstein have been wonderful colleagues in the Department of Government, and the intellectual atmosphere they have created has helped immensely to clarify the ideas outlined here. Audra Simpson, Angela Gonzales, Chuck Geisler, Mil Muskett, and other members of Cornell's American Indian Studies program helped me to think more carefully about these arguments in a variety of ways. Discussions with the students in my graduate seminar on cultural difference in Spring 2006 contributed a great deal to the substance of Chapter 8, while students in other courses on indigenous rights were similarly helpful, with Sepeyeonkqua Myles and Whitney Mauer deserving special acknowledgment.

Sandy Thatcher has been highly supportive as an editor, and Kristen Peterson has been very helpful in answering my sometimes peculiar questions. Both anonymous readers for Penn State Press were extremely helpful in their suggestions for framing the book's central arguments, and John Morris has added elegance to the words themselves during the final stages of the editing process.

Finally, my greatest debt is to David Mapel, who prodded me to think deeply about issues of authority, ownership, and territoriality, and who read and commented on these ideas throughout their multiple iterations. As is traditional in these circumstances, the usual caveat applies: all errors that remain in the present volume are of course Mapel's.

Elements of this book have previously been published in article form and are reproduced here by permission. The central arguments of Chapter 2 were originally developed in "International Law as a Moral Theory of State Territory?" (*Geopolitics* 6:141–62). Chapters 3 and 4 draw in part on two essays, "Moral Minimalism in American Indian Land Claims" (*American Indian Quarterly* 29:538–59) and "Memory in Native American Land Claims" (*Political Theory* 33:763–85), while Chapter 8 draws on "Authenticity and Cultural Rights" (*Journal of Moral Philosophy* 5, forthcoming).

ONE

THINKING ABOUT AUTHORITY

> Conquest gives a title that the courts of the conqueror cannot deny, whatever the private or speculative opinions of individuals may be, respecting the original justice of the claim which has been successfully asserted. The British government, which was then our government, and whose rights have passed to the United States, asserted a title to all lands occupied by Indians. . . . These claims have been maintained as far west as the river Mississippi, by the sword.
> —Chief Justice John Marshall, 1823

Most of us are familiar with the methods by which the United States acquired its current territory from American Indian nations, and the ways in which it forced these nations to submit to its political authority even on the lands they were allowed to retain. Do these historical processes call into question the authority of the United States in the present day? If not, why not? Most other states have similar histories of fraud and violence, even if the details vary—are their claims to authority also called into question?

What justifies the authority of states over particular populations and territories, and what should happen when this authority is challenged in the present day? These are the central questions of this book.

I. Challenging the State

In this book, I will consider the philosophical justifications that can be offered for political authority over particular persons and territorial spaces. In doing so, I will also evaluate principles of political obligation, theories of property ownership, conceptions of democratic self-determination, notions of cultural rights, and other areas of normative analysis. I will argue that a clear conception of political authority requires a careful understanding of each of these areas of moral evaluation, as well as a complex sense of how they link to one another that is often hidden in day-to-day political debates. I will also argue in favor of procedural rights to political separation, so long as they are suitably regulated by careful plebiscitary and deliberative barriers.

To provide a central structure for this inquiry, I will focus throughout on the challenges posed to stable democratic countries such as the United States, Canada, and Australia by indigenous peoples who claim rights to a partially or fully separate political status. For many American Indians and indigenous peoples elsewhere, the history of violence and expropriation noted above has profound implications for contemporary political arrangements: where indigenous nations never voluntarily transferred their political rights to surrounding states, they retain an unrelinquished and foundational authority over their own members and historical territories and are thereby entitled to a quasi-independent or even fully independent political existence if they choose this. (Where treaties were made but violated, this status remains unchanged—fraud is as impermissible as force where relations of political authority are involved.)

While existing countries often claim that indigenous peoples are "within" state boundaries and therefore necessarily under state authority, for many indigenous authors this is a misdescription of the true situation, one usually made in profoundly bad faith. Taiaiake Alfred (1999, 58), for example, has argued that "to frame the struggle to achieve justice in terms of indigenous 'claims' against the state is implicitly to accept the fiction of state sovereignty." While most indigenous scholars and political actors voice a willingness to draft new political linkages with surrounding states, they insist that this can occur only after these states become willing to negotiate on terms that recognize the fundamental status of indigenous nations as locuses of authority rather than simply ethnic groups or something similar (see, e.g., Turner 2006; Deloria 1974). Most of all, states cannot simply assert that superior power somehow translates into rights to rule, as they have so often done in the past; they will have to acknowledge instead that indigenous nations have final authority over their own populations and territories, and then must seek to negotiate a common moral ground that all sides can accept as tolerably just (see, e.g., Tully 1995; cf. Borrows 2002), exactly as they would with other kinds of political units outside the reach of their legal jurisdiction.

Indeed, some indigenous scholars believe that any attempts whatsoever to negotiate new political relationships with surrounding states are profoundly misguided because these states are congenitally incapable of overcoming their histories of violence and deception. Because states are unlikely to acknowledge the full political rights of indigenous peoples any time soon, these scholars argue that the best alternative is for indigenous peoples to pursue their rightfully independent status unilaterally and thereby avoid granting the pretensions of surrounding states any veneer of legitimacy. Taiaiake Alfred (1999, 137), for example, argues that "Native communities must reject the claimed authority of the state, assert the right to govern their own territories and peoples, and act on that right as much as their capacity to do so allows." In the short run, he believes this will require strategic political behavior and highly contentious (though nonviolent) forms of political protest (Alfred 2005); over the long term, it will require that the citizens of surrounding states completely rethink their views about legitimate political relationships: "Non-indigenous peoples need to be brought to the realization that their notion of power and its extension over indigenous peoples is wrong by any moral standard" (Alfred 1999, 144). Ultimately, in his view, the independent status of indigenous peoples will have to be recognized by surrounding states if justice is to be done; in the meantime, countries that prohibit indigenous peoples from acting on their rights continue the shameful history of injustice they claim time and time again to have repudiated.

How should nonindigenous political philosophers react to these challenges to the claimed authority of existing states? Most of us will probably have strong inclinations either toward or against them, especially where the possibility of full indigenous separation is involved—either we will reject them immediately as mistaken or (less commonly) we will accept them as fully justified. But how should we think of these challenges in a more principled way? The claims states make about the nature of their authority are often somewhat peculiar. Many practices suggest that states somehow rule particular territories first and persons only incidentally (cf. Whelan 1983, 21–25; Stevens 1999, 128–48; Baldwin 1992; Copp 1999). Being born within a state's territory usually makes one legally a citizen, for example, unless some clear and obvious commitment to another state prevents this—although many states also claim the authority to refuse citizenship to people born within their borders when it is expedient to do so, much as a property-owner might eject unwelcome guests from his house. Moreover, states usually claim the right to conscript citizens to defend their territories, even when those territories were themselves acquired through force and fraud (like much of the United States) or are virtually uninhabited (like parts of Australia and northern Canada). But if control of territory is what matters, how did states gain the relevant ownership rights in the first place, especially where they are known to have acquired their current territories through unjust means? Perhaps the relationship runs the other way after all, so that states have authority over territory only derivatively from authority over persons. But then we must ask the obvious question: how can states have such authority over indigenous populations and others that reject them as illegitimate? Is this simply a contemporary version of older apologies for conquest? If not, why not?

Thus, indigenous claims do seem to raise foundational issues about the nature of political authority and the moral acceptability of existing political arrangements. In this book, I will attempt to evaluate the moral character of these challenges and of state authority in general. I will consider claims to both a partially and a fully separate political status but will focus more on the latter—as I will argue below, both kinds of claims seem to involve the same kinds of issues, but claims to full separation often allow us to see the issues with greater clarity. I will not try to consider all of the myriad issues that might be relevant to particular regimes of indigenous rights within existing states, even if some of the arguments I make may have relevance for additional kinds of political protections and exemptions as well. My focus throughout will be on the grounds of political authority themselves: what gives a political structure rights to control a specific territory and population, and what should happen when existing political arrangements are challenged?

By the end of the book, I will suggest that there do in fact seem to be good reasons for existing states to allow indigenous peoples to pursue (or reclaim) an entirely separate political existence where they wish to do so. But, as will become clear, the principles at work here are more complex than they sometimes seem, and they are likely to give neither indigenous challengers nor existing states exactly what either might wish to receive.

II. Abstraction and Resonance

The questions that I will consider about the character of political authority matter for all existing sovereign states. Why, then, focus specifically on indigenous claims against stable democratic countries such as the United States and Canada rather than on challenges to state authority in some more general sense?

One reason is that we need to have *some* kinds of cases in mind to engage in any moral evaluation at all, and we are likely to do so more easily with a relatively limited set of cases. But there are stronger reasons as well. Controversies about the authority to rule particular populations and territories differ wildly in their histories, in the relative power of those on each side, in the reasons each side has for valuing given areas, and in myriad other ways. The disagreement between China and Taiwan about the status of Taiwanese independence differs in important ways, for example, from conflicts over the proper political allegiance of Kashmir—and both are very distant from debates between the United States and the Marshall Islands over ownership of Wake Island. Given this range, those who consider such issues may be tempted to focus on the most violent and contentious cases, rather than on those that are pressed only through argument, not force. If people are not yet shooting at one another, one might wonder, can it matter that much? Obviously it can, and does. If the states we live in are engaged in profound injustices, we need to know this and decide what this fact requires of us.

From a philosophical perspective, the very lack of violence involved in claims for rights to a separate political status by American Indians and other indigenous peoples allows us to see basic principles more clearly than might otherwise be possible. Violent or potentially violent conflicts draw our attention toward dying and killing and toward ways of stopping or preventing the violence. War and terrorism can easily dominate our thinking and can make it far harder to think clearly about peaceful claims for redress against our own states. Not all injustices shed blood or take lives, but they are injustices nonetheless. By focusing on indigenous claims, then, we can largely bracket considerations of violence and the difficult measures that they may require; these claims must be considered as moral arguments, not the mere ideologies of adversaries at war.

There is another important reason for focusing on indigenous claims, one that takes into account the more emotional and personal aspects of philosophical thinking. Instead of being pressed against others far beyond the comfort of our borders, these claims are pressed against the states under which most readers of this book are likely to live. We nonindigenous citizens of the United States, Canada, and Australia often see challenges to sovereignty as the problems of other states, so that we can dismiss controversies elsewhere as the product of hatred, greed, or irrationality. But we cannot be so easily absolved in this case, particularly given the well-documented ways in which democratic states have mistreated their indigenous populations. Since the territories claimed by American Indians and other indigenous peoples fall within "our" current boundaries, we cannot evade their challenge by invoking the dangers of international conflict or the general unwillingness of states to part with territory—we would merely be refusing to consider what justice may demand. Indigenous claims should engage both the reason and passions of nonindigenous citizens within these states: *this* is what it feels like to have the legitimacy of one's borders and political system challenged on coherent moral grounds, and we must know whether our states act rightly or not in denying such challenges. Claims for rights to a separate political status by American Indians and other indigenous peoples are the moral petitions of real people who are our friends, neighbors, and—for now—countrymen, and for that reason alone they deserve careful attention.

III. For Indigenous Readers

This book is written primarily within the tradition of Western academic philosophy, with the expectation that most readers will be nonindigenous. Yet it is also intended to be useful and accessible to indigenous readers as well—after all, it is indigenous rights that are under discussion, and it would be deeply misguided not to invite indigenous readers to take part in a conversation where something of such importance is at stake. Thus, I will try to explain why the book approaches these issues in the way that it does, and to offer some suggestions for how indigenous readers might most fruitfully engage with what might not seem the most welcoming terms of political debate.

The most obvious reason for writing within a nonindigenous tradition is that I myself am nonindigenous, and this tradition reflects the ways in which I know how to think and argue. I am not competent to work within indigenous philosophical traditions in any meaningful way, and my attempts to do so would likely be both shallow and misconceived. (I will make some small attempts in Chapter 8, where indigenous readers will probably see this prediction confirmed.) But there are other ways I might have approached these issues that might been more accessible to most indigenous readers.

One alternative would have been to focus on the status of indigenous claims to sovereignty within the legal systems of the United States, Canada, and other countries to see what the best interpretations of the relevant precedents and constitutional principles might be, and to begin my moral analysis from those points. In the United States, for example, this would include an analysis of the two instances in which Indian nations are mentioned in the Constitution; a discussion of the seminal Marshall cases, in which Indian political organizations were described as "domestic dependent nations"; an analysis of the doctrine of Congressional plenary power; a discussion of the contemporary movement toward self-determination; and so on (see, e.g., Barsh and Henderson 1980; Wilkins and Lomawaima 2001). In Canada, this would involve discussions of the Royal Proclamation of 1763, the various Indian Acts, the Aboriginal rights outlined in Section 35 of the 1982 Constitution Act, and the *Calder* and *Delgamuukw* decisions (see, e.g., Boldt 1993; Macklem 2001). In Australia, the record would be considerably sparser until relatively recent times, with the *Mabo* and *Wik* decisions taking center stage (see, e.g., Webber 2000; Russell 2005).

Readers who are not already deeply entrenched in debates about indigenous rights may wonder why this approach seems attractive at all. Indeed, it may seem both perverse and self-defeating—if state legal systems are what is under challenge, why write as if their legitimacy were already beyond question? But indigenous readers are likely to see this approach as more closely connected to the real political challenges they are seeking to resolve: whether they like it or not, indigenous populations are currently ensconced within surrounding democratic states, and in practice only certain legalistic ways of arguing tend to have political resonance. (In particular, states generally require that indigenous claims be historically grounded and oriented around property title, whatever the actual goals that indigenous groups wish to pursue.) Stepping too far outside of categories of legal analysis thus raises concerns that the inquiry will be socially impotent, whatever its conclusions may be (see, e.g., Hester 2001, 1–2).

Beginning with existing regimes of law also has further attractions if one is concerned about the conditions of fair intercultural debate. As James Tully (1994; 1995) and others (e.g., Williams 1997) have argued, the system of treaty relationships that developed in North America during the early centuries of contact represented in many ways a normative middle ground between worldviews that were otherwise radically divergent. Some elements of these older arrangements have survived in the laws of the United States and Canada (see, e.g., Wilkinson 1987, 120–22) and might possibly be revitalized as a similar common ground in the present day. (In Australia, with no history of treaty-making, the legacies of this old intercultural period are far more attenuated, if they ever existed at all—see, e.g., Chesterman and Galligan 1997.) At a minimum, one might say that the law provides something determinate to argue over, so that each side has an entry point into negotiation that does not require it to work within the full normative traditions of the other side. This is an attractive feature for indigenous peoples, given the demographic and power imbalances involved (see, e.g., Turner 2006; cf. Borrows 2002).

The weakness of this focus, however, is that it already assumes clear answers to many of the central questions of interest in this book. Perhaps most obviously, it assumes that indigenous peoples are the sorts of collectives with which existing states are morally required to negotiate mutually satisfying agreements. Someone who simply denies this will have no reason to want to pursue such a process, and it seems unlikely that moral disagreement on its own terms can serve as a justification without additional support. After all, people have disagreements all the time and often have to find some institutional mechanism, such as voting, to deal with them—so why is this case fundamentally different? Indeed, indigenous peoples usually have very deep and long-standing disagreements among "their own" members. If disagreement is what matters, does this dissolve their capacity to serve as collective agents for the purposes of political negotiation? Thus, the argument for intercultural negotiation is inherently incomplete: it may ultimately turn out that this sort of intensive negotiation between indigenous nations and the states now ruling them is morally required, but demonstrating this requires additional kinds of argument beyond reference to moral disagreement itself.

Such an approach is also radically indeterminate from another direction. Even if states are morally required to engage in negotiations with indigenous peoples, what sorts of baselines should they have in mind for morally tolerable outcomes? Which compromises are acceptable and which are unacceptable? Are states permitted to negotiate in hard-nosed ways and for the positions that seem most conducive to their interests, or are there particular normative goals that they ought to have in mind? Thus, the recognition of moral disagreement can serve as no more than the starting point for the conversation about what a morally acceptable political world might look like, and that conversation will require taking substantive stands on the central issues considered in this book. Even if some elements of existing law can be made to provide a common language for some purposes, they will clearly not be sufficient to cover anything like the full range of reasons that must be offered on either side. However deep one believes the gulfs to be between indigenous and nonindigenous philosophical traditions, both sides will continue to want to draw on the full range of possible reasons, and it is hard to see how this process could be stopped even if one believed it would be a good idea to do so.

Thus, I hope indigenous readers will approach this effort to think through the nature of political authority from within my own intellectual tradition as an unavoidable enterprise in the long run, and one that can provide them with a set of argumentative tools to be used for other purposes if the arguments themselves prove unacceptable. Even if the philosophical foundations of this tradition are flawed at the deepest, most pervasive level, indigenous scholars and political actors will need specific points of argumentative access to show where particular errors lie. If even a few of the arguments outlined here can form elements of the most appropriate conception of indigenous sovereignty, they should provide leverage for showing where other elements of the argument go wrong and for suggesting what a better conception might look like. If all elements of the argument prove indefensible, I hope they will at least provide indigenous readers with a set of rhetorical resources that might be deployed in useful ways to defend the goals they recognize as justified on other grounds (e.g., within traditional indigenous philosophies). They might be seen as a supplement to the legal and other arguments more often used by indigenous peoples in defending their interests: if judges and other state actors sometimes deploy abstract philosophical arguments to counter indigenous claims that would otherwise be legally justified, the arguments of this book should give a greater sense of the intellectual countermeasures that might be offered in response. Thus, if necessary, indigenous readers might approach this book as an additional tool for finding their feet within the discourses of those who endanger their rights, and thus for responding more effectively to the forces that persistently threaten them.

My hope is that the book's arguments will prove valuable for more than simply strategic purposes. But the effectiveness of moral arguments depends on whether they persuade those who hear them, and this is something readers will have to decide for themselves. The book is thus intended as a contribution to a much larger set of debates on indigenous sovereignty, on the assumption that only when the moral arguments for and against particular understandings of political authority and self-determination are carefully outlined will indigenous peoples have a fair chance to rebut those that are most misguided or to defend themselves using a full palette of argumentative resources. At each stage, my argument deserves to be viewed with caution by both indigenous and nonindigenous readers alike—each step of the argument, as is always true in investigations of this type, represents a potential point of error and contention, particularly where expectations about human nature, human desires, and social possibilities play a central role. Errors will doubtless creep in, and in a project of this type, where the stakes involve the character of the political units in which each of us must live our lives, they deserve to be defused as quickly and decisively as possible.

IV. Outline of the Book

In the next chapter, I will outline the basic principles justifying authority over particular populations and territories within existing international law. (Those deeply versed in the relevant debates can likely omit this chapter without harm; readers less familiar with them are strongly advised not to.) Although international law, like all kinds of law, is itself subject to moral evaluation, it can nonetheless serve as a valuable starting point for thinking about these issues, and it provides several interesting avenues for determining what is morally at stake. As I will argue, international law's principle of territorial integrity suggests that authority is somehow linked to ownership of geographical space. The legal principle of self-determination, on the other hand, seems to suggest an alternative basis for authority, but is itself ambiguous between two possibilities. On one reading, the principle of self-determination requires that states govern all territories through democratic mechanisms and that they relinquish authority if they refuse to do so; on another reading, states lose such rights if they rule "peoples" that would prefer to pursue a separate existence. The remainder of the chapters are divided into linked pairs as suggested by these competing possibilities: in Chapters 3 and 4, I consider the relevance of ownership to authority; in Chapters 5 and 6, I consider how the quality of governance might matter; and in Chapters 7 and 8, I consider whether groups should have the right to choose separation simply because they would prefer it.

Many indigenous arguments seem to suggest that contemporary political authority is somehow linked to ownership of land itself, and so in Chapter 3 I consider in depth what rights to ownership might be and how they might be justified, whether these rights are held by individuals, groups, or political societies. I argue that conceptualizing property rights as a form of social convention would provide limited support for such indigenous claims, but that some notion of natural property rights might offer substantially more. I consider in depth what such natural property rights would have to consist in, what their limits might be, and what implications they might have for the present day. In particular, I engage the arguments of Jeremy Waldron against the continued relevance of historical ownership, and conclude that even if many of Waldron's objections are correct, indigenous peoples might still retain substantial rights to many public lands, which countries like the United States, Canada, and Australia currently have in great supply. If authority is closely linked to ownership, then, the implications seem substantial—settler states may be required to turn over considerable territories to the governments of indigenous peoples.

As I argue in Chapter 4, however, the relationship between property ownership and political authority is more complex than simple historical arguments might suggest. The most obvious question is how political societies can come to own their territories in the first place. One possible method is through original contracts in which land was collectivized at a society's founding. But such contracts do not seem to exist in any real cases, and, for additional reasons outlined in the chapter, they would have limited moral force in the present day anyway. States or other political units might also claim strong ownership rights if they could demonstrate that each of their members had agreed to hold property in this way, so that the absence of historical contracts would be irrelevant. But once again, no political units seem to receive such unanimous acceptance from those they rule. I conclude that the relationship between ownership and authority must therefore be a mediated one—while states may have rights to rule persons and groups who own property that is protected by natural rights to ownership, states themselves are owners only in regard to public lands, and for that reason a lack of historical transfers does not necessarily call into question the authority of existing states. Even if indigenous peoples are entitled to the return of some historical lands, then, there may be nothing politically that follows from this fact.

In Chapters 5 and 6, I consider how political authority can be justified if ownership or consent cannot provide its justification. Drawing on the work of Immanuel Kant as a starting point, in Chapter 5 I argue that the alternative to consent or ownership must lie in natural moral duties, which must be formulated as coercible duties to aid others in protecting themselves from violence and other forms of wrongdoing. As this chapter argues, such duties are both more familiar and more complex than they may initially seem. The chapter closes with some suggestions about the criteria that make duties subject to enforcement by coercive means (as is necessary if states as we know them are to be justified), and with some questions about how the exact limits of such duties can be recognized.

In Chapter 6, I consider why these duties to aid might justify the authority of states rather than of some other kind of social organization, and what they might tell us about the moral status of specific, actually existing states. I consider first the alternatives to states as political organizations exercising mandatory, nonconsensual authority over everyone within a particular territory, and suggest that states generally seem the best solution in most cases, but not all. For very small populations with strong cultural bonds, I argue, forms of communitarian anarchism may be viable—although it seems doubtful that many indigenous populations could attempt them fully under present circumstances. I then consider what abstract arguments about states as a type of organization might tell us about the acceptability of specific existing states, and suggest that there must be a presumption in favor of the continued stability of stable democratic states, but that this presumption can be rebutted in many circumstances.

In Chapters 7 and 8, I consider what these circumstances might be. In Chapter 7, I argue that there may be some relatively limited justifications for self-determination implicit in the costs of our duties and the difficulties of fine-tuning the balance among rights in diverse contexts, but that neither of these seems likely to justify the risks of political failure involved in claims to full separation from existing states. The strongest argument for self-determination relies instead on the difficulties of evaluating state effectiveness as a whole, and I argue that the populations living under a particular set of laws are generally the best judge of their quality. Drawing on arguments about deliberative democracy, I argue that virtually any group should have a right to choose full or partial separation from the state now ruling it, so long as it can pass multiple referenda that are structured to foster deliberation about specific features of the change in advance. I also argue that the boundaries for such units can be partially specified in procedural ways, and that enclaves and very small territories may be viable as well, particularly if one can show clear reasons for allowing some populations such options even where they would not be possible for all. I close the chapter by considering some of the difficulties and ambiguities involved in procedural rights for choosing a partially separate status, such as a loose form of federalism, arguing that the same deliberative standards must be central here as well, despite increased complexities.

In Chapter 8, I consider the role of nationalism and cultural difference in claims for self-determination. I argue that claims of nationalism can generally be dealt with by the procedural mechanisms outlined in the previous chapter, and that nationalist attachments generally do not raise new issues of concern. Similarly, I argue that "neutral" forms of cultural difference—essentially, those that do not threaten the protection of rights—can likewise be taken care of through procedural mechanisms without alteration. Cultural difference may also involve much deeper issues, however, and some groups may wish to pursue very different kinds of political orders, some of which may not give legal protection to "rights" as we know them. I argue that groups should be allowed to experiment with alternative forms of political life (such as the communitarian anarchism mentioned in Chapter 6) if the members who seem likely to be most vulnerable in this alternative system approve of it, but probably not otherwise. I conclude the chapter by outlining the reasons why existing states should not be fearful of most indigenous forms of cultural difference. I argue that they should instead find in indigenous viewpoints potentially valuable alternatives to dominant patterns of thought, alternatives that cannot be explored fully if groups are prohibited from attempting to put them into political practice.

In Chapter 9, I conclude with a summation of the view of political authority outlined throughout the book, and argue that existing states should generally treat indigenous peoples as if they still retained a foundational moral status grounding rights to fully or partially separate political existence, so long as they are willing to choose political structures that will protect the rights of their members or are otherwise able to demonstrate a firm social consensus on alternative arrangements. Surrounding states also seem required to return substantial amounts of public land to indigenous peoples, over which these peoples will then have the right to exercise political authority. "Inherent indigenous rights" are thus best seen as a shorthand for the more complex arguments of the book as a whole, and while such rights will not justify all of the claims indigenous peoples might want to make, they will nonetheless ground more than existing states seem comfortable admitting. The book closes with some considerations regarding the design of international law and the future of nonterritorial political orders, suggesting that whatever the future may hold, groups will still likely need procedural rights to change their political circumstances when they are profoundly dissatisfied.

ically, political boundaries, and indigenous claims to a separate political
TWO

INTERNATIONAL LAW

There are many places where one might begin thinking about the question of authority, political boundaries, and indigenous claims to a separate political status. As I noted in the last chapter, one place would be with the constitutional law of countries like the United States, Canada, and Australia to determine what kinds of rights indigenous peoples have within these systems. Yet, as I also noted there, this approach would beg the question in important ways. If the claims of American Indians and other indigenous peoples to a separate political existence are seen simply as legal claims within already-determinate structures of authority, then these claims seem automatically defused—they will have force only insofar as each legal system allows it. As should be clear, it is often the very legitimacy of existing political structures that indigenous peoples want to question (even when they seek only a partially rather than fully separate political status).

A more wide-ranging approach would be to focus on existing international law to see what tools it might offer for thinking about the character of such claims. American Indian sovereignty advocate Ward Churchill (1999, 15–26), for example, argues that decolonization for indigenous peoples is the natural conclusion of the principles that mandated the withdrawal of European powers from their overseas empires after the Second World War. In his view, all colonized peoples deserve the same treatment, wherever they may be: "Those nations whose inherent rights are impaired or denied in such fashion retain an open-ended prerogative—indeed, a legal responsibility—to recover them by all available means. It is, moreover, the obligation of all other nations, and the citizens of the offending power itself, to assist them in doing so at the earliest possible date. Although the matter has been subject to almost continuous obfuscation, usually by offenders, there are no exceptions to this principle in the Laws of Nations" (41). This seems a reasonable argument, with its focus on ensuring consistency for all those who are colonized. It is convenient to say that the age of colonialism passed with the dismantling of the overseas empires, but the United States, Canada, Australia, and many other contemporary democracies are equally the products of colonialism and still sit astride territories and peoples who were subjugated by the same mechanisms. How can consistency require anything less than an end to this illegal occupation where indigenous peoples desire it?

Yet perhaps things are not so simple. In this chapter, I want to consider more carefully the principles governing decolonization in the post–World War II era, to see what support they provide for claims by indigenous peoples to a separate political status, and to discover whether these legal principles are morally plausible in their own right. I do not want to conflate legality with morality, since international legal principles are themselves subject to moral evaluation. But international law deserves to be taken seriously as a set of moral claims that happen to be instantiated in a legal regime. (Indeed, given the lack of international enforcement mechanisms, it is hard to see international law as anything stronger than this.) Existing international legal principles provide a kind of common language for many of those debating questions about political boundaries, and also represent a set of principles that have been tested in varying circumstances and debated by a wide variety of social actors. As I will try to show, these principles are ambiguous in important ways and probably do not apply directly to the conditions of most indigenous peoples, but they still provide an important place to begin thinking about these issues.

I. Principles of International Law

Since Churchill focuses on rights for American Indian nations to escape the legal authority of the United States entirely if they choose, in this chapter I will focus primarily on the question of full separation, leaving questions about some type of partial separation for near the chapter's end. As I will argue, partial claims invoke some of the same logic involved in full separation and therefore face some of the same problems.

But first, a disclaimer about the following discussion is probably necessary. Although it is easy to speak of "international law" as if it were a determinate set of principles, in practice it is more difficult to determine what its content actually is, especially since the sources of international law are themselves complex and often competing. They include international customary practices, declarations by the United Nations and rulings by the International Court of Justice, the wording and clauses of treaties, the rhetoric and practice of individual states, and the opinions of international legal scholars (see, e.g., Brownlie 1998, chap. 2; Von Glahn 1996, 10–21; Cassese 1986, chap. 7). Given these complex sources, scholars often disagree about what the rules really are, not only in their specific applications but also in their basic content, and in many cases it is difficult to determine where international law ends and other kinds of moral or prudential arguments begin. While there seems to be a rough consensus among international lawyers that the principles to be discussed here have real meaning for international legal practice, having been ratified by the United Nations and utilized in a variety of situations, particularly during decolonization (see, e.g., Kaikobad 1996; Cassese 1995; Castellino 2000; Musgrave 1997; Halperin et al. 1992, 16–25), scholars of international law remain divided over their interpretation at many points. I will try to make clear the terms of these disagreements and the implications derived from competing interpretations, but I will inevitably exclude many nuances of these intensive debates.

Existing international law provides two central principles for determining the legitimacy of state control over particular geographical spaces and populations: the principles of territorial integrity and self-determination. The first principle grants states the right to continue ruling those territories they now control, while the second holds that peoples (whatever that term might mean) have rights to political arrangements reflecting their desires as distinct communities—including the right not to be colonized. International law has tried to defuse the fundamental tension between these principles through the principle of *uti possidetis,* which fixes international boundaries in cases of decolonization as the existing boundaries formerly used for administrative purposes by the colonizer itself. As I will try to show, this principle represents an uncomfortable half step between territorial integrity and self-determination, but rejecting it leaves some very hard questions about how rights to control particular territories and populations should be understood. The remainder of this book will take up many of these questions in detail.

Territorial integrity, which holds that only a state's internal political processes can change international boundaries once these have been legally determined, is probably the least controversial of international law's principles on political boundaries, as well as the oldest. This principle derives directly from international law's foundational premise of state sovereignty, which provides the logical foundation for an international legal system in the first place (see, e.g., Cassese 1986, 9–11; Brownlie 1998, 153–55; Von Glahn 1996, 102–7; Musgrave 1997, 180–81). As a system of law intended to regulate the relations of states, international law would be radically ineffective unless it recognized rights for states to continue to exist, and having sovereignty at all entails sovereignty over particular territorial spaces. While an extensive body of human rights law now limits the kinds of absolute authority over internal matters that states once claimed, international law remains fundamentally a system of law constructed by and for states. Territorial integrity thus remains the default position where political boundaries are concerned—states have rights to rule the populations and areas they now control, except where some specific legal principle takes countervailing precedence. For the purposes of the current inquiry, this means that countries like the United States and Canada have rights to continue to rule the populations and territories they now control unless some principle can be found that overturns this presumption.

One such principle, on which Churchill's and many indigenous arguments place heavy emphasis, is the earlier ownership of a particular territory by another sovereign entity. Currently, international law recognizes several means by which states may acquire rights to rule particular geographical spaces, including the occupation of lands currently unclaimed by any state, voluntary transfers from other states, disposition by the international community, unprotested occupation of lands formally "owned" by another state, and accretion along waterways or coastlines (Von Glahn 1996, 296–303; Brownlie 1998, 153–55; Detter 1994, 330–41; Van Dervort 1998, 336–38; Chen 2000, 118–20). The first two means are the most relevant historically and for the purposes of this book. When such areas existed, states could acquire legal title over territories claimed by no other sovereign (*terra nullius*) by occupying them and exercising effective sovereignty. Many indigenous claims make reference to such original occupation of historical territories; Churchill's claims for independence assume that American Indians had legitimate rights to govern particular territories in unproblematic ways. Conversely, colonizing states often claimed that the territories indigenous peoples occupied were insufficiently populated and organized, and so classified as *terra nullius* for legal purposes even if they were not literally uninhabited (see, e.g., Cassese 1986, 42–43; cf. Lindley 1926, 4–45; Keal 2003, 50–52, 87–112; *Western Sahara* 1975, 38–40). In the Europeans' view, they had encountered not states with sovereignty, but dispersed bands that had few fixed abodes and little political structure and for that reason were incapable of exercising governance over the lands where they lived.

In other cases, particularly in North America, colonizing states relied on the second method of acquiring territory—voluntary cession by another sovereign political body. This strategy acknowledged indigenous peoples to have at least some legal and political status. The United States acquired the majority of its current territory through this mechanism, and British claims over New Zealand were also explicitly treaty-based (see, e.g., Orange 1987; Ward 1999). Even today, surprisingly few indigenous peoples contest the value of treaties of cession in transferring authority; they more often argue that the terms of cession have been violated, question the authority of the signers, or challenge ambiguous wording.[1] In most cases, their arguments are entirely accurate.

While this may seem at first glance to provide solid grounding for indigenous claims to regain a separate status, the international legal relevance of violated treaties and fraudulent cessions is less certain than it appears. Historically, conquest was recognized as legal means of acquiring control over territories and populations as well, and remained so until the creation of the United Nations. Older international law simply accepted that states would fight and that territories would often change hands by force. Although conquest is now formally illegal, contemporary international law continues to regard territories acquired in earlier times as legally justified despite their method of acquisition (e.g., Bederman 2001, 110–13; Van Dervort 1998, 337–38; Detter 1994, 331–32). Even since the creation of the United Nations system, some recent conquests have been recognized by international actors despite formal prohibitions (Von Glahn 1996, 303–11), and states created through forcible secession are usually granted legal title to territory as well (Brownlie 1998, 45–46; Von Glahn 1996, 71–78; Cassese 1986, 26–28), although in both cases territories are sometimes subject to claims of "residual sovereignty" by the original state (e.g., mainland Chinese claims over Taiwan).[2]

Most states, then, rule at least some legally accepted territories acquired through violence or under the threat thereof, and international law has not been particularly responsive to those who claim treaties of cession were fraudulent or coerced. Rights to control geographical spaces and the populations that inhabit them have thus been historically viewed as alienable and transferable property rights—but also rights that can be acquired through de facto control if this persists long enough. In its basic intent, the principle of territorial integrity seeks to minimize conflict by providing orderly mechanisms for territorial change, and by ratifying faits accomplis when these fail. Its overarching goal is a pragmatic stability, in seeking to minimize war and to maintain some semblance of an international order. Since states can sometimes claim the same territory based in different interpretations of the law or of the conditions of acquisition, the principle of territorial integrity does not and cannot eliminate all potential for conflict, but its generalized preference for the status quo at least tries to reduce the pretexts for international violence.

Taken by itself, the principle of territorial integrity thus seems to create a generalized case against indigenous separation, although its accompanying treatment of sovereignty over territory as a transferable property right leaves a few uncertainties. But territorial integrity is no longer international law's final word on control over territory and populations. In the post–World War II era, title to most overseas colonial territories has been abandoned under the newer principle of self-determination. The principle, articulated in several UN documents, grants "peoples" legal rights to develop states reflecting their desires as particular historical communities. The *Declaration on Friendly Relations* (1970), among other United Nations pronouncements, articulates this principle: "By virtue of the principle of equal rights and self-determination of peoples enshrined in the Charter of the United Nations, all peoples have the right freely to determine, without external interference, their political status and to pursue their economic, social and cultural development, and every State has the duty to respect this right in accordance with the provisions of the Charter" (in Brownlie 2002, 32). Colonized peoples have a legal right to decide their future political allegiance in any of three ways: by formally joining the state of their colonial rulers (incorporation), by joining another state that will accept them (irredentism), or by choosing independence. This is something like the choice that Churchill believes most indigenous nations have not yet been allowed to make.

During postwar decolonization, the UN developed a list of colonial territories that were eligible for self-determination, and specific international treaties designated further areas. The broad outcomes of this process are familiar: the number of units in the international system rapidly tripled as states were created in the former colonial zones of Africa and Asia, and virtually all of these states passed a so-called saltwater test as overseas colonial possessions. Yet because no clear legal principle articulates this test, it has at best a weak basis in custom rather than UN law or international legal rulings (see, e.g., Duursma 1996, 77–84; Musgrave 1997, 149–51; Tomuschat 1993, 2–5; Brownlie 1998, 44–45; cf. Cassese 1995, 327–30). The relevance of this legal silence for American Indian and other indigenous claims should be obvious: there can be nothing magical about bodies of salt water, and if we take these principles seriously, they must be applied everywhere. The case for indigenous separation seems revived.

Yet the waters muddy again when we consider how self-determination actually worked during the process of decolonization. Allowing colonial territories to form independent states was not a simple process, since many of the "peoples" involved had never lived within a state or statelike institution prior to colonization, and where statelike entities had existed, colonization had often radically altered political circumstances. Somehow boundaries had to be drawn between potential states if decolonization were to occur, and the option chosen was the principle of *uti possidetis,* initially used by South American states to set their own boundaries after throwing off Spanish rule (Ratner 1996, 592–601; Brownlie 1998, 55–59; Van Dervort 1998, 356; cf. Castellino 2000, 109–21). This principle fixed the boundaries for self-determining units as the administrative boundaries used by the colonial state (*Case Concerning the Frontier Dispute* 1986, 564–67; Kaikobad 1996, 38–44). According to the *Declaration on Friendly Relations:* "The territory of a colony or other Non-Self-Governing Territory has, under the Charter, a status separate and distinct from the territory of the State administering it; and such separate and distinct status under the Charter shall exist until the people of the colony or Non-Self-Governing Territory have exercised their right of self-determination in accordance with the Charter, and particularly its purposes and principles" (in Brownlie 2002, 32). "In general terms, the new state succeeds to all the recognized boundaries maintained by the administering state before power is transferred to the territory" (Kaikobad 1996, 39; cf. Cassese 1995, 190–93), regardless of the precolonial contours of political life or the fit between colonial boundaries and cultural or geographic divisions. In a few instances, colonizing states combined administrative units to link together cultural groups into the same state (e.g., Italian and English colonies were merged to create Somalia), but this generally involved nothing more sophisticated than the mixing and matching of administrative units and subunits (see Ratner 1996, 599n68).

After an exercise of self-determination (generally through decisions by national political leaders recognized by the colonial state, but sometimes through plebiscites as well), a colonial territory choosing independence became a fully sovereign state, enjoying all of the rights and duties associated with that status. Peoples choosing to annex themselves formally with the colonial state or with some other existing state, on the other hand, were seen as making an irreversible decision that was legally binding for all future times by dissolving themselves into the larger political unit (e.g., Kohen 2001, 172; Kaikobad 1996, 26–33; Cassese 1995, 73–74; Roth 1998, 223–25). According to the *Declaration on Friendly Relations,* "Nothing in the foregoing paragraphs shall be construed as authorizing or encouraging any action which would dismember or impair, totally or in part, the territorial integrity or political unity of sovereign and independent States conducting themselves in compliance with the principle of equal rights and self-determination of peoples as described above and thus possessed of a government representing the whole people belonging to the territory without distinction as to race, creed or color" (in Brownlie 2002, 32). As a matter of principle, territories ceded through self-determination have no international legal claim to withdraw from a chosen state, although domestic law may allow them this option if central governments permit it (cf. *Reference re Secession of Quebec* 1998).

Thus, self-determination, within the bounds of *uti possidetis,* now provides another way for states to lose or gain legal rights to control territories and populations, one that reverses earlier titles gained by other means. But this leaves us with a vitally important question: how do we decide which territories or populations have rights to choose their future in this way? Exactly what does the right to self-determination consist in?

II. Self-Determination and Cosmopolitan Democracy

Many scholars of international law view the principle of self-determination with skepticism or outright worry. Marcelo Kohen (2001, 170) notes that "The relationship between territorial integrity and self-determination is an abiding problem. . . . It is probably the most striking model of seemingly contradictory rules in international law." More strongly, Thomas Van Dervort (1998, 330) describes the principle of self-determination as a "potential source of instability [that] could undermine the entire purpose of the UN system to promote international peace and security." For both, the fundamental problem lies in defining clearly what a "people" with such rights might be. Historically, bargaining between states and in the UN was necessary to designate units as eligible for self-determination within the boundaries provided by *uti possidetis.* But on what basis were such designations made?

Scholars of international law are divided between two possible standards, one involving democratic governance and the other, discussed in the next section, involving national or historical communities. By the first standard, self-determination is justified only for colonial units that are not allowed to govern themselves: "The distinguishing feature was that colonial peoples were put under a separate and subordinated regime" (Kohen 2001, 171). Nothing of importance is contained in the term "people," which merely refers to the set of persons inhabiting such a territory. The standard is instead the relationship of political domination by the metropole, including lesser legal protections for colonial subjects.

On this interpretation, there is no reason to be concerned with how states originally acquired rights to rule particular territories and populations. Instead, we should focus on ensuring that no territories are administered by colonial powers that treat inhabitants as subjects rather than citizens. The relevant standard seems at least potentially easy to apply, since "separate and subordinated" territories seem generally recognizable through the careful investigation of lines of authority, voting rights, and other markers. This interpretation of the principle seems mostly unconcerned with how new international borders are constructed during decolonization, so long as all the populations being mistreated in this way are included. Seen in this light, the standard of adopting the colonial administrative boundaries (*uti possidetis*) seems appropriate enough—the overriding goal is to end colonial subjection, and secondarily to avoid needless conflicts over how new borders should be drawn. The fundamental assumption is that it makes no difference what boundaries are chosen for the new country, nor what disparate populations are included: "Since a cosmopolitan democratic state can function within any borders, the conversion of administrative borders to international borders is as sensible as any other approach and far simpler" (Ratner 1996, 591).[3]

If we accept this understanding of self-determination, there are probably few reasons to consider rights to full separation by American Indians and other indigenous peoples, unless we believe that they are currently living under a "separate and subordinate" political regime. This was absolutely true of many countries in the past, where indigenous peoples were barred from voting and the large majority of other citizenship rights and were subject to being forced onto reserves, where their lives were strictly regulated by bureaucrats intent on assimilating them to colonial worldviews. While indigenous peoples often asserted their "separate" status, none asked to be subordinated in this way. During these periods, these groups would clearly have had rights to separation under this interpretation of self-determination.

But conditions are clearly different now. In the United States, Canada, and most other stable democracies, indigenous peoples are allowed to vote, own property, and exercise the same rights as everyone else. This is not to say that these states are perfect—far from it. Indigenous peoples remain generally poor, alienated, and limited in their political influence. But this does not necessarily ground any rights to a separate status. It could just as easily require exactly the opposite sort of policy—to end whatever kinds of separate political structures prevent indigenous peoples from merging fully into democratic political life on the same terms as everyone else. Indeed, the United States tried to do just this in the 1950s, and most American Indian communities rejected this effort. The United States can thus plausibly claim that it tried to remove the legal barriers creating colonial circumstances and that it was rebuffed in its attempts, so its obligations in this regard have been discharged. It can also plausibly argue that, since American Indians are eligible to leave reservations in search of better living conditions and opportunities if they wish to (as in fact the majority have), then it cannot be held fully responsible for those who choose to remain behind in poverty, any more than it can be held fully responsible for any other persons who refuse to go where the jobs are (cf. Flanagan 2000). At a minimum, Indians would seem to face relatively heavy burdens in demonstrating that their legal relationship with the United States is sufficient to constitute colonialism as this interpretation of self-determination understands it. (Many indigenous readers will probably disagree with this description of the effectiveness of the United States in meeting its responsibilities toward its American Indian population, which suggests some important questions about who has the right to judge. These will be taken up in chapters to come.)

Even if one can make a case that American Indians are suffering under colonialism in the relevant sense, this will still not ground any rights for the return of historical territories, since this interpretation of self-determination is quite comfortable with the doctrine of *uti possidetis*. In the United States, this would limit self-determining territories to the boundaries of reservations as they now exist, and in Canada to band reserves.[4] Since many indigenous claimants are very interested in the return of at least some historical lands, the reasoning behind the principle of *uti possidetis* probably deserves some further exploration. After all, we are considering the possibility of exit from stable democratic states like the United States and Canada—do the same justifications used to defend *uti possidetis* in the international realm apply here as well?

The most obvious arguments for this principle stem from concerns with reducing pretexts for international violence. Since neighboring states have reasons in any instance of decolonization to want borders drawn to their benefit, particularly to give them control over valuable resources or certain populations, *uti possidetis* provides one powerful mechanism for restraining them and nipping conflicts in the bud. Once territories are defined in this way and thereafter protected by the principle of territorial integrity, any state that begins lobbying for changes to its neighbor's boundaries can reasonably be seen as having dangerous intentions. In the words of Steven Ratner (1996, 591) (who is no supporter of the principle): "Absent such a policy, all borders would be open to dispute, and new states would fall prey to irredentist neighbors."

Even at the international level, however, we should not overstate the value of *uti possidetis*. While it may succeed in limiting violence during the process of decolonization, it may actually serve to generate more violence in the long term. International law grants belligerent rights to secessionist and irredentist movements that demonstrate the capacity to control territory through violence (Walzer 1992, 96), and generally recognizes new boundaries as legal once they have been forcibly changed, allowing militarized groups alternatives to *uti possidetis* (Ratner 1996, 590). Nor is insisting on *uti possidetis* for former federalist subunits necessarily conducive to reestablishing peace once conflict has caused a state to fragment. Ratner (591) attributes some of the violence in the collapse of Yugoslavia to the lack of flexibility created by *uti possidetis:* "The assumption by states of its applicability from the outset prevented any debate over the adjustment of boundaries and limited the universe of possible choices to one—leaving those people on the 'wrong' side of the border ripe for 'ethnic cleansing.'" More strongly, he suggests that "*Uti possidetis* thus represents the classic example of . . . an 'idiot rule'—a simple, clear norm that offers an acceptable outcome in most situations but whose very clarity undermines its legitimacy in others" (617). Given the violence of civil wars compared to international wars since the end of the Cold War, it seems reasonable to believe that international law might find some more effective mechanism for determining international boundaries.

While much more could be said about the costs and benefits of *uti possidetis* as a mechanism for limiting interstate war and other forms of militarized violence, these considerations apply only weakly where the claims of indigenous peoples are involved, since these peoples lack sufficient numbers or resources to pose any real military threat to the states now ruling them. *Uti possidetis* may ultimately be a defensible element in a set of international laws intended to regulate the interactions of heavily armed states, but it may not be the most appropriate mechanism for determining boundaries in all cases, even if we accept the basic understanding of self-determination in which it has a natural place. Even if democratic governments that protect human rights can be constructed among the most disparate populations and within any territories, states with certain demographic structures and geographical shapes may still do better than others, and it is hard to say why this should not matter when conditions allow for it. Indeed, there is nothing in international law that would *prevent* states like the United States and Canada from using some more sophisticated method for determining the boundaries for any indigenous groups that could show sufficient mistreatment to have rights to separation.

But this raises another question: if the background conditions that justify *uti possidetis* in international law do not necessarily apply for indigenous peoples within stable democracies like the United States and Canada, should the requirement that groups seeking separation demonstrate severe mistreatment also be abandoned in these cases? Why not simply let groups who wish to exit do so, particularly if they were brought under the state's authority by dubious means? Indeed, some people believe that this is what international law has demanded all along.

III. Self-Determination and "Peoples"

Not everyone accepts the interpretation of self-determination outlined above. Perhaps this should not be surprising, since the terminology of "self-determination of peoples" seems to suggest something more robust than merely an end to separate and subordinate political status. In its original incarnation, the terminology of self-determination was used to restructure the borders of several European states along ethnic lines after World War I, and the easy carryover of the terminology into decolonization seems to imply something similar, as does the use of the term "peoples" (a term that scholars such as Kohen feel continually required to defuse). Moreover, although it was hoped that the new states resulting from decolonization would be democratic, the principles governing decolonization did not require this; decolonization continued even after it became obvious that few states would really have this character (see, e.g., Cassese 1995, 71–74; cf. Roth 1998, 223–34; Franck 1992). The relevant change during decolonization was often not from subordination to self-government, but from rule by colonial powers to rule by domestic tyrants, which was often regarded as improvement because at least the new tyrants were homegrown. It is difficult to escape the conclusion, then, that the principle of self-determination has something more than simply cosmopolitan democracy as its goal.

It is particularly difficult to ignore the reference to "peoples" in the principle of self-determination, especially in a project concerned with moral arguments and indigenous groups. Many American Indians assert something more than simply a right not to be misgoverned by the United States (although this remains a tenuous achievement). They view efforts to deny them a separate status as a more profound violation of their inherent right to control their own future, and often assert that their peoples are suffering the same kind of colonialism that occurred in Africa and Asia, except that it has lasted longer and continues into the present day. For many indigenous groups, the term "self-determination of peoples" should be understood in the plain sense of the words—as a right held by culturally distinct communities that have been incorporated into a state against their will. The states that currently rule such groups, on the other hand, frequently insist that term "peoples" not be applied to them, or the term "self-determination" to their aspirations, fearing that acceptance of these terms will license movements for independence (Anaya 1996, 77–88) or, at a minimum, greater localized self-government. At the very least, then, this interpretation of self-determination seems to fit more comfortably with the day-to-day meaning of the legal terms involved and has a different resonance for many political actors (on both sides) than legal scholars supporting the alternative view would prefer.

For many political actors and some legal scholars, the principle means exactly what it sounds like it means: that all "peoples" have rights to self-determination. But this poses an obvious question: how does one recognize a "people" in which the right inheres? As many scholars note (e.g., Buchheit 1978, 9–11; Kohen 2001, 171; Duursma 1996, 73–77; Roth 1998, 22–26), absent some clear territorial standard such as *uti possidetis*, it seems possible to conceive of the relevant "self" in a great many ways. "Peoples" are generally seen as groups sharing both objective and subjective traits, centering around shared cultural characteristics and a sense of communal solidarity and exhibiting at least some degree of territorial contiguity (cf. Anaya 1996, 77–80; Margalit and Raz 1990; Musgrave 1997, 154–67). But while this definition makes the central concept clear enough, it provides only broad guidelines that are very difficult to apply in most realistic cases.

It is unclear, for example, whether objective (e.g., shared language) or subjective (a sense of "nationhood") elements should be given greater significance; whether degrees of cultural distinctiveness matter; how the subjective elements are to be recognized; what is to be done when characteristics such as language, religion, and history overlap in complex ways; and so on.[5] Somehow it must be determined which kinds of social and cultural divisions are relevant in defining a group as a "people," and the legal principle of self-determination by itself provides no guidance about how this should be done. It is moreover unclear if a population must be a certain size to be considered a "people," if all groups that meet this description are so entitled, or if this depends on the degree of the groups' contiguity or some other factor. In the absence of *uti possidetis*, the principle of self-determination by itself provides little insight into how a "people" is to be recognized, and it is not at all obvious how this term might be given more definite content. Even in the case of American Indians and other indigenous groups, which may seem relatively easy to define as "peoples," the immense variety of their contemporary circumstances means that the difficulties remain severe (cf. Frantz 1999). Many of these groups have intermarried with nonindigenous populations for generations, have adopted broad elements of mainstream culture, and have very different visions of who is "indigenous" and who is not (see, e.g., Simpson 2000).

Moreover, even if some acceptable definition of a "people" can be found, the "self" in question may still face what Lee Buchheit (1978, 28; cf. Miller 1995, 111–12; Kofman 1998, 31) calls the problem of infinite divisibility. Consider the former Yugoslavia once again. If Croats as a nation were entitled to exit Yugoslavia, then minority Serbs seemed to have equally persuasive claims to secede from an independent Croatia, and Croats within these new territories to secede yet again. Taken to its ultimate conclusion, the principle of self-determination can potentially lead to geographically interspersed peoples being separated into a bewildering multitude of geographically noncontiguous microstates (cf. Newman 1997), a possibility that poses deep dangers for any kind of stable political life. Even in the United States, many American Indian reservations have large (and sometimes majority) nonindigenous populations as a result of historical policies of land redistribution, creating the potential to foster similar kinds of problems.

Nor is some version of *uti possidetis* (e.g., for existing reservations or other governmental subunits) a natural way to reduce these difficulties, at least if this interpretation of self-determination is taken with full seriousness. Its implausibility is particularly clear if we consider the way in which the doctrine has functioned in international practice. In most incidents of decolonization, *uti possidetis* was used to demarcate the population of a given territory as a "people" for legal purposes, thus conveniently resolving all questions by making the "self" simply a product of the colonial state's past policies. If the self-determination of *peoples* is to play any real role in determining the character of political boundaries, this clearly will not do—if the decisions of peoples are supposed to matter for shaping political borders, "peoples" cannot simply be defined as whatever populations happen to fall within an existing governmental subunit. Whatever characteristics are necessary to define a group as a "people" in a substantive sense will rarely match exactly with colonial administrative boundaries, and in some cases "peoples" so conceived will spill across the boundaries of multiple states. Much the same could be said in the case of many indigenous groups, whether one intends to take existing reservation boundaries as fixed or some other kind of existing subunit; taking this interpretation of self-determination seriously seems to require some more complex effort to match boundaries and peoples.

It is the potential for violence and endless controversies over boundaries implicit in any such process that leads many legal scholars to reinterpret the "self-determination of peoples" as a focus on cosmopolitan democracy, so that where borders lie and who they include become more or less irrelevant. They reasonably fear that a central political role for "peoples" will provoke and legitimate extreme nationalism, leading to explosive disagreements about who is really a member of the nation (cf. Levy 2000, chap. 3) and the potential for ethnic cleansing and genocide. Yet, as I have already noted, simply demonstrating that something may be a reasonable fear within a regime of international law does not necessarily entail that established democracies like the United States and Canada cannot achieve something more nuanced in regard to their indigenous populations. It may be that other mechanisms for redrawing boundaries beyond *uti possidetis* can be successful, such as negotiations with the group's leaders or sophisticated methods of voting (see Chapters 7 and 8). At a minimum, it seems premature to insist that these difficulties are equally prohibitive in all cases. This understanding of self-determination seems particularly important given the claims to cultural difference made by many indigenous peoples—any theory of authority that ignores cultural difference entirely seems likely to run roughshod over too many complex realities. There are thus obvious reasons to worry about too much reference to "peoples"—but also reasons to worry about too little.

Given the potential for chaos in a massive wave of secessions and other changes to authority structures across the world, many legal scholars and indigenous activists argue that self-determination grounds rights to fully independent statehood only if existing countries fail to offer cultural minorities and indigenous peoples substantial rights of self-government within the countries' current boundaries (e.g., Anaya 1996, 77–88; Neizen 2003, 197–207).

At first glance, this looks like an intermediate position, but it actually concedes less than it appears. It leaves a very important question unanswered, or answered only implicitly: who has the right to decide which groups are eligible for such protections and to decide whether those offered are sufficient? A great deal depends on this question. If the "people" itself is the relevant judge, this argument is back where this interpretation of self-determination started—groups that declare a need for customized rights are entitled to them, and if they fail to receive them to their satisfaction, they have rights to exit their current state. This is very much the choice that Churchill, as outlined at the chapter's beginning, believes all indigenous nations should have anyway—deciding to stay with the status quo constitutes an exercise of self-determination just as deciding to exit does.

If, on the other hand, only the government of the existing state has the right to decide what forms of self-government should be offered and when they are sufficient—so long as they do not force these groups into a "separate and subordinate" legal status—then indigenous claims for a separate political existence remain quite weak. Leaving this sort of authority with the central government, so long as it is tolerably democratic, is what the earlier interpretation of self-determination had in mind all along. Thus, the apparently intermediate position of insisting on federalist arrangements for indigenous peoples proves to be mired in the uncertainties gripping the notion of self-determination itself. The conflict between these two understandings remains unresolved, as does the fundamental uncertainty about how political boundaries should be understood in moral terms.

IV. Ownership and Self-Determination

If the principle of self-determination leaves much unresolved, so does international law's uneven treatment of political authority over geographical space as a kind of transferable property right. Despite the historic legality of conquest and the sporadic acceptance of boundaries resulting from conflict in the present day, most states continue to press their territorial claims in the language of ownership (albeit often with opportunistic reference to differing grounds of acquisition). Historical ownership is clearly important for American Indians and other indigenous peoples, as are their claims that many lands now lost to them were never legally transferred. But, given the discussion of self-determination above, we might wonder: is the presence or absence of historical transfers really so important after all?

Self-determination is usually taken in existing international law to require a one-time restructuring of state boundaries, after which the status quo must be protected under the principle of territorial integrity. The territorial boundaries of states created during decolonization were justified through this process, with acts of self-determination (theoretically) creating rights of territorial integrity at all subsequent times (cf. Kohen 2001, 172). Territories that chose incorporation with the colonial state or another state were seen as making a binding decision from which they could not later withdraw. States that chose independence, on the other hand, gained clear legal title to their existing territories against both external and internal claimants. After an incident of self-determination, the process of territorial change was effectively ended.

If we understand authority over geographical space as a transferable property right, then the claims of American Indians and other indigenous peoples for a separate political status seem to depend on exactly what rights were exchanged in treaties and other historical transactions. While much depends on our judgment about how freely these transfers were made, this interpretation would seem to leave some indigenous groups with extremely inclusive rights to reclaim authority over historical lands (particularly in Australia, where no treaties were ever made), while leaving some other groups with no remaining rights at all. But is this really the right framework for thinking about something so momentous as political authority? Should single historical choices really matter so much? For international law, the one-time nature of this principle reflected a deep concern with international order—the goal was a single massive round of alterations to international boundaries, and then nothing more. But do similarly strong prudential reasons for one-time-only changes hold where indigenous peoples are concerned, particularly if the historical transfers were made a very long time ago, long before their real outcome could be known?

The obvious response may be that, prudential considerations aside, these actions resulted in a transfer of ownership (with accompanying sovereignty) from indigenous peoples to the states that now rule them, and that this is the end of the matter. Just as individuals can transfer their property and thereby leave their descendants unable to reclaim it, so indigenous political organizations had rights to transfer ownership of the territories they governed to states and must be held to these terms whenever such arrangements were made. (States might find this an appealing argument, until they remembered that most of the lands they rule were never transferred to them.) This is, I suspect, more or less the way that most people think about political rights to particular territories, because the parallels to individual property rights seem so natural. Yet these parallels may be deceptive—property rights in ordinary life may rest on very different moral justifications than apply where transfers of state authority are involved.

Indeed, international law's understanding of territorial ownership is overly consequentialist and therefore concerned with political outcomes rather than absolute ownership. As Ian Brownlie (1998, 52; cf. Cassese 1986, 376–77; Musgrave 1997, chap. 10; Kaikobad 1996) notes, property rights form a stable "traffic system" that allows states to recognize each other's territorial boundaries, to invest in infrastructure and defense construction over time, and generally to ensure domestic and interstate order. When this order breaks down, the international legal system usually finds ways to ratify new boundaries in hopes that future conflicts can be prevented or at least blunted. And it is not only considerations of peace and order that can cause ownership rights to dissolve—the entire process of decolonization required states to abandon overseas holdings that were acquired through means legal at the time of acquisition (e.g., conquest and forced cession). Even in international law, then, ownership rights over geographical space are far from absolute. Why wouldn't they be far less so where American Indians and other indigenous peoples are concerned, since the difficulties of maintaining peace and order may be much less severe in these instances?

Of course, this argument will probably make those on both sides of debates about the status of indigenous peoples nervous, since indigenous peoples often want to make strong historical claims about original ownership, while states will look askance at anything that threatens their perceived rights to territorial integrity. For ownership to play a fundamental role in either set of claims, we would probably have to posit some stronger notion of ownership than that found in international law. Some philosophers and political actors argue that nonconsequentialist, natural property rights exist that have no purpose beyond protecting what individuals or groups have legitimately acquired (e.g., Nozick 1974). If such rights could be shown to exist and to form the basis for political authority, such a strong focus on historical transfers would probably make sense. But can such rights really be defended, and are they really linked to the right to rule territories and populations? That remains very much to be seen.

As with self-determination, then, considering international law's treatment of control over territory as a sort of property right leaves much as yet undecided: What sort of property right might this be, and how might the history of such transactions matter? Is there some sort of statute of limitations on past expropriations (Buchanan 1991, 88–89), or do they retain their relevance forever? If past expropriations retain their relevance, what would it mean to rectify them? These important, unsolved questions and many others will form the topic of the next two chapters.

V. Paths Ahead

So far this inquiry has generated more questions than answers. Existing international law provides at best ambiguous grounding for claims to separate status by indigenous peoples, although it calls our attention to some important possibilities for moral evaluation. In trying to balance multiple types of moral considerations under difficult circumstances, international law is necessarily forced to make some difficult compromises. Whether these compromises are made correctly given contemporary international circumstances is a difficult question, and it is not entirely clear which considerations matter the most in answering it.[6] (Indeed, uncertainties about the principle of self-determination leave it unclear exactly what those compromises really are.) International law scholars themselves struggle with these questions, and, perhaps unsurprisingly, virtually all express serious worries regarding at least some aspects of contemporary law (see, e.g., Halperin et al. 1992, 4–9; Musgrave 1997, 257–59; Brownlie 1998, 41–47; Castellino 2000, 132–44; Cassese 1995, 315–33). Most importantly for the current project, many of these compromises may not be necessary or appropriate when we think about the status of American Indians and other indigenous peoples, given their very different situation, lodged within stable, cosmopolitan democracies. International law deserves respect as a tolerably functional system of law, but it is not perfect, and not at all the final word on political authority over populations and territories.

Thus, existing international law on territory, in suggesting three broad options for thinking about the rights of governments to rule particular groups and geographical areas, provides a stepping-off point for further exploration. The first option is to conceive rights to rule particular geographical areas as some sort of transferable property rights. In the next two chapters, I will explore this idea in more depth, considering what property rights are and whether such rights can plausibly be linked to political authority. The second and third options, found in differing interpretations of the principle of self-determination, suggest radically divergent possibilities. For the first of these, the relevant feature of states seems to be their role in protecting basic rights and guaranteeing democratic governance. In Chapters 5 and 6 I will consider the view of authority that must underlie such a view. The alternative possibility focuses on national differences and moral pluralism and suggests that states ought to protect or express a group's wishes. In Chapters 7 and 8 I will consider these issues as they may apply to states, one chapter considering the importance of popular desires for particular political arrangements and the other focusing on the moral plausibility of cultural claims.

In short, we need three types of intellectual tools to think clearly about political control over territories and populations: a theory of property rights, a theory of state authority, and a theory of self-determination. In the chapters to come, I will offer particular versions of each, while also trying to make clear the implications of views different than those I outline in depth. My goal is less to rebuild our thinking about political authority from the ground up than to disaggregate a set of moral arguments often encountered in political life, so that each can be viewed in a clearer light. How these pieces should be reassembled, and whether they support claims for a separate political status for indigenous peoples, are questions that will take the remainder of the book to answer fully.

THREE

THE LIMITS OF OWNERSHIP

The most sweeping potential challenge to the current political shape of countries like the United States and Canada is that posed by unextinguished indigenous ownership rights. If such rights exist, and if ownership is strongly linked to political authority, the implications seem profound: countries like the United States and Canada may have to return a great deal of territory and its accompanying authority to indigenous political collectives and thereafter allow these groups to pursue whatever future seems best to them.

For some defenders of indigenous rights, this kind of thoroughgoing reconstruction is exactly what morality requires. Ward Churchill (1999, 382–91; cf. Alfred 1999, 120),[1] for example, has argued that the United States is morally bound to return territories equivalent to all lands acquired without treaties to American Indian nations, and then to allow these returned lands to form the new political territories of any groups that desire full independence. This is far from a trivial amount of territory, as the source Churchill draws upon makes clear: "From the close of the American Revolution to 1900, the United States took possession of more than two billion acres of land claimed by indigenous tribes and nations. Half this area was purchased by treaty or agreement. . . . Another 325,000,000 acres, chiefly in the Great Basin area, were confiscated unilaterally by Act of Congress or Executive Order, without compensation. An estimated 350,000,000 acres in the contiguous forty-eight States, and most of the State of Alaska's 375,000,000 acres, were claimed by the United States without agreement or the pretense of a unilateral action extinguishing Indian title" (Barsh 1982, 7–8). According to Churchill's calculation (1999, 383), this comes to approximately one-third of the territory of the contemporary United States.

If this understanding of ownership and authority can be vindicated in all its details, the implications are obviously immense. But even a partial vindication of some of its key elements could overturn many of the presuppositions made by countries like the United States and Canada about the scope and character of their authority. For that reason, doing justice to indigenous claims requires a careful investigation of historical ownership and its potentially continuing relevance in the present day. Although international law frequently finds ways to treat acquisitions by conquest as legitimate. I noted in the last chapter that more exacting standards may be appropriate where challenges to the authority of our own stable democracies are concerned. This seems to be precisely the case here: to know what our own states ought to be doing in regard to indigenous challenges, we need to know what property rights are and what (if anything) might happen to expropriated ownership rights over the passage of time. We must also know how such ownership might ultimately be tied to the unambiguously territorial authority exercised by existing state structures.

Since the issues involved here are complex, I will subdivide them between this chapter and the next for easier evaluation. In this chapter, I will evaluate the degree to which indigenous peoples might retain ownership rights over the territories historically expropriated through force and fraud by existing states. In doing so, I will try to see what the strongest viable case for the continuing relevance of past ownership might be, in the interests of ensuring that the analysis takes indigenous claims with appropriate seriousness. My basic presumption throughout this chapter will be that political rights over territory are simply property rights to specific areas, rather than some other kinds of principles more metaphorically framed in the language of ownership. In the next chapter, I will explore the potential relationships between property ownership and political authority in more detail and will suggest that these relationships are more complex than they sometimes seem. Yet the basic conclusion reached at the end of this chapter will remain unchanged: indigenous peoples may continue to have rights to substantially more land than existing states prefer to concede, and insofar as political authority is linked to ownership, this may require extensive revisions of existing political arrangements.

Before proceeding any further, I want to sound a note of warning about the language of "ownership" as used in this context. Although many indigenous scholars use this language comfortably, others use it only with reservations, often explicitly as a political tool for pursuing goals that seem to them justified on other grounds. For the latter, the notion of ownership fails to take seriously the deep interconnections among different individuals and communities and among humans and other parts of the natural world. In the strongest versions, these alternative conceptions can point toward very different conceptions of the human role in the larger natural order. Native Canadian John Borrows (1999, 72; see also Borrows 2002; Deloria 2003), for example, describes the relationship in these terms: "Our loyalties, allegiance, and affection are related to the land. The water, wind, sun, and stars are part of this federation." One cannot be in federation with something one "owns"—one must view it as worthy of respect in its own right. Nor should one reduce this language to some form of environmentalism or something else immediately familiar; insofar as indigenous philosophical traditions really do differ in fundamental ways from Western frameworks, efforts at translation may be far more difficult and imperfect than expected (Mehta 2000; cf. Hendrix 2007).

Yet despite these concerns, many indigenous scholars continue to use the language of ownership because it remains such a foundational element within the intellectual frameworks of surrounding populations and therefore provides potentially powerful leverage for pursuing goals that seem to them justified within indigenous traditions on other grounds (cf. Hendrix 2005b; Turner 2006, 151n2). Whatever the motivations of indigenous actors who invoke property ownership, the challenge for nonindigenous philosophers remains the same: to determine what "our own" theories of property tell us about the historical rights of indigenous peoples, and more broadly about the political rights of states and indigenous political organizations. In this chapter and the next, I want to explore what can be said about historical property rights using the Western theoretical resources commonly associated with the notion of ownership, to find what those claims can support. When the argument is about property rights as they are usually understood, these two chapters should help to clarify what can and cannot plausibly be said; if the argument is really about something else, these other arguments are probably best dealt with separately and their potentially divergent implications explored on their own terms. I will try to do this to some degree within Chapter 8's discussion of cultural difference, but, as I will argue there, debates across—or about—cultural traditions are always complex and uncertain, and the decisions about what compromises (if any) are being made in deploying the language of ownership seem ultimately the kind that must be left up to indigenous actors themselves.

I. Social Conventions

What does it mean to talk about ownership in any circumstances? It is now standard to note that a "property right" is really a complex collection of rights, moral powers, immunities, and duties (Honoré 1987, 165–79), but I want to leave most of those complexities aside here. Most of us have a general sense of property rights as moral claims to do more or less what one wants with whatever one owns, so long as this does not cause too much harm to others. Specifying the character of these rights more exactly should not be necessary for the purposes of this chapter.

Property rights, whether held by individuals, states, or indigenous peoples as collectives, can be justified in either of two broad ways: either as social conventions intended to achieve particular goals or as "natural" rights that exist regardless of social context. For reasons that I will outline, conventional property rights seem ill-suited for making strong claims about the contemporary relevance of historical ownership, although they leave room for some ambiguity. Claims based in natural rights, on the other hand, promise to have moral force whatever the social circumstances but are subject to persistent objections, some of which may be difficult to surmount. I will argue that ultimately neither theory of property can support the absolutism about historical transfers that Churchill's arguments invoke, although natural rights seem able to ground more limited claims for the return of historical properties in ways that could remain extremely important.

For many people, property rights are understood as useful social conventions that can be altered as necessary to achieve important social goals, rather than natural rights that exist regardless of context. The basic model here is roughly legalistic, and those who make such arguments often have in the background some conception of what enforcement mechanisms might look like. The basic assumption is that property rights are a socially created mechanism for achieving a variety of moral goals, and not some kind of inherent or free-standing claim to control particular resources. What matters are the overall social consequences of having one regime of property rights rather than another. But this provokes an obvious question: what sort of social consequences should we be concerned with, and for which people over what time line? It does not tell us very much simply to say that property rights should be structured to achieve important moral goals.

Jeremy Waldron (1994) has suggested that there are two broadly competing ways to conceptualize the goals of property rights as social conventions, which he calls the "Humean" and "Rousseauian" approaches, after the philosophers Hume and Rousseau. The Humean approach is concerned with immediate social consequences, and primarily with limiting violent social conflict. Its basic preference is for ratifying the status quo, whatever it may be, if this will allow an end to conflicts over who owns what—any set of property holdings that emerges as socially stable should be protected, no matter how it came about or what its character may be. "Provided a settled pattern of possession emerges, we simply draw an arbitrary line and say, 'Property entitlements start from *here*'" (91–92; emphasis in original). Since more theoretically detailed conceptions of ownership will invite people to argue over specific principles of distribution or acquisition, it is better simply to cut off all such argument. Indeed, we have already seen some elements of this approach in international law's principle of territorial integrity, which generally finds ways to ratify whatever international boundaries seem the most conducive to continued peace (although the principle of self-determination suggests that rather different principles are also at work).

There is clearly something appealing about this approach, since peace and security are often difficult to secure both within and between states. But just as clearly, this strategy sacrifices too much to peace and security and may often fail to secure these goals. After all, the effects of past injustices do not magically fade away over time, nor does knowledge that they occurred, at least within any tolerably free society. American Indians and other indigenous peoples are acutely aware of the methods by which they were put into their currently marginalized position, and many other groups across the world are similarly conscious of how history has affected their current prospects. Seeing these injustices ignored may not always lead to outright warfare, but it can often lead to a variety of social conflicts, often with very high social costs to all those involved (Waldron 1994, 115–17). Moreover, peace and security are scarcely the only goals that we care about; most of us also care about some notion of human equality or basic rights, and simply ignoring history may condemn many persons to permanently subordinate social positions. Since this is the circumstance of many indigenous peoples, is it at all fair simply to say that social weakness has rendered their claims moot?

Given the failings of this approach, it makes sense to look for one that pays greater attention to how structures of property ownership actually affect the lives of all persons involved. The Rousseauian approach (Waldron 1994, 85) holds that any acceptable regime of property rights must focus not only on peace but also on ensuring that each person's moral interests are protected as well as possible. While such an approach takes into account basic facts about the world and human nature, it is often pitched at a very high level of abstraction: "Rousseau's position is that the distribution of property ought to be subject to the general will of the whole society: society is entitled to establish a new distribution (or ratify an existing one) on the basis of broad principles of justice that reflect each person's status as an unconditional and equal partner in a contractarian social union" (85). The Rousseauian approach thus gives little weight to existing property arrangements: it maintains that if these arrangements do not protect as many moral interests as possible, they should be redistributed. Further, whatever unconditional or equal partners involved in social interaction would agree to should be brought about, however many changes this may require to the status quo; simply controlling a particular resource right now says nothing about whether a person or group has moral rights to it.

This kind of abstract formulation can easily become both cryptic and extremely complicated in determining what kind of contractarian social union is involved and who the parties choosing might be (e.g., Rawls 1971). I will try to bring these abstractions down to ground level by focusing on the core claims motivating this understanding of property ownership. The central question of Rousseauian accounts is usually something like the following: "What system of property can be created that will minimize economic inequalities while also leaving sufficient room for the exercise of human freedom?" This approach's basic decision procedure for evaluating regimes of property rights and economic outcomes can likewise be simplified into some version of the Golden Rule. In evaluating extreme poverty, for example, a Rousseauian might paint a detailed portrait of what poverty is like and then ask, "Would you want to live in such circumstances?" Most people would probably want opportunities to escape deep poverty through labor if the poverty was their own fault, and some kind of aid if it was not. These basic decisions clearly do not determine the full details of an ideal regime of property ownership, but they help set the fundamental goals of such a system and may alert us to particularly profound injustices in the way that property holdings are currently distributed. The Rousseauian approach thus differs from the Humean in its concern for contemporary poverty, and it provides at least a rough idea of what goals a system of property rights might want to pursue.

What about historical property rights? Most of those who take a Rousseauian approach, including Waldron himself (1992), are extremely skeptical of claims for the return of historical properties, at least when these properties were expropriated long ago. In part, this reflects their general skepticism about the way claims for strong property rights are used by powerful political actors to justify existing economic inequalities within stable democratic states, but it also reflects a principled sense that claims for historical ownership cannot be defended.[2] Using the kind of simplified test I suggested above for poverty, a Rousseauian approach to historical claims would ask something like the following: "Would you think it was fair if historical properties were returned to the descendants of the original owners, if this would make those who lost the resources poorer than those who regained them?" Those who answer "no" must admit that they care more about contemporary poverty than about historical claims, and for that reason should support a property system that focuses on poverty rather than past ownership. Such a test does not decide the argument once and for all, but it does ask us to put ourselves in the shoes of those on both sides rather than take any received views of ownership for granted. Coupled with the uncertainties of historical property claims themselves (see below), this convinces many people that historical property rights cannot be justified. Waldron (1992; cf. Lyons 1981) is very clear about his own feelings on the matter, arguing that indigenous peoples usually deserve far greater resources to remediate their current poverty, but none because of what their ancestors once owned.[3]

Since a Rousseauian approach must eventually take complex social factors into account in determining a final regime of property rights for a just society, it is possible that a derivative case for returning historical properties does exist, at least within a limited time frame. An ideal regime of property will probably need some way of punishing theft and creating deterrent effects, for example, and returning stolen properties and punishing those who took them seems necessary to achieving this. (Of course, punishment may be deserved even if it lacks deterrent effects, so that this is not simply a matter of ownership.) But would these concerns with preventing future events of injustice provide reasons to return *all* stolen properties, no matter how long ago they were taken? This seems unlikely (Waldron 1992, 16), particularly after the thieves themselves have passed away. Still, we should not reject this possibility with absolute finality; a compelling argument for deterrent effects from returning lands stolen long ago would belong firmly within a Rousseauian approach to property, if such an argument could be found.

A more compelling argument that might or might not be at home within a Rousseauian theory of property would focus more deeply on strategies for dealing with current injustice. In practice, nothing resembling the redistribution of existing holdings called for in most Rousseauian accounts appears imminent, so it may be that indigenous peoples are justified in trying to reclaim any lands to which they still hold legal title as the best mechanism for remediating their current poverty (see Hendrix 2005b). Whether a Rousseauian account of property should integrate allowances for such strategic action is not entirely clear to me, but it seems plausible that it might, given the real conditions of the world in which we live. As I have noted elsewhere (Hendrix 2005b), this kind of strategic thinking is a distinctively inferior option to honest argument about moral principles, but may sometimes be necessary nonetheless.[4]

Whatever we think of these possibilities, however, it seems clear that most of those who adopt a Rousseauian approach do not believe that historical claims can be justified on their own merits, even if there is some chance that returning historical lands could be justified by its deterrent effects or its strategic value under conditions of injustice. This is not what many indigenous peoples seem to be arguing for—they seem to have in mind historically grounded claims that are important on their own merits, and that deserve to play a role within a regime of property rights for that reason alone.

At least some philosophers agree, and object that property rights are not mere mechanisms for achieving the goals that "rational contractors" might have for their society (cf. Simmons 1994). For them, any talk of redistributing resources or ignoring histories of expropriation fails to acknowledge that specific properties are naturally tied to certain persons and not others (e.g., Nozick 1974). On this view, redistributing property is something like redistributing body parts—possible, but an incredible violation of the person so affected (Miller 1982, 284–85; cf. Cohen 1995, 243–44). In short, some people believe rights to ownership are natural rights and ought not to be reshaped with some idealized social contractors in mind. These rights must instead be protected; and where properties were stolen, they must be returned if possible, and if not possible, some suitable form of reparation must be offered.

II. Natural Property Rights

For the rest of this chapter, I will consider whether natural property rights of this type are morally defensible. I will draw on the work of some of their proponents, but will also try to offer stronger arguments where these are available. My intention will not be to make a definitive ruling on the validity of natural property rights, but to see if a plausible case can be made for them where arguments for them may break down. Waldron's own objections to such rights will play a central role in examining the limits of these arguments. As I will try to show, his critiques are often quite cogent but are likely not sufficient to destroy arguments for natural rights once and for all.

While a great deal could be said about what "natural" might mean in connection to moral rights, I do not want to engage in that debate here. Although the term has a theological history, I want to consider only a secular interpretation of such rights. Using a rough-and-ready definition, we can hold that rights designated as "natural" must meet at least four conditions. First, they must be rights that are held or at least can be held (as for property) by persons in all times and places (cf. Simmons 1994, 75; Christman 1986, 156–59; Steiner 1977, 41–42). Second, they must always have important moral weight, even if they may sometimes be outweighed by other moral considerations (cf. Simmons 1992). Third, their scope and content must be substantially definable without reference to existing legal practices (cf. Lomasky 1987, 199–29; Steiner 1994). Fourth, criteria for recognizing right-holders must exist that are usable in a wide variety of social situations. The universality of these rights is particularly important—to qualify as natural in the relevant sense, they must be rights that can be held by twenty-first-century Americans in complex market economies and that could also have been held by individuals in precontact indigenous nations.[5]

Some would deny that any such rights exist, but this position seems to me mistaken on its own merits and self-defeating for the case at hand. Moral prohibitions against wrongs like torture and rape seem to me reasonably formulated as natural rights, since these acts should be regarded as profound violations in virtually all circumstances. Such actions not only cause great suffering to another person but show a profound disregard for the person's humanity as well. Whatever foundational premises we use for deciding when acts are prohibited, it seems exceedingly likely that these acts will be shown to be wrong, even if there may be extreme cases in which these prohibitions might be overridden. Of course, not everyone will agree that all humans are worthy of moral respect or that anyone should really care about the suffering of others, but I can give no quick answer to such extreme challenges here. Every moral theory has to start somewhere, and I think most plausible foundation should be the belief that all persons are deserving of certain protections simply by virtue of their common humanity.

But is an invocation of natural rights question begging in a project concerned with the moral claims of American Indians and other indigenous peoples? I do not think so, but there is at any rate no possible value for the present inquiry in endorsing some view of strong moral relativism. Empirically, I think that the common caricature of indigenous peoples as concerned with the good of the community over the good of the individual is considerably overstated. While I will say more about this in chapters to come, it seems to me that the usual objection to "individual rights" in indigenous communities arises not against the idea that all persons are entitled to respect by virtue of their basic humanity, but against the assumption by states that legalistic, bureaucratic mechanisms external to the indigenous group must be used to enforce these protections (see, e.g., Alfred 1999, 139–41). But even if I am entirely wrong in this factual judgment (a distinct possibility, as with any of my claims about indigenous nations), it would still seem that if indigenous peoples seek the return of historical lands solely on the basis of prior ownership, it would be of little benefit to them to reject the notion of natural rights to property. (They need not make such historical arguments at all, of course.) An argument for divergent values will not help here. What is needed is some set of claims that are binding on everyone regardless of cultural membership, so that claims for the return of lost property will have moral force against anyone who is presented with them.

For purposes of this discussion, then, I want to proceed on the assumption that at least some natural rights are defensible. Most fundamentally, any list of natural rights would include prohibitions against killing, maiming, or otherwise damaging someone's physical body—what is often referred to as the right to "life." If it is to play any role in this project, a list of natural rights should also include some notion of rights to individual liberty, since, as I will argue, the strongest justification for natural property rights must focus on the linkage between the ownership of material goods and the practice of individual liberty. Exactly how much room for liberty should exist can remain for the moment an open question, although it has to be relatively broad if it is to be important in its linkage to ownership.[6]

Natural property rights are usually understood as relying on an "entitlement" conception of ownership, of the sort most closely associated with the work of Robert Nozick (1974). Under an entitlement theory, the overall social pattern of property is not a subject for moral concern, as the Rousseauian approach contends it should be. Instead, what matters is the means by which particular holdings were acquired—if properties were originally acquired from nature without injustice and have been transferred freely by their owners up until the present time, then those who now hold them have natural rights to do so. If holdings were expropriated at any point, on the other hand, then justice requires that these properties be returned to their original owners or (where this is not possible) to their heirs. For Nozick, redistributing properties that were acquired through legitimate means allows people to interfere in things that are not their concern and constitutes a way of treating persons and their property as mere means to social ends, rather than as equals whose choices should be respected fully. For Nozick, natural rights must be conceived as a kind of protective box around each person that must be respected if each person is to live his or her own life.

But this could be seen as a form of question-begging itself—why do rights to material goods belong within this protective box, rather than, say, perpetually outside of it, available to be redistributed at any time, as the Rousseauian approach might be taken to suggest?[7] It cannot be simply that individual property rights are socially valuable in creating wealth, since a Rousseauian approach could admit this to be causally true and still hold that property should be redistributed whenever this would improve the condition of the worst off. Simply stating that property rights are conducive to the creation of wealth tells us nothing morally—what is important about creating wealth as such? Indeed, a focus on total social wealth would make natural property rights *weaker* than most of their defenders believe they should be, since natural rights also presumably allow individuals to squander their resources in nonproductive ways, and any theory requiring individuals to be industrious would seem to license exactly the kind of interference Nozick rejects. At any rate, this focus would be of no help in defending claims for the return of historical property holdings, since attempts to do so might have very disruptive effects on existing economies. So the role of property rights in creating wealth is mostly beside the point here. While such wealth may be a pleasant by-product of natural rights to property, it cannot serve as their fundamental justification.

While Nozick is sometimes less clear than one might hope, his central contention seems to be that particular holdings express uses of natural liberty that themselves deserve protection. The importance of material goods for the project of living one's life is probably obvious once it is pointed out—if individuals are going to act as they choose, they will have to do so in the world, and the world is made largely of material objects (along with other people). Using and altering these objects in particular ways is necessary if individuals are going to develop long-term projects and if most are to pursue their conception of a worthwhile human life. (Those who do not believe a worthwhile happy life requires extensive material resources are free to do without them.) While some individuals might choose to use material objects only as economic resources within a market economy, many will also use them to create works of art, or to engage in gift-giving as a way of demonstrating affection, or to destroy them in the process of scientific inquiry. If individuals want to pursue long-term projects of this type, they will have to have protections against the interference of others, who could easily frustrate their goals if material goods were simply free to anyone to take. Yet individuals must also have the right to exchange particular goods when they wish to do so; this, too, allows each person to pursue his or her goals more effectively.

Importantly, this focus on liberty demonstrates why initial indigenous holdings would have been protected by natural property rights. Consider the acquisition of previously unowned lands from their natural state: those who begin living on those lands first seem to gain property rights to them immediately because they have begun to use these lands in expressing choices about the lives they will lead. Moreover, the transferable nature of property rights allows persons engaged in collective projects to do so without interference, since individuals can either pool whatever properties they hold or become members of collectives that already exist when they come on the scene. It is thus a mistake to see natural property rights as fundamentally individualistic; the contrast to private holdings is not group holdings, but holdings redistributed by force against the wishes of those involved.

Seen in this light, Nozick's contention that property rights deserve to be within the protective box surrounding each person seems quite forceful—the redistribution of property entails not only the redistribution of material goods, but the alterations to them that are shaped by a variety of individual and collective purposes (cf. Lomasky 1987, 120–22).[8] A focus on respecting liberty can also provide reasons to allow persons to sink into poverty through their own actions. Some people will end up living disastrous lives and thereby end up with few resources, but if we want to respect their liberty (including their errors), we seem to be under no obligation to return whatever property they have lost (even if we may have duties of a different kind to prevent them from outright starvation and homelessness—see Chapters 5 and 6). On this view, respecting human liberty means respecting the results of human action in the material world, and if claims to liberty deserve to be ranked as natural rights, the property rights resulting from them seem to deserve exactly the same protection.

For my purposes, I will be leaving aside some important objections that could be raised against this argument, regarding the unforeseeable results of choice (e.g., Cohen 1995) and the role of bad luck in determining outcomes (e.g., Dworkin 1981).[9] At a minimum, the important link between liberty and property suggests that any viable moral system must provide substantial rights for individuals to control material resources and must allow real opportunities for individuals to sort themselves into different levels of wealth. But for purposes of the current discussion, this link between liberty and ownership should give us pause—if liberty and ownership are so tightly linked, why should this link support claims for the return of *historical* properties, as Nozick suggests it does? After all, the reason to consider natural rights rather than some Rousseauian account was that such rights are purportedly strong enough to require reparation for past injustices, if possible by returning the properties that were taken. Why might that be so? Nozick, unfortunately, more or less just asserts that historical properties must be returned if possible, as if this were the natural conclusion from a theory holding that the expropriation of property is profoundly wrong. He provides very little meaningful argument for this principle, and indeed even expresses some uncertainty about how far back in time it might apply.[10]

There may be good reasons for this uncertainty. According to Waldron (1992, 15–20), it is exactly the link between liberty and ownership that provides a powerful argument *against* returning properties historically owned by indigenous peoples. The problem is that these intensive linkages fade if resources were taken long ago, because people usually readjust their way of life to the circumstances they find themselves in. Thus, even if indigenous peoples were historically exercising their liberty through the use of certain lands, they have not been able to do this for a very long time, while other persons (born after the original injustice) have created lives in which these lands play an important role. Severing these bonds thus threatens to repeat the original injustice rather than rectify it. In Waldron's words, "Historical entitlement theories are most impressive when moral entitlement is conjoined with present possession. Then it seems plausible to suggest that continued possession of the object might be indispensable to the possessor's autonomy and that an attack on possession is an attack on autonomy. But when the conjunction is disrupted, particularly when, as in the cases we are considering, it is disrupted for a considerable period of time, the claim looks much shakier" (Waldron 1992, 19). This seems at least a plausible description of the contemporary situation for many historical indigenous lands—other people have now built their lives on these lands, and for that reason it does not seem unreasonable to suggest that these historical claims have now expired.[11]

Is this objection right? Perhaps surprisingly, I think that it is, but that historical property rights may nonetheless have considerable moral relevance. Waldron is almost certainly right that historical expropriations can lose their relevance within any theory that takes seriously the purpose of property in human life. It is hard to conceive of any reason for trying to trace back ancient patterns of wrongdoing through every single human on the planet, to try to reconstruct the world as it might have been had no one ever committed theft. Whatever the first humans did to one another in a long-forgotten prehistory can hardly have any moral relevance now. But it does not follow that a theory of natural property rights should care only about the present, nor that property rights cannot persist through the passing of generations. Indeed, Waldron himself hints at the reasons why this might be so. He admits that his argument "may not apply so clearly to cases where the dispossessed subject is a tribe or community, rather than an individual, and where the holding of which it had been dispossessed is particularly important for its sense of identity as a community" (Waldron 1992, 19), such as for sacred lands. This seems reasonable enough—if property matters for the practice of liberty, then it should be particularly hard for rights to fade or be overridden where groups have been lobbying for the return of historical lands for a long time and continue to give those lands an important place within their understanding of the world. Attachments to particular pieces of land can sometimes have a very long life.

If Waldron is willing to admit that that is so, however, he should also admit the other side of the coin—that not all persons who hold properties today have integrated them into their lives in any fundamental way, and that not all historically expropriated properties are now held by individuals. In thinking about contemporary attachments, consider, at the extreme, someone who buys an undeveloped property on former indigenous lands with no intention of ever building on it or even of visiting it with any frequency. The person simply happens to have some extra money and has always liked the idea of owning property in some isolated spot. (Perhaps the person comes to it for a weekend once every few years rather than going to the nearby campground he or she previously visited.) Is this property being used in the practice of individual liberty? To some degree, yes, but it is hard to say that anyone has integrated it deeply into his or her way of life. Although any theory of natural rights should allow individuals to leave their property unused, the way in which these possessions are regarded seems to make a great difference for the expiration of past ownership rights. One who purchases lands in their natural state on the open market and spends every free moment there contemplating nature or writing philosophy can plausibly claim that removing these properties would disrupt his or her life in unfair ways. But one who simply owns these lands uncritically may not be able to say the same thing.

But wouldn't trying to determine how intensively particular people are using their property take us into exactly the kinds of impossible comparisons and decisions that lead to never-ending conflict of the type that the Humean approach to property warns us about? Waldron seems to believe that it will and that in most instances we must take a relatively Humean line toward contemporary property holdings: whatever properties people now hold within existing market economies are assumed to be legitimate, without reference to their history, except perhaps in the case of sacred lands. (Remember that he makes no such presumption about the *amount* of property these people hold, since he wants to remedy contemporary poverty whenever possible.) I do not see, however, why a theory of natural property rights should simply legitimate the legal status quo. Having legal rights to own a property is not the same as having a justified natural right to do so, and if natural rights to ownership are closely linked to the practice of liberty, it seems plausible to believe that some people now control properties to which they lack moral title, and that in some cases different people may have overlapping moral title to the same property. While we cannot easily sort particular properties from one another, we can nonetheless make some broad generalizations and can likely develop some midrange solutions as well.

Rather than assuming that existing holdings are prima facie legitimate, a theory of natural property rights might more plausibly assume that historical rights of ownership remain valid in all cases where they have not been overwritten by contemporary use. Historical ownership also seems to leave a secondary claim in cases where the current owner chooses to abandon a property for one reason or another. While Waldron seems right that we should want a hard-and-fast rule that individual homes and most other kinds of individually held properties cannot be directly returned to indigenous peoples, there is no reason why indigenous peoples could not have rights of first refusal for any lands that became available on the market (since the current owners are obviously no longer attached to them). It may also be appropriate for states to provide indigenous peoples with funds for doing this, or for making offers on properties that they would like to buy but that are not yet up for sale.

Commercial properties seem entitled to somewhat lower protections, since they usually matter as assets for making money rather than for the particular resources themselves, especially for large corporate holdings rather than family businesses. Here it may be reasonable to enact a stronger solution by providing indigenous peoples with opportunities to force the sale of particular properties that are especially important to them, once again potentially with funding from the relevant state.

The barriers for publicly held lands would seem far lower yet, or even nonexistent, and it is here that direct transfers emerge as the dominant option. It is true that some public lands (e.g., parks) are fundamental to collective social practices and others are probably necessary to serve as ecological reserves, but many public lands in the United States, Canada, and Australia are not put to any particular purpose, or are leased out for various commercial uses. In this case, it is hard to imagine that historical property rights have expired—after all, no people using these lands have any reasonable claim to have based their lives around them (since they knew from the beginning that the resources were never theirs), and for that reason no new set of rights has come along to override the original ones. Nor would this involve only a small, trivial set of lands—the United States, Canada, and Australia all hold massive quantities of such lands. In the United States, for example, almost one-third of the total landmass is held as public land, most of it not committed to any specific purpose (Barsh 1982, 75–78)—the same percentage that Ward Churchill (1999, 383) claims was never transferred by treaty!

Despite the likelihood that many historical property rights have faded under the most plausible derivation of natural property rights, then, it would seem deeply mistaken to suggest that all such rights have lost their relevance. The most obvious holdings to which they apply fully are public lands, followed at some distance by commercial properties, and then on to individual homes and farms where historical property rights have a far more residual character. This is probably weaker than some indigenous peoples have in mind when they assert historical property claims, but it is also far stronger than many nonindigenous persons seem willing to admit.[12] Yet this leads to an extremely important question: do indigenous peoples continue to hold residual property rights to everything they once claimed to own, or are their rights to something more limited?

III. Labor and the Lockean Proviso

We should not immediately conclude that indigenous peoples necessarily retain residual property right to all lands they once claimed to own. To determine what historical ownership might require in the present day, we have to answer a number of questions. The first is how much property indigenous peoples could legitimately have owned prior to expropriation, regardless of how much they claimed to own; the second is the degree to which some version of John Locke's famous proviso on property ownership might have reduced initial holdings over time; the third is how multiple and overlapping kinds of injustices should be dealt with in a world with multiple strands of historical wrongdoing. I will deal with the first and second over the remainder of this chapter, and with the third more fully in the next.

Consider first the question of what lands particular indigenous peoples might have had historical rights to control. In North America, it is easy to say that the entire continent was collectively held by its indigenous population prior to contact, but this may not be correct, and in any case the United States and Canada often face competing claims for historical ownership by multiple groups. We thus need some way of determining which groups had rights to control which territories, and this in turn requires some more fundamental explanation of how the limits of particular acquisitions are to be recognized. I have already noted that natural property rights seem best justified through their linkage to individual liberty, and that holdings should be protected that are being used in particular ways of life. But there are various ways in which one can use resources, and varying degrees of intensity in such use, and for that reason ownership claims may be more plausible for some properties than for others. How, then, do we recognize when properties are being used with sufficient intensity to justify exclusive rights of ownership against everyone else?

Most of those who defend some theory of natural property rights draw on the seventeenth-century work of John Locke, who famously argued that persons could claim previously unowned parts of the natural world by "mixing" their labor with it. Since they own their bodies (and therefore whatever labor they engage in), this kind of mixing brings the resources thus altered within the protective box that natural rights form around a person, making these resources thereafter off limits to all others until the owner chooses to transfer them freely.[13] "Though the earth, and all inferior creatures, be common to all men, yet every man has a *property* in his own *person:* this no body has any right to but himself. The *labour* of his body, and the *work* of his hands, we may say, are properly his. Whatsoever then he removes out of the state that nature hath provided . . . he hath mixed his *labour* with, and joined to it something that is his own, and thereby makes it his property" (Locke 1980, § 27; emphases in original). For Locke, land could be claimed only by laboring on it in this intensive way: "*As much land* as a man tills, plants, improves, cultivates, and can use the product of, so much is his *property*" (§ 32; emphases in original). Locke believed the ways in which indigenous peoples were using lands generally were insufficient to justify ownership, giving them instead only limited property rights arising from particular acts of labor: "Thus this law of reason makes the deer that *Indian's* who hath killed it; it is allowed to be his goods, who hath bestowed his labour upon it, though before it was the common right of every one" (§ 30; emphasis in original).

However, if natural property rights are justified by their relation to liberty, as I have argued that they should be, then this standard is too narrow. The most serious failing of Locke's account is obvious when we consider someone whose understanding of a good life requires that the properties of most value to them be left in their natural state, as is true for the sacred lands of many indigenous peoples. Requiring labor to mark particular properties off would be self-defeating for such cases, yet these lands cannot simply be available to the first person who wants to labor on them. The Lockean story of mixing labor seems to focus too narrowly on the physical act of altering the natural world, rather than on the basic moral nature of humans as persons whose projects can be illegitimately hindered. This mistaken focus is perhaps not surprising (Locke himself was invested both politically and economically in colonialism—see Armitage 2004[14]), but it seems erroneous nonetheless.

Yet the Lockean explanation does offer one substantial advantage in recognizing what individuals or groups own. In practice, it is considerably easier to recognize properties altered through intensive physical labor than lands that are integrated into individual or collective plans of life in other ways. In the absence of obvious changes to the natural world, outsiders may face serious uncertainties in determining what resources are already owned and therefore whether they will be interfering in someone else's life. This is a substantial problem within a theory of natural rights, since individuals should be able to have at least a rough sense of what treating each other justly consists in. If we were starting from scratch in acquiring properties, the best solution would probably be to require that persons claiming particular parts of the natural world take steps to delineate their claims clearly, either by telling others directly what the limits are or finding some mechanism for marking their boundaries. (Requiring others to do intensive research themselves puts unfair burdens on them—they have their own lives to live, after all, and cannot be required to spend all their spare time sorting out what is already owned but remains unaltered.)

Since, in evaluating claims to historical ownership, we cannot require history to be rewritten, the best we can probably do today is to accept what indigenous peoples historically said about the limits of their territories, along with whatever information they can provide about how those lands were historically being used, including documentary data from the era of expropriation. This would not tell us when particular ways of using these lands were sufficient to ground exclusive ownership rights against everyone else, but it would make it clearer what relative importance these lands had, and therefore some idea of the relative strength of their inherited claims to these areas. In cases when competing groups claim ownership of the same lands, this would not always be sufficient to determine who had the stronger case, but there is probably no way to avoid these uncertainties entirely, and this would at least help to solve many. At any rate, this uncertainty is a problem for Locke's labor standard as well (see, e.g., Nozick 1974, 174–75). The only difference is that ambiguous alterations created through labor are easier to recognize visually than ambiguous uses that leave the resources unaltered.[15]

Ultimately, the degree to which relatively minor uses of liberty justify ownership probably depends at least in part on the total resources that are available. European colonists to the Americas often argued that indigenous peoples held more land than they could reasonably use. That argument points to a general concern about ownership, whether it is justified by labor or in broader ways. On Locke's labor standard, the question may arrive more slowly because people will only manage to alter smaller areas through labor, but it arrives nonetheless: when are people claiming to own more than they can legitimately have rights to? If there were an infinite supply of lands and other natural resources always waiting to be acquired, there would be no difficulties—individuals or groups could claim as much as they wanted, and there would always be plenty left for others. But this is obviously not what the world is like. How, then, should one deal with the inevitable finitude of natural resources?

Most of those who believe natural property rights exist hold that they must be limited by some version of the so-called Lockean proviso on ownership, generally formulated as the requirement that all acquisitions leave "enough and as good" for others to acquire. Although this limitation is putatively taken from Locke,[16] his own formulation is not actually that helpful, since it proceeds as if resources *were* infinite: "Nor was this *appropriation* of any parcel of *land,* by improving it, any prejudice to any other man, since there was still enough, and as good left; and more than the yet unprovided could use. So that, in effect, there was never the less left for others because of his inclosure for himself: for he that leaves as much as another can make use of, does as good as take nothing at all. No body could think himself injured by the drinking of another man, though he took a good draught, who had a whole river of the same water left him to quench his thirst: and the case of land and water, where there is enough of both, is perfectly the same" (Locke 1980, § 33; emphases in original). Locke may have believed that lands were effectively infinite in the Americas during his day, but this is little help for those of us who recognize that they were not and who want to consider the proviso's meaning in more realistic circumstances.

The most literal understanding of this Lockean proviso in conditions of limited resources would be to require that each person have opportunities to acquire *equal* amounts of property, or at least property of equal usefulness. (Groups would presumably hold as much as the total allowable to their membership.) This kind of equality seems to follow from the basic character of natural rights—if all individuals are morally equal and property expresses uses of their liberty, then all persons should be able to acquire previously unowned resources in a way that reflects this equality. But it is not a standard that can be easily applied in the real world, at least not directly. Such equality would be difficult to ensure even in a world where all resources had been thoroughly catalogued, since we would have to figure out how to compare different kinds of resources—forestlands, for example, are probably more useful than deserts for most purposes, but how much more? Is one square mile of forest equal to ten of desert, or a hundred, or a thousand? More acutely, this kind of comparison is complicated by the varying preferences individuals have—some people will simply like deserts more than forests, or vice versa, and these desires have to fit on any scale of usefulness that is concerned with ensuring "enough and as good." Since most people share basic preferences such as avoiding hunger, we could undoubtedly make some rough comparisons here, but this would never be a simple matter even in the best of circumstances. And in the real world no one has anything approaching complete information about the total value of all the world's resources; precontact indigenous groups could have had only the roughest idea of how the resources they held compared with those of others, had they wished to compare them in this way.

Nor is it immediately obvious what providing equal chances to acquire resources might mean once we admit that human life is not simply a one-generation affair in which everyone arrives fully grown in an area at the same time. Even when individuals and groups entered entirely unoccupied lands, they could not easily have limited their acquisitions to ensure that there would be "enough and as good" for people who would arrive in the future, because they could not easily guess how many people there would be (Waldron 1992, 23; cf. Wolf 1995, 798–99). To see the implications of the proviso most clearly, it may help to work through the details of a hypothetical example. Imagine that ten explorers find a new island and occupy half its area. What happens if fifty refugees arrive a few years later? Should the fifty divide the unoccupied half equally among themselves, or must the original ten readjust their holdings? Neither option is very appealing—either the recently arrived fifty must get far less than the first-arrivers simply because they were a few years late, or the first-arrivers must rearrange the lives they are living, a result that hinders the purpose of natural property rights in the first place. Saying that those who arrived first should have left "enough and as good" for others is of little help here—there *were* no others when they set about establishing patterns of ownership.

Matters become even more complex when we admit that most newcomers do not arrive with the randomness of refugees, entirely unexpected and effectively without histories; new generations are instead created through the decisions of living people. Imagine the citizens of our hypothetical island once again. Some families will choose to have many children, while others will choose to have only a few or none at all. Must those who chose to have only a few children now transfer property to those who chose to have more? This seems distasteful, because no one should have to pay for the expensive decisions of others—parents should always have the first responsibility to provide for their children, even if they must impoverish themselves to do so. But many parents will nonetheless have more children than they can provide resources for, and the children clearly cannot be punished for this—they had nothing to do with it, and so came into the world as de facto refugees. Thus, the Lockean proviso seems to intervene here as well. Somehow these children have to receive some resources from others to give them a fair chance, which once again threatens some awkward disruptions of existing property arrangements.

Does this mean that the only solution is to redistribute holdings in land with every generation, taking a little bit from everyone to ensure that children have opportunities to acquire something? It would be if the only valuable resource on our hypothetical island (or in the world) were land, and if that land could not be labored on to produce more goods. But of course neither is true. Indeed, land itself has fairly limited value apart from the resources it provides, and these resources can often be traded back and forth between individuals with relative ease. Moreover, intensive labor (along with some technical knowledge) can often induce land to yield greater resources for exchange than would occur in its unaltered condition (which was one of the reasons for Locke's strong valuation of labor). Labor also allows metals and other imperishable resources to be extracted from land and altered through hard work into artifacts like shovels, hammers, and other tools that might be highly valued on our hypothetical island. Once our society is up and running, much of its wealth will not come directly from the extraction of natural resources, but from various goods produced through intensive labor. Even if labor is not necessary to ground rights to original acquisition, then, it can have a strong causal effect on what kinds of material goods individuals ultimately end up having.

Since these goods are produced by labor rather than given by nature, they are not subject to redistribution under the Lockean proviso.[17] Since there were no hammers waiting to be claimed when the first group reached the island, for example, no one in later generations can complain of not having received "enough and as good" if he or she does not have one. This suggests that newcomers, whether arriving as refugees from outside or as children, are entitled to receive something equal in value to the *prelabor* value of the resources that would otherwise have to be directly and awkwardly redistributed to them.[18] They will not have to be made rich or given holdings equal to what everyone else now has; they will simply have to be provided with a starting point, and the degree to which this brings them close to actual equality will depend on how much wealth the society has managed to generate through past labor. Where most of a society's wealth comes from present and past labor, the Lockean proviso will be consistent with newcomers beginning from a position of substantial inequality.[19] And where most wealth comes from natural resources in their raw form rather than from labor, the proviso will bring these newcomers much closer to equality. In most cases, children will manage to receive what they are entitled to through inheritance, but when they do not, others will be required to redistribute some of their holdings to make sure that they are given a fair start.

The question, then, is how these responsibilities to newcomers would be apportioned, whether on our hypothetical island or elsewhere. While there may or may not be reasons to require those who have more total wealth to contribute a greater share, it seems clear that everyone must contribute something and that those who have chosen not to alter their land extensively through labor or to acquire a surplus in other ways will have difficulties in doing so. They will have to find some other way of meeting these responsibilities under the proviso, and the most straightforward way is simply to give up some of what they now own.

So what does all of this suggest once we move from our hypothetical island into the real world? Although interpreting the proviso's implications in real circumstances is never easy (leading many to reject natural property rights as unworkable), the implication seems to be that existing property claims are always complicated by considerations of fairness toward newcomers, and that these limitations are especially sharp for those whose wealth comes primarily from natural resources in their unaltered condition. This suggests that those who claimed that indigenous peoples initially held more land than they could claim ownership over probably have something in their favor (cf. Simmons 2001, 246–48), at least so long as there were some in need, as seems to have been true.

Yet we should not move from this apparent implication of the proviso to the claim that anything like European colonization as it occurred was morally permissible. European colonists clearly were not justified in taking land through force and fraud with very little regard to established patterns of indigenous life, nor did they have any claims that indigenous peoples should create immense empty tracts for them rather than simply allowing them to fill gaps in indigenous use patterns. Nor could European states claim that indigenous holdings were somehow uniquely egregious in regard to the proviso. Given the relatively rigid class structures of Europe, most of them maintained by political power rather than market transactions, Europe's first order of business should have been to provide something for its own poorest members, rather than first to hold out the promise of cheap lands elsewhere as a way of profiteering and defusing domestic tensions. After the American Revolution, when these European class systems were left largely behind, the best arrangement would have been for the United States to have made arrangements to acquire excess indigenous lands through treaties or below-market purchases, and then to have redistributed these lands for free to those who would otherwise have started out life with nothing. There were some hints of this process in this case, particularly in homesteading laws, but these were always incomplete and at any rate very rarely took indigenous interests into account.

So it is not entirely absurd to believe that the Lockean proviso required indigenous people to transfer some of their land to those who would otherwise have inherited nothing, but it *is* absurd to believe that the historical process by which this dispossession actually took place was anything close to justified. Indeed, there is considerable evidence that indigenous peoples were quite willing to share their land with settlers so long as those settlers were willing to honor established patterns of use and to treat indigenous inhabitants with respect (e.g., Williams 1997). The failure of the process, it seems fair to say, owed far more to European greed and aggression than it did to indigenous unwillingness to share with those in need.

So all of these counterfactual histories suggest that Waldron (1992, 23–25) is right in arguing that some reductions of indigenous holdings would have been necessary by the present day had no injustices ever occurred, and that contemporary indigenous peoples would not have inherited rights to everything their ancestors once claimed even in a fully just world.[20] What this suggests, in conjunction with the earlier argument that property rights can fade with changing usage patterns, is that indigenous peoples may not be entitled to the return of all historical lands even where this could be acquired without displacing anyone (e.g., as in some underpopulated areas), nor that they are necessarily entitled to monetary compensation sufficient to buy back all the lands that were expropriated. But exactly what these limits are is difficult to say—determining the proviso's specific implications is far from straightforward, even if we know that it would have required some reductions. As I will try to show at the end of the next chapter, other considerations may make this decision easier, but these uncertainties cannot be removed entirely. For the present moment, it seems fair to conclude that indigenous claims for the return of historical lands seem to remain extremely relevant, even if they may ultimately be more limited than they first appeared.

Before closing, I should also note the dangers that the ambiguities and uncertainties in the Lockean proviso may pose for the accuracy of my conclusions. Indigenous readers should rightly treat my claims throughout this book with caution, but the uncertainties present in the Lockean proviso may create special dangers that my conclusions will be unfairly weighted against their interests. This is always a danger in any moral argument, particularly when principles cannot be specified with much exactness. I hope I have not made such an error, but I am sensitive to the dangers of doing so nonetheless.

IV. Property, History, and Indigenous Understandings

I have not shown, of course, that all morally serious people must accept natural property rights; what I have tried to show is what a theory of natural property rights can plausibly say about the contemporary relevance of historical ownership. Since this is a relatively compressed discussion, there are certainly places in which additional subtleties could be introduced or alternative answers to certain questions considered, but it seems sufficient to suggest that arguments for historical ownership should be taken very seriously. If indigenous peoples want to make claims using the language of property, they will probably have to be justified in something like this way and will probably include something like these limits and possibilities.

These conclusions may remain too weak for some indigenous scholars, or the foundations used to support them may have unwanted implications for other aspects of political or social life that are not worth incurring (e.g., in allowing excessive room for individualism or economic inequality), but this is likely something indigenous actors will have to decide for themselves. (In practice, indigenous scholars seem to think carefully about these issues each time they make public arguments.) It may be that indigenous actors will be better off in the long run to forgo the leverage offered by the language of ownership and to focus instead on persuading surrounding populations to accept alternative conceptualizations of relationships with the natural world (see, e.g., Borrows 2002), but the prospects of succeeding in such attempts should not be overstated (see Hendrix 2007). How these trade-offs should be negotiated—and how deep the gulfs really are between Western notions of ownership and indigenous relationships to land—are not ultimately decisions that I am correctly placed to make. While I will offer some thoughts in this regard in Chapter 8, they will be no more than this, and nonindigenous readers should not misinterpret them as anything stronger. It may be that some other language will be more useful in capturing what indigenous philosophers have in mind over the long term; I hope I have at least outlined here what can plausibly be said within the language of *ownership*.

In the next chapter, still using the language of ownership, I will consider how this concept might or might not help us to make sense of political authority over persons and over particular territorial spaces. As I will try to demonstrate, ownership and authority are linked to one another in important ways, but not in the straightforward manner that much of our ordinary debate about political territory seems to suggest.

FOUR

OWNERSHIP AND SOCIAL CONTRACT

Although I will assume in this chapter that something like the set of natural property rights outlined in the previous chapter is defensible, the spirit of such ownership matters more here than the specifics. If natural property rights in some form are defensible, then the possibility that indigenous nations have claims to regain some historical lands has potentially important implications for existing political boundaries. If authority derives from ownership, as many indigenous arguments seem to suggest, then settler states have no moral rights to govern many of the lands they now rule.

But is political authority really linked to ownership in this way? If so, what is the link between the rights to control holdings within states and the jurisdiction of the state itself (cf. Buchanan 1991, 107–9)? In this chapter, I will investigate the potential links between natural property rights and political authority and will argue that the links are less direct than they may seem. As I will try to show, questions about the political status of indigenous peoples cannot be answered by direct reference to historical ownership, but must be evaluated through some approach that looks more carefully at the bases of political authority in the present day. This more mediated linkage does not imply that historical ownership is irrelevant, however—in fact, historical ownership likely provides grounds for revising many existing political boundaries if indigenous peoples have rights to a fully or partially separate status for other reasons.

I. Original Contract

It is not surprising that many people regard authority as somehow linked to ownership. As I noted when discussing international law, states often talk as if they owned the lands they control in unproblematic ways, and the ways in which jurisdiction over territory has historically been traded between states suggest that some kind of ownership really is at stake. Indeed, most states could easily be accused of subscribing to a double standard—they outlaw separatism on the ground that the country "owns" the territory on which it sits, while ignoring the claims of indigenous peoples who point out that many of these lands were not given willingly.[1] So a great deal of ordinary language and political practice seems to suggest that political authority and ownership are somehow closely related, without ever really specifying what this relationship might be.

In the first part of this chapter, I want to consider the possibility that political authority is justified simply by ownership and that the property rights involved are the same natural property rights considered in the previous chapter. As I noted there, arguments for natural property rights do not assume that such rights must always be held by individuals; groups can also hold these kinds of rights when they are engaged in collective projects. But simply because groups can hold such rights does not demonstrate that any of them actually do hold such rights. Demonstrating this requires some explanation of how the relevant kinds of collective projects came about and how they have been maintained through time.

For political philosophers, the best-known attempt to link ownership with political jurisdiction is probably that associated with John Locke, who not coincidentally was foundational in defending the natural property rights outlined in the last chapter. According to some readings, Locke (1980, § 95–122) argued that states historically acquired ownership of their territory through an "original contract" made by individuals previously living without a government; these founders transferred the property they already owned to the new political community, and the government of that community thereafter had partial rights to all land within its boundaries.[2] As Charles Beitz (1980, 491) notes, "the original contract is not only an agreement among human beings to obey a government, it is also an agreement to submit their property to the government's jurisdiction."

While these original contractors could in theory have transferred their property entirely to the new political unit, Beitz argues that Locke had something more limited in mind. Those who transferred partial rights to their property retained the everyday right to buy and sell, but transferred to their state many of the other rights associated with ownership of their lands: "The founders mutually agreed to restrict their rights in their land in various ways designed to insure that anyone who came on the land would be obligated to obey the government's laws. Perhaps they promised neither to violate, nor to permit others to violate, the laws while on the land; more importantly, they transferred to the government the right to demand the compliance of anyone else who comes upon the land" (Beitz 1980, 492–93). On this story, neither states nor individuals hold full rights to any properties within a particular territory. The state has a kind of partial ownership and might be conceptualized as a senior partner in regard to all of the individuated parcels within its boundaries. Individuals retain the right to buy and sell their land and to alter it in a broad variety of ways, but they have transferred whatever elements of ownership are necessary to ensure political control by the state. Whichever properties states acquire partial rights to in this way form their political territory; lands they are not part owners in are beyond their political control.

Since partial property rights have been transferred, those who come after the founding generation are only eligible to inherit property with political authority attached, rather than the full rights their forebears once owned: "One's choice is to accept the inheritance together with the obligations that travel with it, or not to accept it at all" (Beitz 1980, 490; cf. Gale 1973). For the same reason, states have rights to enforce their laws against anyone who visits within their boundaries, since these persons would violate the state's property rights if they failed to acknowledge its authority. If individuals want to escape the authority of a state, they must sell or abandon whatever lands they partially own within its boundaries and pursue a life elsewhere—they cannot demand that the lands they "own" be put under the authority of some other state, because the elements of property rights associated with political rule were already transferred away long before. Only the state, which holds those rights as owner, has the authority to give away or sell rights to political rule. (Since its political rights are only partial, however, it can presumably transfer political jurisdiction without requiring those who retained the "individualized" portion of property rights to leave.)

I suspect that many of us think about the relationship between political jurisdiction and individual ownership in something like these divided terms. Yet this Lockean story is not as plausible as it may initially sound. While it seems to be a reasonable account of how state ownership *might* come about, in the absence of actual historical transfers it is no more than a story. As A. John Simmons (1992, 312n11) notes, any theory that purports to derive political rights from historical events has to care about whether those events actually happened: "Surely ... whether or not such rights have been transferred to government in any particular society is a matter for historical inquiry, not *a priori* pronouncement." Would we find actual incidents of transfer from property-owning individuals, with the terms of the transfer clearly specified, in the histories of any real state? This seems doubtful. At best, we might find a few incidents of quasi-contracts drafted under conditions of duress (Simmons 1979, 80–100; 1993, 232–48; cf. Brilmayer 1989), and even these would be rare; in most instances, states have simply enforced obedience without bothering to ask.

Even a promising case like the founding of the United States cannot be seen as an authentic original contract in this sense. Many of the colonists would have preferred to remain under British rule, and their forcible inclusion in the country (or flight into Canada) creates multiple complications if authority must be based on transfers of ownership. Indeed, even if all of the colonists had willingly joined the United States, most of those involved would not have held justified property rights to the areas they inhabited anyway, since these had often been stolen from indigenous peoples not long before. So if we want to talk about an "original contract" even in this most promising of cases, we cannot mean this as a literal transfer of property—at best, "original contract" can be shorthand for some more complex relationship.

Since the primary difficulty with this argument is factual, it would be a mistake to state definitively that *no one* in the United States or elsewhere holds these kinds of divided property rights. If the United States had legitimate rights to acquire property for its citizens (very much an open question at the moment), then those parts of the American West that it acquired without injustice might legitimately have been owned first by the country as a whole. By extension, American citizens who came to occupy them later might have acquired something like this kind of partial and divided property rights to their individual holdings. If so, the United States would have a reasonable answer if any of these persons sought political independence with their holdings—it could say that these persons held only limited property rights that did not allow for such exit. But if we cannot show that the United States had rights to rule and acquire property in the first place, I am not sure this is a plausible characterization. Otherwise we would have to regard the whole enterprise as an unjust conspiracy, and anything resulting from it would likewise deserve condemnation.

What about the collective property of indigenous peoples? The conclusion that virtually no states can be traced to original contracts makes the relevance of searching for such contracts less obvious, since indigenous nations will have to acknowledge some further ground for authority if they accept that the states surrounding them have authority over their nonindigenous citizens. Still, this need not be fatal; it may be that original contract is only one basis for authority or collective property among others (albeit perhaps the best one). So it is worth considering whether indigenous peoples can plausibly be characterized as having been "founded" through these kinds of initial agreements. If so, their rights of ownership might have a superior status to whatever justification the United States can provide for authority over the rest of its citizens.

But could we find any examples of such contracts? Although it is more difficult to rule on this question for indigenous peoples, once again there are reasons for doubt. The obvious empirical difficulty is the relative lack of clear historical data. While oral histories and early colonial documents provide substantial information about some foundings, such as that of the Iroquois Confederacy by Deganawidah, these usually involve alliances and mergings between preexisting groups rather than an initial Lockean agreement between previously independent individuals. Since few indigenous leaders had the massive coercive capacities characteristic of states with which to enforce their will, it is more easily conceivable that indigenous groups were founded through something resembling initial voluntary agreements. Even so, we can do no more than speculate that a few such cases may have occurred. Speculations like this are a doubtful basis for something as important as collective ownership of property, particularly if this ownership is also going to justify political authority.

There are also good reasons to doubt that indigenous peoples would historically have seen the need for this kind of transfer of ownership from individuals to the collective. While some indigenous peoples seem to have made arrangements for permanent and transferable ownership of land, most apparently did not, instead allowing a wide variety of redistributions of usage rights on the basis of need (probably much beyond what the Lockean proviso would have required). There is, of course, nothing entirely unfamiliar in such practices, since most states have historically regarded land as subject to political redistribution as well, but it still seems unlikely that indigenous peoples ever regarded themselves in anything like idealized Lockean terms. (Indeed, thoughts of original contracts among initially unaffiliated persons would probably seem strange to anyone not already influenced by Lockean ideas.)

But even if we would find such transfers, either for states or for indigenous peoples as collectives, would this really accomplish what might be claimed for such contracts? Probably not, if we accept some version of the Lockean proviso on ownership as outlined in the last chapter. Although it is difficult to determine exactly what the Lockean proviso means, some things can almost certainly be ruled out, and transforming collective ownership smoothly into political authority is one of them. To see why this is so, imagine an extreme case, in which a society was contractually founded several hundred years ago by a few thousand people in the grip of religious fervor. Each of them joined willingly, transferring their individual property to an extremely strict theocracy, which was intended to provide citizens with only some limited control over material goods. (The contractors, let us say, believed human nature to be generally sinful and shortsighted and thought this was the best hope for reducing the incentives to selfishness.) Now step forward to the modern day, when several million people live within the theocracy's extensive territory, universally in deep poverty. The theocracy allows exit, since it claims to own only the land rather than the citizens themselves, but most of them are too poor to leave, and the theocracy does not provide them with resources to do so, since no citizens inherited rights to take anything back from the collective.

Would the Lockean proviso be met in this strange situation? Even if the proviso is difficult to interpret with any exactness, it nonetheless seems hard to imagine that it is. (It may also be hard to imagine that anyone would actually transfer property in this way, but we should not allow that to give us an easy escape from the question.) Even if all persons are provided with goods in quantities equal to "enough and as good," the fact that they are persistently unable to control how these goods are used suggests that the proviso's terms are not met at all. Despite the material goods these people are guaranteed by the theocracy—let us assume it ensures that each person has a house and nutritious if bland food—it seems difficult to say that any of them actually own *property*, particularly if ownership is strongly linked to uses of natural freedom, as I argued in the last chapter. Thus, the Lockean proviso raises requirements not only about the quantities of material goods that individuals have access to, but about the degree to which those goods are actually under their control and subject to their choices.

This does not suggest that collective ownership is generally impermissible, of course, or else we would be in the strange position of arguing that historical transfers from individuals to organizations were somehow less legitimate than transfers of individuals amongst themselves, and thereby moving into some very different framework for understanding ownership. What it does suggest is that collective property rights can only form part of a larger pattern of property holdings, in which individuals have a chance to acquire "enough and as good" in material goods that they can actually use as they will—in other words, to acquire goods that they own more or less completely, without the interference of others. This leads to a striking conclusion: if collective ownership is really what justifies political authority, then newcomers must have rights to acquire property free from all political authority when they wish to do so (cf. Tideman 1991; Steiner 1998, 64–69). Moreover, states cannot simply eject those who refuse their authority from the state's collectively held territory; if these individuals must somehow receive "enough and as good," their present state will have just as much responsibility to help provide for them as everyone else and will be most directly placed to ensure that they receive property in the right way. This suggests that states must allow individuals within their borders to either purchase or receive in direct transfer some lands that are free of all political authority, if they wish to pursue this option.

There are doubtless multiple ways that states, indigenous peoples, and other kinds of collectives that want to exercise political authority could try to meet these requirements without entirely sacrificing territorial contiguity (for example, by making arrangements that only lands along their margins would be given up, or by creating ungoverned "state-of-nature zones" where dissenters could go—Beran 1987, 104), but none of these seems likely to be sufficient. At one level, it may violate the proviso if individuals are able to acquire property holdings only at great distances from the places where they grew up. But even if this is not a problem, nothing will stop these individuals who wanted to acquire property free of political authority from creating their own kinds of collective ownership in their own turn. (They might, for example, want to form strict theocracies.) So if political authority is really founded on ownership, there will be nothing to prevent state boundaries from shifting quite often or to prevent new states from coming into existence on the margins of the old with each new generation.

I suspect this is not what any of us have in mind when we think of political authority, even if a few people might find the possibility exhilarating (e.g., Simmons 1993; cf. Beran 1987). I also suspect that most people will not be terribly impressed with such arguments, since they did not believe that so much really hung on original contracts anyway. As I will argue below, this reaction is probably because state control over particular geographical areas is not really justified by ownership in any strong sense, and because "state ownership" is only a conceptual shorthand for a more complex relationship between individuals and particular structures of authority. Before proceeding to this argument, however, I will consider another method by which states might come to own their territory. This is the possibility of widespread individual consent to contemporary political orders, which renders concerns about rights to acquire property free of all authority under the proviso much less pressing. As I will try to show, this method too, whatever its natural appeal, must ultimately fail.

II. Ownership and Contemporary Choices

If original contracts are absent in practice and of dubious value in principle, the natural alternative is to argue that such historical foundings were never so important anyway; what matters instead is how living people in each era have felt about the authority of a particular political society. Democratic states often claim to rule with "consent of the governed," and if existing people really accept the political orders in which they live, it seems unimportant what the history of a particular state may have been. One might conclude that, whatever the injustices in the foundings of a particular state, they have been washed away by the consent of those who have come after.

But this suggestion plays off the ambiguity between two meanings of "consent of the governed." For many people, this phrase invokes democratic principles, suggesting that authority is legitimate when it reflects the wishes of democratic majorities. But while democratic governance matters a great deal (as I will argue in Chapters 6 and 7), this argument evades the central question where the justification of authority is concerned, because it assumes that democratic processes allow minorities to be ruled against their will. Can we plausibly describe the rule of the United States over American Indian nations as justified by "consent of the governed" if these nations reject their current status? This seems unlikely. An argument about democratic voting, then, is not really an argument about consent to be ruled; it is instead an argument about how laws should be made once authority has already been established through some other means.

If we want to take "consent to be governed" literally, we must show that each individual has consented to particular political arrangements, and that those who refuse to consent are allowed to live their lives free of political authority, or even to form new political units among like-minded persons if they so desire.[3] If states really wanted to ensure this, they would have to reorganize themselves in fundamental ways. As A. John Simmons (1979; 1993) and others note, the clearest way to receive unambiguous consent is to present each individual with a choice situation where the options are transparent to all involved and where the choice is not at all coerced. If, for example, states approached all prospective "citizens" on their eighteenth birthday with a carefully written, exhaustive contract detailing the legal relationships between citizens and the state, while offering each person lands free of authority if he or she desired this, then those who chose to consent would clearly be bound. But of course no state offers anything like this unambiguous, noncoercive choice—most simply enforce laws against everyone within their territory, whether these laws have been accepted by specific citizens or not.

Although state authority cannot be based on universal consent in contemporary circumstances, we should not therefore conclude that many states lack the consent of most of those they rule. Many people try in a variety of ways to offer consent, and these ways seem binding even they are not linked to clear mechanisms for escaping political authority. (Individuals may value their country in the absence of an ideal choice situation, much as partners in an arranged marriage may also love one another.) Consider, for example, the Pledge of Allegiance in the United States. Reciting the Pledge cannot be taken as a clear contractual act, because refusing to do so does not allow one to escape authority in any way.[4] But it would nonetheless be absurd to deny that many people recite these words with intentions to actually accept political obligations—how else could one explain the social pressure faced by those who refuse to recite along with surrounding crowds? It is very hard to tell, since the markers are so ambiguous, which specific persons have attempted to offer their consent through the Pledge. But it seems mistaken to deny that many people have tried to commit themselves politically in this way and many others.[5]

So the point is not that *no one* consents, but rather that *not everyone* does. Some people simply refuse the authority of the state now claiming to govern them, and many would gladly form some other state or live without one if given the chance to do so. Given the complications of the Lockean proviso, these people cannot simply be ejected from the state's territory without receiving some alternative lands, but they cannot be ruled either. If consent is really the sole basis of political authority, all these people have to do is refuse to consent whenever states try to solicit this—states must thereafter withdraw any claims to rule them, and this is the end of the matter.

This may sound like a promising basis for indigenous claims, since indigenous groups often deny the authority of the United States over them, but on closer inspection it is less appetizing. At one level, the finding that the United States cannot justify its authority over its nonindigenous citizens raises questions about what principles indigenous peoples really want to advocate—unless indigenous peoples are willing to see the authority of United States over its nonindigenous population fragment, they will need to acknowledge other justifications for authority that may have implications for their case as well. But what if indigenous peoples are untroubled by these disruptions to the authority of surrounding settler states? Can indigenous nations really be justified on the basis of consent if states cannot?

Since consent theories focus on how authority over individuals becomes justified, they have no obvious role for preexisting political collectives created in other ways, meaning that indigenous peoples must meet the same standards as states in demonstrating rights to govern their purported members. Could indigenous nations claim this kind of consent?[6] Clearly they could not in current circumstances, because the acts available to individuals for demonstrating it are all too indeterminate. The most obvious marker, at least in the United States, would be those who choose to retain a tribal affiliation, since no one is legally required to do so. But this leaves uncertainties—what exactly are individuals consenting to, given the contemporary intermediate status of American Indian political units? Are they consenting to tribal governance on its current terms, or to something stronger, such as to the group's traditional methods of governance or some reconstituted version of them? Are they consenting to a particular kind of political organization, or to some more diffuse notion of "groupness"?

For indigenous nations to ensure that they are based on the consent of each member, then, they would have to make the conditions attached to membership absolutely clear, would have to provide property on noncollective terms for those who refuse, and so on. These actions would obviously pose the potential for further fragmentation of the territories and assets now held by indigenous groups and of those that may be owed to them in regard to historical lands. While it remains possible that indigenous nations could reform themselves based on consent in this way, the authority thereby gained would be relatively fragile, and all existing mechanisms of governance would have to be suspended until the status of individual members was sorted out in fully determinate ways.

Faced with the potential for severe fragmentation found in consent theories, most people will probably feel drawn to some middle position that gives political structures greater stability over time. Even if original contracts are usually missing and contemporary consent is always incomplete, does it really follow that political boundaries must be changed whenever a few malcontents want this? There is something obsessively specific about trying to trace political authority and collective ownership back to the choices of every single individual—wouldn't it be more useful to look for some account of political authority that has greater contact with the exigencies of real politics, where greater stability is often extremely valuable?

I believe that it does make sense to look for ways to justify this greater stability, and that consent cannot ultimately provide the grounding for a morally tolerable kind of political life (see Chapter 6 for a further defense of this claim). But we should be very clear about what is at stake in moving away from original contract or ongoing consent. If political authority is not literally justified by property rights that have been collectivized, then the linkage between political authority and ownership of land is more attenuated than it may seem. Political jurisdiction over particular territories will have to be justified on some other grounds than ownership, and we will need some explanation of what the relationship between individual property rights and political jurisdiction might ultimately be. At most, we will be able to speak of "state ownership of territory" as shorthand for some more complex moral relationship that rests on neither collectivized ownership nor universal consent.

To see the importance of the distinction involved, recall Ward Churchill's suggestion in the previous chapter that returning lands historically unceded by treaty would necessarily carry with it political authority over those lands. If the rights of political units to control particular territories are not automatically coupled to natural property rights, then it does not automatically follow that any transfer of political authority would be involved; the political question would have to be answered on some other grounds. It might be that the transfer of these lands would provide a justification for returning them to the control of indigenous political units, or it might not. Alternatively, it might be possible that the boundaries of indigenous political units could be expanded without any transfers of actual property rights.

In the remainder of this chapter and in chapters to come, I will consider an alternative justification for authority that gives neither consent nor natural property rights a foundational role, although both individual preferences and patterns of ownership will play important secondary roles. This justification will derive from natural moral duties that are posited to preexist all political structures and that bind individuals and groups whether they would prefer to be bound or not.[7] (In being prepolitical and universal, these duties are "natural" in the same sense that property and other rights were posited as natural in the last chapter.) This justification asserts that states and other types of political units (i.e., indigenous nations as governing organizations) are necessary to the achievement of fundamental moral goals—particularly in ensuring that all people are protected from violence and other forms of wrongdoing—and that individuals are required to contribute to their maintenance for this reason. Particular distributions of political authority will be subject to evaluation based on how well they achieve this goal.

I will defend this understanding of political authority in Chapters 5 and 6. Here I will limit myself to evaluating the relationship that this argument entails between natural property rights and political jurisdiction. As I will show, that the relationship is mediated does not entail that none exists or that indigenous peoples can have no claims to extend political authority over lands they once controlled. The relationship between historical ownership and contemporary political boundaries remains important, even if it is less direct than it may sometimes seem.

III. State Authority and Public Lands

If ownership is not going to serve as the fundamental justification for political authority, it is probably not essential to have any particular position on the character of property rights at the nonpolitical level. What I will say about political duties in future chapters will be entirely consistent with a conception of nonpolitical ownership as natural rights, or as Humean or Rousseauian social conventions, or as just about anything else. But since I have been discussing property rights as natural rights with a substantial historical component, I want to continue to do so through the remainder of this chapter, to see where these kinds of rights might fit if they are justified on their own terms. As I will try to show, their implications might be very interesting even if they do not provide the fundamental justification for political authority.

The natural duties I will outline in chapters to come are duties to aid others in protecting themselves from violence and other forms of wrongdoing. These duties, I will argue, justify states or something resembling them as a necessary mechanism for meeting their requirements. So would states justified in this way need to hold any property themselves, in the sense of the term I have associated with everyday individual ownership? If states are justified by their role in protecting everyone's moral interests, including their rights to property, it seems that whatever they hold must be fairly limited (or else their "protection" will be self-defeating). But what could they legitimately acquire in this regard?

It seems clear that they will have to acquire some properties in this sense, since they will need to own some public lands if they are to serve in this protective capacity. If states are to provide a workable judicial system and police protection, for example, they will need some public buildings such as jails and courthouses. If natural duties require us to support states, then they will also require that we help them in gaining control of these kinds of holdings. In the absence of a market, this would have to occur through direct transfers; in the presence of markets, on the other hand, these duties seem to require support through monetary taxation instead, so that states have funds to support their operations and to acquire the properties that are necessary in doing so. (Taxation is clearly preferable to direct redistribution, since it allows individuals to have more control over what they will do without and allows states to better seek out the right kinds of property for purchase.) The degree to which such duties would allow states powers of eminent domain is a more difficult question, but I will assume here that states are justified in exercising such authority, so long as they exercise it only in cases of real need rather than of mere convenience.[8] States can also presumably use market mechanisms to acquire properties that are not fundamental to their basic function, so long as they do not use taxation to do so—they can, for example, finance the purchase of properties through user fees, lotteries, or other mechanisms that individuals contribute to only if they wish. Although these options raise some interesting possibilities about what states might pursue in this regard, I will leave them aside here.

If states are justified in funding the acquisition of necessary properties through taxation, how much property would this entail? The answer depends on how widely we construe the rights and moral interests that individuals have. Consider something like national parks and wilderness areas as mechanisms for facilitating environmental protection, for example. Presumably the Lockean proviso puts limitations on the degree to which contemporary individuals can destroy the future viability of the world for generations to come (since they will also need chances to live a tolerable life), but should these kinds of properties be legitimately owned by a state in fulfilling its basic function of protecting individual rights? It seems to me that they could and should, but exactly how trade-offs should be made between different kinds of risks over the long term is not entirely clear.

Wherever we set this limit, it seems likely that many of the public properties owned by actual states could not be defended as directly necessary to fulfilling their role in this way, nor were they financed by user fees or similar voluntary measures. Does this mean that these holdings are illegitimate? Perhaps not, if one can show that these kinds of holdings are *indirectly* conducive to the protection of rights by playing an important causal role in fostering an environment in which rights are more likely to be protected. If we believe a sense of shared nationality facilitates the protection of rights (Miller 1995), for example, then certain historical monuments may be permissible or even required. Moreover, any tolerable state will likely have to be governed by a roughly democratic set of governing institutions, and this probably provides reasons to allow more extensive moral latitude for public ownership. Since democratic citizens will have to feel empowered and in charge of their collective life, it probably makes sense to permit them a few moral misjudgments in how much property they allow states to acquire, so long as these are relatively limited.

There is certainly a great deal more that could be said about how these limits should be conceptualized and what they might imply for specific circumstances, but the upshot of the argument is that states justified by natural duties would never have claims to actual ownership of most of their territories. They would be morally required to own some kinds of properties, and morally permitted to own others, but the total of the two would have to remain fairly limited in regard to the holdings of their citizenry—otherwise they would begin to infringe too much on the holdings of their citizens.[9]

Would these same kinds of limitations apply to indigenous nations? Insofar as they want to act as political organizations with authority akin to (or the same as) that of states, the answer would seem to be yes, at least so long as natural property rights exist that should be protected by whatever political organization exists. This is not a conclusion that I feel entirely comfortable stating, but it does seem to follow logically from the argument so far. If one could demonstrate ongoing consent to collective ownership in unambiguous terms, strongly collectivized property would not raise any concerns, but in the absence of such a demonstration, it seems that indigenous nations must ensure that publicly controlled properties within their territorial boundaries will remain relatively limited, or restructured accordingly when they are not.[10] In practice, it is probably easy to understate the degree to which indigenous individuals now hold individualized property rights within the boundaries of their own political units (at least in the United States), and I want to avoid any caricaturing of indigenous peoples as inevitably hostile to such rights, but the conclusion that indigenous political units are limited in this way may nonetheless be a troubling one.

The best way to avoid this conclusion if it is unwanted, I think, would be to begin from premises very different from those on which natural property rights rely—but the likely cost of doing so is to abandon what seems to be the most plausible defense of historical ownership within the resources of Western philosophical thought. I do not want to claim that such alternative arguments are impossible, or that they have not already been made, but they do seem to me difficult to reconcile with the apparent weight given to historical ownership in many indigenous arguments. In Chapter 8, I will try to suggest the shape of an alternative argument for a very different conceptualization of relationships among individuals and parts of the natural world, but this argument will invoke a very different set of premises than those usually attached to discussions of property and ownership. Ultimately, then, whatever discomforts come from the conclusions about property rights that I have reached here probably arise from using the language of ownership rather than making these claims in some other way, and whether these costs are worth bearing is a decision that only indigenous groups themselves can make.

IV. States and Trusteeship

If states justified by natural duties would be entitled to hold only relatively limited property rights for themselves, how should we conceptualize their right to exercise jurisdiction over particular geographical spaces? These rights are clearly not the same ownership rights held by individuals and nonpolitical collectives, since political authority is intended to protect these more prosaic rights. Indeed, a strictly conceived natural-duty justification of political authority seems to suggest that states should have whatever boundaries are most conducive to their effectiveness in protecting individuals from violence and other kinds of wrongdoing (cf. Waldron 1993).

While it will take the whole of Chapters 5 and 6 to outline the character of these duties fully, the fact that they are adopted as an alternative to consent should make it clear that they assume no direct relationship between individual preferences and political boundaries. Since political authority is decoupled from individual preferences in this way, a very strict natural-duty argument might permit or require boundaries to be shifted around individuals or whole populations despite their wishes. Imagine, for example, that I go to sleep one night as an American citizen and wake up in the morning as a citizen of Canada, after the two states determine with absolute certainty that this change would allow them to protect their citizens more effectively. On a strict natural-duty account, I would have no complaint about this, even if everyone in my area disagreed with the change. For a natural-duty account, then, no intrinsic moral relationship exists between an individual and his or her government—it is simply the government he or she lives under right now, and nothing deeper. (Publicly owned lands would pose some problems when boundaries are reshaped in this way, but it would be distracting to consider how this could occur in such instances.)[11]

In practice, recognizing when particular states are really performing their role well is far more difficult, and it should give us pause whenever populations become severely dissatisfied with the political arrangements they live under. In Chapters 7 and 8, I will argue that a natural-duty justification of authority should allow an important secondary role for self-determination, so long as the process is regulated by careful procedural safeguards. While the details of this argument cannot be outlined here, it should be obvious that any role for a principle of self-determination creates a stronger relationship between populations and the political units that rule them—particular states are charged as trustees for specific groups of citizens rather than others (cf. Buchanan 1991, 107–9).

If states are trustees in this sense, then the relationship between individual property rights and specific political boundaries is stronger than it would be under a more narrowly construed understanding of natural duties. Even if states are permitted only to hold limited public properties themselves, they are in a unique position as the political bodies specifically charged with the protection of their citizens' rights, including their property rights. If citizens hold justified property rights to the land they inhabit, then the continued support of these citizens justifies strong state rights to territorial integrity, even if portions of their territory are neither held as public land nor occupied by day-to-day inhabitants. We might imagine, for example, a state where a few citizens own vacation homes on a small island far from the rest of the state's territory. A trustee state could legitimately govern these islands, because they are owned by its citizens. Even if these islands are never actually occupied, other states have no claim to extend jurisdiction over them, unless the current state abjectly fails in its foundational purpose of protecting rights.

If states are trustees for their citizens and their citizens' property in this sense, then they can also make claims on behalf of individuals who were deprived of their property by other states or political units, either for the return of those property rights *simpliciter* or for the alteration of jurisdictional boundaries when required. Consider indigenous claims for the return of historical lands. If some lands were actually returned, this would create a large and partially contiguous block of properties in many cases. If some principle of self-determination allowed indigenous groups to reclaim their historical independence, this kind of trusteeship would also allow them to extend their authority over such newly regained lands. (Even if these properties are owed to individual Indians as the inheritors of shares in historical holdings, it would make sense to return these lands to these nations as collectives first, after which they could sort out more specific holdings among their individual members.)

We can also imagine an opposite case, in which a trustee state would have rights to rule a particular population but not the area where these people now live. If, for example, a state ruled a population that had recently and egregiously displaced a set of property owners from a wide territory, that state would be required to return these lands to their rightful owners, even though it had authority over the particular citizens involved. (For reasons discussed in the last chapter, this case does not describe most nonindigenous citizens in the United States, given the passage of time and other factors, but even here some recent expropriations might fall under this description.) In either case, the result of this shift would look very much like a change in "state ownership," and one might plausibly speak of it this way so long as the more complex relationship for which it is shorthand is kept clearly in mind.

To recapitulate, the relationship between natural property rights and political authority produces two justifications for political control over particular geographical spaces. The first kind is more straightforward—states own public lands in order to fulfill necessary functions and as decided by democratic populations. Only in this simple case are states literally the owners of any property. The second justification involves separate elements that resemble "state ownership" only in conjunction. States have rights to rule the particular populations for whom they are trustees, and these populations either have property rights to the areas they inhabit or they do not. They may also have property rights to areas that they do not now control. In instances where disjunctions occur, states will be required to return lands to the groups holding justified property rights to them and to change their boundaries accordingly. Property rights, then, can matter a great deal for evaluating existing relationships of authority—even if states are not the owners of their territory in any simple sense, the contours of ownership may play a large role in determining the character of particular political boundaries.

V. Repairing Historical Wrongs

The remainder of this book will be dedicated to arguing for the conception of political authority sketched here and to determining the character of rights to self-determination, so it would be premature at this point to rule on the question of whether indigenous peoples ultimately have rights to political independence from the states now ruling them. But it should be clear that where property rights have not been dissolved by the passage of time, states justified by their role in protecting rights will endanger their authority if they fail to return expropriated properties to their rightful owners. Before concluding this chapter, then, I should revisit the question of how much land American Indians and other indigenous peoples might be entitled to regain in current circumstances, whether these properties will ultimately form the territories for independent political units or something more limited.

How much land might American Indian nations and other indigenous peoples be entitled to receive in the present day if we accept some version of natural property rights? While Churchill argues that all lands unceded by treaty should be returned, the arguments of the previous chapter suggested several reasons why any lands returned must be more limited. The first problem, as Jeremy Waldron (1992; 2003) notes, is that historical ownership can fade after a long term of nonpossession. This suggests that indigenous nations have lost rights to directly reclaim lands that are now occupied by nonindigenous property holders, at least in most instances. (Particularly important sacred lands might be a partial exception—see Hendrix 2005a.) On the other hand, nothing about this kind of contemporary occupation would prohibit states from reacquiring many of these lands for indigenous peoples through market mechanisms, or from providing indigenous peoples with the resources to do so themselves. So this limit, while it reduces the prospects for direct transfer, may have less effect than it seems.

The second kind of limitation on the return of historical lands comes from the reductions to original ownership required over time by the Lockean proviso. As I noted in the last chapter, the proviso suggests that those who acquire substantial resources from their natural state face special burdens in justifying these holdings over time, given the proviso's requirement that those with property provide some to those who would otherwise be left without "enough and as good." But, as I also noted, it is not easy to determine exactly how much of a reduction this might have required had these lands not been expropriated by other means; the proviso's requirements in general are difficult to interpret with any specificity. So we can say that American Indian holdings would have been reduced, but cannot say with certainty by how much.

In the remainder of this chapter, I want to consider a third complication, one with a somewhat different character from the other two. So far I have presented a simplified model of historical expropriations, proceeding as if the expropriation of indigenous lands could be easily isolated from other kinds of injustices in determining what may be required in the present day. But this kind of simplification, however necessary it may be for purposes of clarification, is also artificial in important ways. In the real world, history contains myriad complex and often overlapping injustices, which greatly complicate our judgments about what contemporary justice might require. Given these complexities, it seems likely (albeit surprising) that indigenous peoples have *benefited* from injustices committed against others in a variety of ways. This has to be taken into account in determining what properties indigenous nations may be entitled to regain.

Ideally, an entitlement conception of ownership would want us to trace all justified property holdings back to original conditions of just acquisition while demonstrating that no expropriations occurred between the original acquisition and the present. If history had proceeded in that way, then each contemporary person would have rights to own whatever he or she inherited, plus or minus whatever that person was able to gain through his or her own trade and labor and minus whatever limited amounts were necessary to meet his or her obligations under the Lockean proviso. In short, some people would hold large amounts of property while others would hold very little, and no one would have any complaints about the ultimate results of these freely made transactions. But this is not the kind of world we live in—ours *has* included expropriation and fraud, and not only against indigenous peoples.

Consider, for example, the effects of slavery in the United States, along with the extended period of segregation that followed it. Clearly it is no accident that African Americans as a group remain far poorer today than most of their fellow citizens (see, e.g., McCarthy 2004; cf. Thompson 2002). In the case of slavery, the problem was not expropriation of land, but of labor—slaves were forced to work without gaining anything from that labor beyond mere survival, and their "owners" were thereby able to create fortunes that in turn formed the basis for business investments and all sorts of further transactions of wealth. These kinds of transactions, by shaping the kinds of goods that were produced on the market, therefore shaped relative prices and by extension gave illegitimate advantages and disadvantages to third parties who had themselves committed no injustices (Waldron 1992, 12). Given these effects on prices and goods produced, simple involvement in this kind of tainted market economy ends up giving some people more property than they would otherwise have, and some less.

Slavery and segregation are clearly not the only injustices that have tainted contemporary property holdings, even if they are the most easily recognized. Many people throughout history have been victims of simple force and fraud, while others have suffered through adverse legal regimes such as unjust tax laws. (Whatever just tax law might consist in, the laws have been sufficiently variable to ensure that some people have been treated unjustly by them.) Nor do these tainting effects stop at national borders. In an era of worldwide markets, injustices in one place can affect market prices far away and so call into question the holdings of those who might never have known of the original injustice at all.

Given this complexity, it is not easy to recognize whether any individual involved in a market system is on balance the victim or beneficiary of historic injustice. In broad terms, it seems reasonable to conclude that those who are relatively wealthy have likely benefited from historical injustices, whether they were aware of this or not, while those who are generally poor can have likely generally suffered from historical injustices, if not directly then through the distortions caused to market prices and so on. But this is far from a perfect gauge—consider someone who starts out life in extreme poverty and is able to become wealthy by inventing something valuable or creating works of art with a very wide appeal. Is this person on balance a beneficiary or a victim of past injustices? It is not easy to be confident one way or the other.

This ambiguity carries over to the contemporary holdings of indigenous peoples. Although they have often been less fully involved in markets than other groups, most indigenous peoples are nonetheless deeply enmeshed in the present day, and this necessarily complicates the force of their claims for the return of historical lands. This is particularly clear in the case of those few American Indian groups in the United States that have recently become relatively wealthy through gaming operations—the wealth received in this way seems owed at least in part to nonindigenous individuals who have suffered from past injustice, and once enough of this wealth has been acquired in this way, we can no longer regard the group involved as on balance the victims of historical injustice. They seem instead to have become those who have *benefited*, even if they never intended to do so, and if they have sufficient wealth, they seem required to give some property to others rather than to receive it. Other kinds of involvement in market relationships at both the level of indigenous individuals and that of indigenous groups as collectives create the same kinds of complexities, albeit in less acute form because they are usually less profitable. Since most indigenous peoples remain relatively poor, it is probably fair to say that they remain on balance the victims of historical injustice rather than its beneficiaries, but these considerations nonetheless weaken the force of claims for the return of expropriated properties, and in the case of extremely successful casino-operating groups may be sufficient to obviate them entirely.

In the face of so much uncertainty about the legitimacy of contemporary property holdings, what should be done? Many philosophers, adopting some kind of Rousseauian understanding of property (see Chapter 3), simply decide that we are better off ignoring history and focusing instead on the future. But even those who want to defend an entitlement theory of ownership acknowledge the need to use simplified mechanisms for dealing with historical expropriation. Robert Nozick (1974, 153n), whom I discussed in the last chapter as a forceful advocate of an entitlement conception of ownership, concedes that widespread redistribution is probably appropriate in such circumstances. The clearest solution, if we assume that everyone's property rights could be equally tainted, would be to redistribute everything equally as a way of starting over once and for all. But realistically, this attempt would do far more harm than good, since it would pervasively disrupt existing economic structures and plans and likely leave everyone worse off in the long run.[12] Achievable solutions will almost certainly involve something more limited and will always represent an incomplete attempt to deal with the difficulties of history.

What, then, does all of this tell us about indigenous claims for the return of historical lands? We should not conclude that it makes such historical claims irrelevant once and for all. When indigenous groups remain relatively poor, as most do, they seem entitled to something to raise their economic circumstances closer to the level of wealth typical for the society surrounding them. And this has important implications: if they have residual property rights to their historical lands, simple monetary payments are not the most appropriate solution for them (cf. Simmons 2001, 242–43). When their historical lands are publicly held and therefore easily returned to them, it is these specific lands to which they retain property rights and that they should regain. Only when such lands are really unavailable do alternative arrangements become reasonable.

If the amount of current public holdings in the traditional lands of particular indigenous groups is very large, how much land should be returned in this way? (This is not a mere hypothetical in the United States, Canada, or Australia, each of which holds extensive public lands.) Much will depend on the contemporary wealth or poverty of the indigenous group involved, but it does not seem absurd to envision something like a doubling of the contemporary indigenous land base in many circumstances, and probably more for those groups that are most extremely impoverished.[13] This is far less than all of the lands that were historically expropriated, and less than some indigenous peoples may be satisfied with, but it would nonetheless be extremely significant. If indigenous peoples have rights to self-determination that allow them partial or full separation from the states now ruling them, the implications are more profound yet—structures of authority will need to be extensively reconstructed, and the result will likely be a political order with a far clearer indigenous cast to it. It is to questions about the nature of political authority and self-determination that we now turn.

FIVE

DUTIES TO AID

In the last chapter, I argued that political authority cannot be derived from ownership in any straightforward way, nor, given existing circumstances, can it be derived from "consent of the governed." I argued instead that political authority, whether that of existing states or indigenous peoples, must be justified by natural moral duties that somehow override the preferences of specific individuals for one political order or another. Yet there should be something troubling in the claim that natural duties allow individuals to be ruled despite their wishes; this apparently uncaring attitude toward the desires of those ruled has created severe injustices in the past, not least against indigenous peoples. Given that this principle seems almost custom-made for abuse, one could legitimately suspect that its adoption here is simply a show of confusion or bad faith.

I hope it is something more than this, but as always the claims of this chapter should be treated with caution—my own perspective as a nonindigenous citizen of the United States likely poses strong temptations toward problematic conclusions in ways that may be difficult to recognize. In this chapter and the next, I intend to investigate carefully the content of the duties posited in the previous chapter, as well as the route by which they might provide a justification for political authority (whether of states or indigenous peoples as political collectives) rather than for something more limited. To think about these issues, I will use the work of eighteenth-century philosopher Immanuel Kant as a jumping-off point. My goal will not be detailed exegesis of Kant's texts or an attempt to determine once and for all what Kant "really thought," but to see what justifications he offers for political duties and how plausible they might be on their own terms. As has been true throughout this book, my goal will be to understand these questions through the theoretical resources of Western philosophical traditions, rather than trying to determine what indigenous understandings of the relevant duties might be or how they might compare to Kant's arguments. While I will try to make these comparisons in Chapter 8, there are few guarantees that I will do so well; I hope these chapters will nonetheless help indigenous readers to see where my arguments diverge from their own, and by extension where my errors lie.

As I will try to show, there are actually multiple ways to understand Kant's intentions when trying to justify political authority, and tensions and uncertainties will probably plague any attempt to derive authority from natural duties that override individual preferences for one political order over another. I will argue that the relevant duties must be conceptualized as *coercible* duties to aid other people in protecting themselves from violence and other forms of wrongdoing, a troubling conclusion that nonetheless seems difficult to avoid. Given the apparent lack of alternatives, I will consider in the next chapter what such duties might tell us about particular ways of organizing political authority and about the claims of authority currently made by existing states over indigenous peoples.

Any viable duty-based justification of political authority will have to show that individuals can be ruled despite their wishes in at least some situations, and demonstrating this is no easy task. If the arguments of this chapter or the next fail, we will be back to individual consent, with all its difficulties, or else will need to probe more carefully into indigenous conceptions to see whether they offer options not considered here (see Chapter 8).

I. Natural Duties and Moral Disagreement

Indigenous readers who know Kant's work well will have reasons for skepticism because his arguments are extremely conservative toward the stability of existing states. For Kant, it is irrelevant how particular political orders came about—indeed, whether countries were founded through original contracts or conquest or something else is not only irrelevant, but dangerous to consider: "Whether a state began with an actual contract of submission . . . as a fact, or whether power came first and law arrived only afterwards, or even whether they should have followed in this order: for a people already subject to civil law these subtle reasonings are altogether pointless and, moreover, threaten a state with danger" (Kant 1996, 95). The basic implication is obvious: individuals and groups should be ruled by the state now exercising authority over them, however that state came into being. This includes indigenous peoples—whatever injustices were perpetrated against their ancestors have no relevance now, and living persons have no rights that political arrangements should be different.

Why does Kant reach this view? Unfortunately, it is not entirely clear what Kant's intentions were, and he himself seems undecided in some places. There are multiple ways of understanding his argument, and each of them points in a different direction for understanding and evaluating authority. Since I am interested in thinking about natural duties rather than ruling on Kant's "real view" once and for all, I will take each of these possibilities as a potential method of defending such duties. As I will try to show in this chapter and the next, none of them proceed as smoothly toward Kant's conservative conclusions as he believed. Whatever Kant's own firmest commitments, a natural-duty justification of authority is neither so straightforward nor so conservative as it may appear, and does not justify the claims of existing states over their indigenous populations without far more discussion.

Let me begin with the least plausible interpretation of Kant's argument. At points, Kant seems to suggest that something in moral disagreement itself requires all persons to live under the authority of some state, despite their particular wishes. In this vein, he notes that people will naturally disagree about the moral principles they should follow and about how to organize their social lives. At times, he seems to suggest that since all people are fundamentally equal, the moral principles that each of them accepts will have equal footing as well. Until some system of law is established, there is no way of deciding between these multiple views: "However well disposed and law abiding men might be, it still lies *a priori* in the rational idea of a such a condition . . . that before a public lawful condition is established, individual human beings, peoples, and states can never be secure against violence from one another, since each has its own right to do *what seems right and good to it* and not to be dependent upon another's opinion about this" (Kant 1996, 89–90; emphasis in original). Notice that Kant does not say only that each person will *in fact* do whatever seems right and good to that person—he says that each has a *right* to do so. The only way to end this disagreement is to create a system of shared law, which will then govern everyone's relations rather than their own individual judgments about how social interactions should occur. Those who refuse to submit willingly to this legal order must be coerced into doing so, whatever their wishes.¹

While this seems like a plausible argument at first glance, things are not really so simple. What happens once everyone has been brought under the authority of a state, by force if necessary? Kant argues that laws must be created to reflect the "general will" of the society, which is justified virtually by definition: "The legislative authority can belong only to the united will of the people. For since all right is to proceed from it, it *cannot* do anything wrong by its law" (Kant 1996, 91; emphasis in original). But what exactly is a general will, and how is it related to real-world structures of governance and actual policies? Kant cannot mean simply that a majority should always get its way—majorities can sometimes end up supporting extremely oppressive laws (as indigenous peoples within democratic states are all too aware), and for that reason no theory presuming that a majority is *always* right can have even minimum plausibility.

In fact, it would be surprising if Kant really meant something like this, because many of his voluminous writings are dedicated to showing in great detail that certain kinds of moral arguments and principles are better than others. Kant argues at length that we should act only in ways that reflect the basic freedom and equality of others, and this seems to provide clear grounds for condemning any laws that fail to do this, no matter what their source. Indeed, Kant makes clear that the general will does not always reflect what people really want, so that it cannot simply reflect the will of the majority: "For if the law is such that a whole people could not *possibly* agree to it . . . it is unjust; but if it is at least *possible* that a people could agree to it, it is our duty to consider the law as just, even if the people is at present in such a position or attitude of mind that it would probably refuse its consent if it were consulted" (Kant 1991, 79; emphasis in original). This is all somewhat mysterious. What kind of will is involved here, if not the actual will of those being ruled?

The most plausible solution (for which there is ample textual evidence) is that Kant believes real people will make a variety of errors in deciding what morality requires, but also believes that certain principles of social organization would be accepted if all of those involved were thinking clearly and honestly. (Alternatively and less demandingly, certain principles would be easily rejected if they were thinking in this way.) This is not an implausible claim, and virtually any kind of moral argument has to presume something like this idealized agreement, or else the practice of offering reasons for particular moral judgments makes no sense. The problem is that this kind of test is necessary for evaluating moral principles in general and has nothing uniquely to do with law or political authority. Thus, saying that laws should reflect the general will in this sense is akin to saying that state laws should reflect those moral principles that are most defensible to rational people after intensive discussions and careful thinking. It is undoubtedly true that we want laws to be defensible in this way, but this tells us far too little about specific state policies. Which laws and principles would be accepted in this way, and how are they related to the decisions of real populations operating through state authority? Once we outline these ideal principles clearly, we can use them to evaluate the characteristics of real states and may discover that many specific laws are unjust or that the boundaries of existing states should be revised. So we are still left with the questions of how moral disagreement can play a central role in justifying authority and how reference to a general will can help in real cases.

The short answer is that neither can be of much assistance.[2] If actual political processes reliably produced a general will in the more fundamental sense just outlined, it would be obvious why all persons were obligated to maintain those processes and why any questioning of present arrangements would be necessarily dangerous. Where existing political processes are not so reliable, however, we need some other sort of argument that makes no claims about the inherent acceptability of political decisions. Indeed, suggesting that the coercive structures of state authority can be used to resolve moral disagreements through law does not even take disagreement seriously, since it offers no substantive reasons for those who reject these arrangements to change their mind—it offers them only coercion. Appealing to the dangers posed by moral disagreement, on the other hand, may have much more purchase. But an argument about dangers requires relative judgments about the quality of actual states and does not automatically justify the continued existence of those that now exist or the continuance of their policies.

II. Natural Duties and Human Nature

At any rate, the argument from moral disagreement is probably the least plausible interpretation of what Kant really intended, even if his claims that citizens should never question the continued existence of their state do not seem defensible in any other way (see especially Kant 1996, 96–97). In many places, Kant seems to have in mind a more appealing justification for authority: that it is necessary to prevent violence and other forms of wrongdoing. In this argument, moral disagreement plays only a secondary role—it is one of the causes of conflict, but far from the only one.³

At many points, Kant asserts that humans are naturally conflictual and that this conflict will eventually persuade people to submit to state authority, if only out of self-interest: "Universal violence and the distress it produces must eventually make people decide to submit to the coercion which reason itself prescribes (i. e. the coercion of public law), and to enter into a civil constitution" (Kant 1991, 90). The real problem here seems to be not that people disagree about moral principles, but that all of us have a tendency to do things we know are wrong when we can avoid punishment, and governments must be designed to counterbalance that tendency. In Kant's words, "In order to organise a group of rational beings who together require universal laws for their survival, but of whom each separate individual is secretly inclined to exempt himself from them, the constitution must be so designed that, although the citizens are opposed to one another in their private attitudes, these opposing views may inhibit one another in such a way that the public conduct of the citizens will be the same as if they did not have such evil attitudes" (112–13). This seems like a reasonable conceptualization of the human tendency to harm others in ways we know to be wrong, and it does seem wise to plan for the worst in human nature. But why do these facts create a *duty* to live under the authority of a state, rather than simply a strong motivation for each person to join one through consent? If the dangers are really this high and people will recognize this, why not just allow them to affiliate themselves with a political organization for self-protection, rather than forcing them to do so?

There seem to be two possibilities here: either individuals can force others into a common political system as a form of self-defense, or else each of us is required to live under state authority as a way of helping others to receive the protections they need. At many points, Kant seems to be suggesting the first, in arguing that the absence of political authority makes every person a threat to every other and that each person therefore has a very broad right to self-defense: "No one is bound to refrain from encroaching on what another possesses if the other gives him no equal assurance that he will observe the same restraint towards him" (Kant 1996, 86). But on this formulation we don't have to wait until someone actually threatens us—each person can be forced into a political system in spite of having done nothing wrong, because there is a good chance that person eventually will: "It is not necessary to wait for actual hostility; one is authorized to use coercion against someone who already, *by his nature*, threatens him with coercion" (86; emphasis added).

Although this is a somewhat subtle point, it is worth noting that this argument does not actually provide a duty-based argument for authority—it says instead that *if* a person feels threatened by others, *then* that person, along with others who desire such protection, will have rights to form a political system that will defend them against those who prefer to remain outside of it. The steps necessary for self-defense need not include actually bringing everyone under the authority of whatever political organization these people create—self-defense seems to allow nonconsentors to be impacted insofar as this is necessary to protect the "insiders," and so would be consistent with leaving many people free from political authority if they could be localized into "authority-free" zones where they would be harmless to others (cf. Beran 1987, 104). Notice also that those who did not feel a need for political protections, or who did not want them on the terms offered, would do nothing wrong in defending their interests by force against those who did want them—and in fact they would have rights to use preemptive violence against these state-making people if they thought it necessary to do so!

Thus, this kind of extensive and preemptive right to self-defense would at a minimum have messy political implications, and it would not show that all persons actually have duties to live under political authority. Moreover, it seems implausible on principled terms. Unless all people have moral duties that somehow require them to live under political authority, an argument like this seems to allow some people's desire for self-defense to override everyone else's moral interests. Most people who write about rights of self-defense believe they must be construed relatively narrowly and that preemptive actions should be allowed only when a person poses an inescapable and imminent causal threat (e.g., McMahan 1994; Ryan 1983), neither of which seems true here.[4] It is one thing to claim that I can defend myself by coercing someone else who is bearing down on me, about to do harm—quite another to, say, hit someone from across the street with a rock simply because that person might be dangerous. If people have such an open-ended right to defend themselves through preemptive coercion against anyone who seems even remotely threatening to them, do they also have rights to directly violate someone's bodily integrity in the interests of self-preservation, say by removing kidneys they suspect they will eventually need from passersby (cf. McMahan 1994)? Clearly not, or else any moral limitations on what we can do to others would be entirely moot. Rights to self-defense have to have some limits, or else trying to determine what moral protections we should all enjoy is simply a waste of time—anyone will be eligible to do anything, no matter how coercive, simply because he or she feels threatened.

So it cannot be simply self-defense that provides Kant's justification for authority, even if the fears of attack it invokes are surely important.[5] Ultimately, the argument from self-defense focuses on the wrong side of the equation—what we need are moral duties demonstrating that people have no right to cause such fear in the first place and, more strongly, that we have positive duties to ensure that other people remain tolerably safe.[6] The most plausible interpretation of Kant's argument, and the one I will argue for throughout this chapter and the next, is that our duties to care for others require that we take positive actions to preserve them, and that this requires us to live under a well-designed regime of political authority. Much of the benefit of a good political organization is that it allows each person's dangerous tendencies to be used for positive ends: "It only remains for men to create a good organization for the state . . . and to arrange it in such a way that the self-seeking energies are opposed to one another, each thereby neutralizing or eliminating the destructive effects of the rest" (Kant 1991, 112).

The narrow interpretation of our positive duties toward others in this regard would be that we must live within a well-constructed state to limit our own bad behavior. Essentially, we have to create the conditions under which we ourselves can be prevented (or at least strongly dissuaded) from causing direct harm to other people. But this formulation still seems too limited, particularly if there are other ways to reduce my own tendencies toward harming people (for example, with some device that administers an electric shock whenever I try to engage in such behaviors). The problem is that this formulation seems to be too narrowly focused on what *I* might or might not do, and to be indifferent toward whether anyone else is actually enjoying any protections or not. While I do not want to state definitively that this self-focused interpretation of the relevant duties cannot provide a viable justification for political authority, taken on its own it seems underwhelming and also a bit callous toward the actual suffering of other people.

The stronger possibility, and the one I want to endorse, goes beyond fears about my own bad behavior to the claim that all of us have positive responsibilities to aid others in protecting themselves. According to Robert Pippin, this is what Kant had in mind all along: "Assuming that I have a duty to respect others as ends in themselves, then, Kant is arguing, I cannot be indifferent to others' *not being* so treated, to their being treated as means in the pursuit of material ends" (Pippin 1997, 82; emphasis in original). Even if we ourselves are able to avoid harming anyone, we nonetheless should be concerned when other people will be victimized without our aid, and we must therefore plan accordingly: "Our obligation to treat other rational beings as ends in themselves entails a further obligation—to do what we can to establish the most favorable conditions under which others are treated as ends in themselves" (82). Each of us has a responsibility to ensure that other people are being treated as humans worthy of respect rather than as simply targets for anyone who wants to victimize them.

While I do not want to spend an extensive block of text arguing for or against Pippin's interpretation of Kant, this does seem to me the most promising basis for arguing that natural duties somehow require us to live under state authority. If these duties toward others exist, then it is not enough if I myself endanger no one's life or other moral rights. I must make sure that everyone else will be tolerably well protected no matter what I myself do. Given reasonable expectations about human behavior, it seems likely that someone's life or moral interests will always be in substantial danger and that mechanisms for deterring and restraining criminals will always be necessary. This broad concern with other people also allows us to intelligibly bring concerns about moral disagreement back into the picture—if there are reasons to believe, as I will argue in Chapter 7, that democratic mechanisms will tend to produce the most justifiable laws in the long run, then each of us has reasons to value democratic rule, even if we recognize clearly the kinds of errors such a system will produce in many specific policies. I will say much more later about these specific concerns and the ability or lack thereof of states to achieve these goals. But it should be clear already that broader duties to aid provide a more robust set of possibilities for justifying particular political arrangements than do more narrowly construed duties.

These duties to aid other people in protecting themselves are nonetheless relatively demanding, and for that reason their moral plausibility deserves to be evaluated in greater depth, particularly if they are to provide reasons for coercing people to live within a state that they personally reject. (I suspect that most indigenous readers will be more responsive to claims that we have strong responsibilities to others than will many nonindigenous readers, although they may contest any claim that states actually help in fulfilling these duties. Those who accept such duties without further argument could perhaps skip to the beginning of Chapter 6 without danger, but the following discussion should be helpfully clarifying even for those who need no convincing.) There are at least four concerns that need to be resolved in regard to such duties. First, it is not entirely clear that there really are such duties to aid others, rather than simply to abstain from certain actions—if I am not directly harming anyone, am I really doing anything wrong? Second, duties to aid may hold only when we can aid others without significant dangers to ourselves, and this point may raise questions about the capacity of these duties to justify something so important as political authority. Third, others may not have rights to coerce us into fulfilling these duties, and if these duties cannot be coerced, state authority will be far harder to justify. Fourth, and perhaps most obviously, states may not provide the best mechanism for rendering this kind of aid in all or any circumstances, and even if states as organizations are capable of doing so, the states we actually have may fail miserably in this regard. I will devote the next chapter to the last concern, which is the most difficult to answer and the most important for the current project. In the remainder of this chapter, I will consider the first three concerns to see what kinds of duties we might really be working with and whether we can rightly be coerced if we fail in them.

III. Duties to Aid

The first and in some ways most difficult question to adjudicate is whether we have any duties to aid others at all, even when there are no costs or dangers to ourselves. Most of us probably accept at least some duties to aid, based on our recognition that other people are vulnerable beings like us who can sometimes, through no fault of their own, find themselves in dire situations from which they simply cannot escape without assistance. In somewhat stiff language, Kant formulates the duty to provide economic assistance to those in severe need in this way: "The maxim of common interest, of beneficence toward those in need, is a universal duty of human beings, just because they are to be considered fellowmen, that is, rational beings with needs, united by nature in one dwelling place so that they can help one another" (Kant 1996, 202). Can we really look carefully at others who are in distress and not feel required to aid them if we can? Perhaps, but this seems like a very strange thing to want to do—if we believe everyone's life is sufficiently worthy of respect that it would be wrong for us to endanger it, surely we must care when others endanger it.

To test one's intuitions in this regard, consider as a concrete example someone walking through a park who sees a child, presumably in the grip of psychosis, attacking another child, whose face is turning blue and who seems to be unconscious. Let us assume that our passerby teaches classes on nonlethal self-defense and is extremely skilled at restraining even fully grown adults without harm to them or danger to himself. If our passerby does nothing and instead continues on his afternoon walk while the child dies, it seems hard to believe that he has treated this child with the moral respect due another human being in a time of extreme danger. If it is wrong to strangle other people to death, it seems bizarre and inconsistent to remain unmoved when someone is suffering this fate and we could stop it with few costs or dangers to ourselves. (Perhaps it is less wrong to allow people to die in this way than to kill them ourselves, but it still seems deeply illegitimate.) I am not sure I have a ready answer for someone who simply denies that we should ever care about how others are treated—but I also fail to see how such callousness could ever be a compelling moral position.

I suspect that very few people would really be willing to reject duties to aid entirely, and at any rate I will proceed as if no one *should* reject them. The more serious worry, I think, lies not in the abstract existence of such duties but in determining their moral limits. Few cases are really as free of danger as the one above, and even in this case it is not impossible that the self-defense instructor could be harmed if his luck is extremely bad. If duties to aid are to have any political importance, they will have to require that we sometimes accept serious risks to ourselves; states, for example, often conscript soldiers and send them to fight, and while we need not accept this as morally legitimate, we must take these kinds of costs and dangers into account nonetheless. How, then, should we conceptualize the limits of our duties to aid?

According to philosopher John Kleinig (1976, 385), the strength of our duties to aid in specific circumstances is conditioned by the *magnitude* and *imminence* of the danger to the threatened person compared to the dangers to ourselves. The magnitude of the harm can itself be evaluated along two further criteria, the *importance* of the moral interest at stake for both parties and the *irreversibility* of the likely damage. On this standard, our passerby would have a duty to help the endangered child, who will die if he does nothing, even if there is some small chance of harm to himself, but he would have no duty to rescue one child's doll if another had stolen it, even if it would require only a momentary delay on his part. Clearly, there is an extremely wide array of cases in between, but these standards at least give us some tools for thinking about these questions.[7]

Perhaps more importantly for current purposes, Kleinig's distinctions can also help us clarify the degree to which duties to aid leave us moral discretion in different circumstances. In cases where dangers are imminent and of high magnitude, such as when someone is suffering assault, our duties will be narrowly focused on the harms to this particular person, but the risks will also usually be far higher. Thus, we will usually have reasons based in our own safety to avoid attempting to render aid. Our discretion here lies in determining what the dangers are, rather than who deserves our aid. Less imminent dangers, on the other hand, allow individuals much more choice about which set of persons to help and involve much more uncertainty about which persons are most in need, but they also allow far greater chances for social coordination and innovative solutions so that the dangers to ourselves of rendering aid can be sharply reduced while that aid's reliability can be increased. In such circumstances, our judgment may often focus on which set of social institutions (e.g., charities or states) to support. Nonetheless, such discretion cannot be entirely open-ended—if some ways of rendering aid are far more reliable than others, our duties presumably require that we support them rather than less effective mechanisms. This may be particular important in justifying states rather than other potential political structures, as I will try to show in the next chapter. I will assume for present purposes that states are appropriate in this way—if not, we must return to consent theory and all of its difficulties, or else find some entirely new way of thinking about the grounds of authority.

IV. Duties and Coercion

Even if one agrees that we have duties to aid others in protecting themselves, and even if these duties require that we make arrangements to aid persons in need, it does not necessarily follow that others can coerce us into rendering such aid, which is necessary if natural duties are to provide an alternative to consent in justifying political authority. If such duties exist but cannot be coerced, then we could legitimately argue that those who refuse to consent to an aid-procuring state are "bad people," but we would be able to do no more than exhort them. All of us are familiar with noncoercible duties in everyday life (such as the duty to love one's children), and they are thought sometimes to be simply matters of personal virtue—things that we really should do but that bring no consequences (outside of a guilty conscience) when we fail in them. Indeed, the quotation above from Kant, about the importance of economic beneficence to those in need, actually appears in a section outlining virtues that are not subject to coercive intervention. So are the duties to aid I am positing here legitimately coercible?

According to Kant's central distinction, duties of right (or, as we might say, justice) can be enforced through law and other forms of coercion, while duties of virtue cannot. But why do particular duties fall into one class rather than another? Kant's (1996, 25) own formulation is puzzling: "One can locate the concept of right [or justice] directly in the possibility of connecting universal reciprocal coercion with the freedom of everyone." As Robert Pippin (1997, 62–63) notes, this could mean either of two things—either that, empirically speaking, coercion can affect whether people actually fulfill a given duty or not, or that coercing the duty must be "morally possible" or something of the sort.

On the first standard, duties of right are simply those where coercion can actually affect people's performance or nonperformance. Thus, for example, Kant (1996, 156) claims that "ethical duties involve a constraint for which only internal lawgiving is possible, whereas duties of right involve a constraint for which external lawgiving is also possible." There are obviously some duties that simply cannot ever be coerced, such as honoring one's parents or listening seriously to the ideas of others, because they involve attitudes of mind that are naturally resistant to direct coercive intervention (at least with present technology).[8] But there are probably also some duties that could be coerced but should not be—for example, there may be mechanisms to keep persons from violating marital duties by cheating on their spouses (cf. 61–62), but it seems hard to believe that such coercion would be appropriate even if it were possible (Pippin 1997, 62–69). Surely there are some duties that we simply should not apply coercion to, even when this is empirically achievable.

The alternative and more plausible possibility is that effectiveness provides only a necessary condition for the acceptability of coercion rather than a sufficient one, because only some duties deserve to be coerced (Pippin 82–91). On this interpretation, one can legitimately use coercion against acts that, "when considered universally would make a . . . society of autonomous agents *impossible*" (Pippin 1997, 86; emphasis in original). In other words, what would happen to human life if everyone were allowed to perform a certain kind of act or omission?[9] This test can be applied to all duties, whether to act positively in rendering aid or to act negatively in abstaining from certain acts. In that light, the coercible negative duties normally attached to individual rights are easy to understand. It would be hard to imagine a society of autonomous agents in which coercion could never be legitimately used against would-be murderers, for example. Of course, we cannot take Pippin's suggested standard of "impossibility" too literally. Even if we can imagine rare circumstances in which a society of autonomous agents might be possible without rights to use coercion against would-be murderers, the extreme unlikelihood that such a society could exist seems sufficient to make the case.

Would a society of autonomous individuals be extremely unlikely if duties to aid others were not eligible to be enforced through coercion? Although giving up impossibility as a standard leaves us with some uncertain questions about when the relevant threshold has been crossed, duties to aid seem coercible, at least in principle, because a universal failure to aid others in need would leave many people unable to protect themselves in a wide variety of circumstances. This may be especially true of certain vulnerable populations, such as the young, the old, and the ill, who would be obvious targets if no one were required to render them assistance in any circumstances (see the next chapter). But since the notion of coercible duties to aid is unfamiliar, the case is somewhat difficult to evaluate in the abstract, and our fuller judgments may depend significantly on the options that exist for attempting to enforce these duties, as well as on other details of practical politics—if attempts at enforcement will prove especially unwieldy, we may want to forgo them even if they seek to achieve valid goals (cf. Wellman 1996). The question of what our options for coercing duties are, and how well they might fare, will thus form the whole of the next chapter (and in some ways the remainder of the book).

One objection can be defused before we go any further, however, and this is the charge that enforcing duties to aid will necessarily do more harm than good, as demonstrated in so-called Good Samaritan laws, which punish persons who fail to render aid. To see the problem here, imagine our self-defense instructor walking through the park once again. This time he fails to save the child despite his absolute certainty that he could have done so with no danger to himself. Although this person is not the direct cause of the victim's death (cf. Mack 1980), it seems reasonable to regard him as a "guilty bystander" (McIntyre 1994) who has committed a serious moral wrong. But could we design a regime of criminal law to punish such people reliably without punishing in the process a far greater number of innocents? It seems unlikely that we can. Criminal guilt, after all, requires at least some degree of intentionality, and it is usually far easier to prove what people did than what they failed to do. How often will we be certain that bystanders recognized the need for their aid, and how will we be able to recognize the kinds of dangers they believed were involved? Over the long term, there would be a very high probability of deciding many cases in the wrong way and therefore of punishing in wildly inappropriate ways.

But while these difficulties may provide an excellent case against trying to punish guilty bystanders after the fact, they are not necessarily applicable against other efforts to coerce duties. Coercing individuals into paying taxes and otherwise supporting a state is quite different—it is largely concerned with the *prospective* protection of rights, and in these cases we will rarely need to prove anything about the motivations of particular persons who are required to fulfill their duties. Arguments against Good Samaritan laws thus do not commit us to rejecting coercible political duties, despite the initial comparisons we may draw between the two cases.

Nonetheless, it would be unwise to dismiss the possibility that attempts to coerce such duties in the political case will also face serious difficulties of achieving their purposes. If enforcing such duties through coercion is what states and other kinds of political organizations are intended to do, it matters a great deal whether they do so effectively enough, and in the right way, to be morally justified by our duties, and it also matters whether mechanisms exist for reducing the dangers that they themselves may pose. Simply arguing that duties to aid are coercible is an important step in evaluating political authority, but it leaves much still to be decided in chapters ahead.

V. Duties and Moral Foundations

Some readers may be unconvinced by this discussion and may deny that any duties to aid exist or that they are ever sufficiently important to allow coercion when individuals fail to meet them. If these duties to aid cannot be defended or are necessarily too weak, any argument that political organizations can claim authority over everyone within a particular territory (in the absence of consent) will have to rely on narrower arguments about self-restraint in the face of individual tendencies toward harming others, or on some version of the self-defense argument. (Perhaps some version of the argument from moral disagreement could also be attempted, although I do not see how it could succeed.) I see both of these alternatives as too weak to me to do the job asked of them, but in the absence of moral duties of the right sort, we will have to fall back on consent, and if so, should begin to consider seriously how this might be achieved with the fewest possible dangers (see, e.g., Simmons 1993, 241–43; Walzer 1970, chap. 5).

As should be obvious from the fact that I have proceeded to this point, I think rejection of coercible duties to aid would be mistaken. While there are deep questions involved here about the fundamental character of moral principles, this view of our natural duties does seem to express the goal of treating all people as valuable in themselves far better than the alternatives might. Those who deny duties to aid others adopt what might be seen as a particularly one-sided view of morality, one that accepts serious inconveniences to ourselves in avoiding direct harm to others but that allows very few inconveniences in protecting others from harm by third parties.

The more serious worry lies not in the existence of such duties, but in our ability to put reasonable and compelling limits on them. The value of moral rights lies precisely in their ability to mark out a sphere for individual action,[10] something that duties to aid seem to threaten by providing a ready pretext for innumerable incursions into this space. Thus, the implications claimed for such duties must be watched with some caution, and their coercibility must be allowed only when the alternatives involve serious violations of rights that cannot be prevented in any other way. In the next chapter, I will try to show that a relatively narrow construal of such duties seems sufficient to justify the authority of states that are necessary to protect rights, and in Chapter 8 I will ask some broader questions about the limits of these duties. At each turn, readers should consider carefully whether the implied extension of our duties crosses the uncertain line into excessive danger (cf. Elfstrom 1983, 711–12), and what the implications might be for our political life if it does.

Although I have been working within Western conceptions of moral and political duties so far, and will do so for the next two chapters as well, I should say something in closing about my interpretation of indigenous conceptions of duties to aid, pending a further attempt in Chapter 8. My sense is that most indigenous viewpoints accept even stronger duties to aid than I have suggested here, but that most are also more wary of attempts to enforce these through coercive mechanisms, particularly given the historical ways in which states have behaved in trying to "help" indigenous peoples by coercively reshaping their values. I hope I can show in the next chapter that such duties to aid can be construed politically in nondangerous ways, but unfortunately I cannot promise that I will not inadvertently provide justifications for this kind of mistreatment. I hope indigenous readers will thus watch these arguments with special care so that they can recognize any points at which my argument goes astray.

SIX

AUTHORITY WITHOUT CONSENT

In the last chapter, I argued that state authority must be justified by natural duties to aid others in protecting themselves, a position adopted as an explicit alternative to consent. Yet simply showing that duties to aid exist, and that they are in principle coercible, leaves an important question open: do states really provide the best mechanism for fulfilling these duties? Given the historical mistreatment indigenous peoples have suffered at the hands of states, the dangers posed by states have to be compared seriously with the benefits. In this chapter, I will evaluate the general case for states as a form of political organization and consider what this case might tell us about the claims of real states over particular territories and populations, including indigenous peoples.

The central arguments in this chapter will be that natural duties really do require us to support states as a type of organization, and that they contingently require us to support stable democratic states where they exist, while requiring a more ambiguous response toward nondemocratic states. But the reasons for supporting the status quo are generally pragmatic ones involving the difficulties of widespread political change, and the presumption in its favor can be rebutted if mechanisms for peaceful and orderly revisions can be found. In Chapter 7, I will defend a procedural conception of self-determination, in which groups seeking a changed political status must pass multiple carefully designed referenda, and in Chapters 8 and 9 I will consider what this might say about the future status of indigenous peoples.

I. Against Authority

In the first part of this chapter, I will consider the value of states as a type of political organization claiming the exclusive right to enforce laws over everyone within a particular territory. This exclusivity is consistent with a broad array of federalist subdivisions, so long as the relationships between levels are clearly articulated and the mechanisms for adjudicating disagreements between them well established (e.g., in a supreme court). I will assume for the moment states that are governed in a roughly democratic way, with most important positions chosen by election, but details are not essential to proceed further—if states cannot be justified as abstract entities, then questions about exact balances in their governing structures are essentially moot.

Some philosophers deny that states are fundamental to fulfilling our duties even in the abstract. According to A. John Simmons (1999, 741–51; 1979, 29–38), for example, duty-based arguments routinely confuse *justifying* a state with demonstrating that it is *legitimate*. On this distinction, *justifying* a state means showing only that such an institutions can be beneficial and that people would do nothing wrong in choosing to create one through voluntary means (i.e., consent). A justification in this sense does not show that such an institution has rights to rule persons who have not agreed to its authority. Only a state with legitimacy has a right to rule real, specific persons: "A state's (or government's) legitimacy is the complex moral right it possesses to be the exclusive imposer of binding duties on its subjects, to have its subjects comply with these duties, and to use coercion to enforce these duties" (Simmons 1999, 746).[1]

The importance of this distinction might be made clearer by an analogy to marriage as a social institution. A justification for the practice of marriage, in Simmons's terms, would outline the value of a long-term commitment to a person one loves and would show why formalizing these commitments might have beneficial effects (e.g., in increasing trust and fostering shared expectations). It would not demonstrate, however, that any real person had ever engaged in this practice, nor show that anyone *must* do so—and certainly would not show that one party can coerce another into this! Justifying the social practice of marriage, like justifying state authority, would show only that such a practice is a good idea, but the only way to know if real persons had such obligations would be to discover who had gone through the relevant ceremonies and procedures. For Simmons, demonstrating that a state is legitimate requires the same attention to the histories of real persons, and this investigation seems likely to demonstrate that many people never agreed to be ruled. (Obviously, I do not mean to imply that marriage involves authority or coercive rights for one party or the other. The commitments involved are quite different; it is only the central distinction between good ideas and actual commitments that I mean to invoke here.)

According to Simmons, natural moral duties are simply too generalized to create the kinds of authority states seek to claim. Since existing states are not justified by original contract or ongoing consent, he argues that "existing governments regularly and systematically wrong their 'citizens,' no matter how many good qualities (some of) these governments may otherwise display" (Simmons 1993, 266). He concludes that the only plausible position in regard to existing states is "philosophical anarchism," meaning, in simple terms, that we should regard state claims of authority as illegitimate but do little to directly undermine them (e.g., through violence) until they can be replaced by more satisfactory political units (e.g., Simmons 1979, 195–201). Simmons (e.g., 1992, 326–52) does accept duties resembling those I outlined in the last chapter, and acknowledges that these require caution in any efforts to revise existing political structures: "[Philosophical] anarchism, then, insists that persons in existing societies are by no means free to do as they please, but rather that they have a wide range of moral duties that will overlap considerably (i.e. require the same conduct as) their nonbinding legal duties" (Simmons 1993, 262). But whatever moral benefits they might provide, existing states simply cannot arrogate to themselves authority in the absence of consent, and any attempt to do so is an impermissible exercise of force. While natural duties limit our responses to the injustices of illegitimate states, they are far from sufficient to grant these states the authority they claim.

How plausible are these objections? Perhaps surprisingly, I think some of them are clearly correct. Simmons is right, for example, in objecting that natural duties cannot create strong bonds between particular states and particular persons. Although states usually claim specialized relationships with their citizens, Simmons is clearly right in arguing that natural duties cannot ground such an intensive linkage. If states were founded on consent, they could legitimately claim such a relationship, since each person would have consented to one state and not states in general. (Likewise, one's commitments in marriage are to particular person, not "spouses in general.") Such a relationship cannot be created by natural duties, which by their nature are generalized toward all persons. If states are essential to fulfilling the duties we owe toward all other people, wherever they may be, it is hard to see how individuals could be strongly tied to one political organization rather than another (cf. Waldron 1993), although there are doubtless important secondary reasons for legal categories of citizenship to remain relatively clear. As I will argue below, this finding may have important implications in showing that state claims to unquestioned territorial integrity cannot be sustained.

Simmons is also surely right in objecting to strong state claims of authority, if authority is understood as the ultimate and unquestionable right to decide what laws should exist. If states are justified by our duties to aid others in protecting their basic moral interests, then laws and policies can be justified only as they help to achieve these goals. Any laws that fail to protect basic moral interests of citizens are at best unnecessary and at worst unjust. (While I have generally assumed that these basic moral interests should be formulated as natural rights, nothing in the present discussion hinges on this exact formulation.) Our natural duties provide obvious grounds for skepticism about particular state policies and claims of authority—if laws and policies are not conducive to this central purpose, we should ask whether they can be justified at all. Exactly how skeptical we should be is a harder question. As I will argue below, our duties likely require that we support democratic states, and this will require us to support or at least tolerate some laws that are indefensible on their own merits.

How limiting is this rejection of state claims to strong authority, however? I believe it is far from radical, even if it does challenge some of the more extravagant claims states make. Few of us would want to endorse rigid views like those of Kant (1996, 96–97), apparently reached from his views on moral disagreement: "The reason a people has a duty to put up with even what is held to be an unbearable abuse of supreme authority is that its resistance to the highest legislation can never be regarded as other than contrary to law, and indeed as abolishing the entire legal constitution." Few people except political elites and philosophers have probably ever propounded such positions seriously, and we are doubtless better off without them. The conclusion that state claims should be approached with caution, however, does not imply that we usually lack good reasons to follow their laws (as Simmons acknowledges), nor that we are morally free to refuse them support. If our duties require that we aid others, and if states turn out to be best mechanism for doing so, then we will have few options in deciding whether and how to support their operations (cf. Wellman 1996). If states are necessary in this way, then our relationship toward them when they enforce some unjust laws will be contradictory in complex but familiar ways—we will be entitled to resist the specific wrongs that they do, but required to preserve the larger system of protection they provide. Even if states are not legitimate in the strong sense Simmons associates with consent, then, it does not follow that they thereby lack good claims to exercise lawmaking and enforcement activities. Deciding whether these activities are justified depends instead on a different sort of question, one that is largely factual: do states really provide the most effective mechanism for fulfilling our natural duties, or could those duties be better fulfilled through some other means?

Simmons argues that states are simply not necessary for meeting the requirements of our duties, because other mechanisms can fare just as well. According to Simmons, questions about the relationship between duties and state policies can be evaluated only on a case-by-case basis: "Only in the *very rare* instance when a government program provides the only way for an individual to do his or her duty can the government legitimately require participation and payment" (Simmons 1993, 265; emphasis added). He believes that states as a whole are not essential in this way, and therefore lack rights to rule those who personally reject their authority: "Even if the problems Hobbes, Locke, and Kant identified can't be solved without states (a point on which I am not fully convinced) all these problems of life without states can be solved without unanimous participation, either at the state's formation or later in its history. States can be made without the participation of all in their territory, and they can be maintained without the participation of all in their jurisdictions" (Simmons 1999, 766).[2] If this is true, then individuals who choose to fulfill their duties through alternative means are doing nothing wrong, and states cannot simply force them to contribute despite their choices. We seem to be back to consent once again.

I believe that Simmons is mistaken, however, both in his claim that states can operate successfully without authority over everyone in their territory and about our ability to fulfill our duties through nonstate mechanisms (cf. Wellman 1996). Consider the ways in which we might aid others in protecting themselves: we might give them weapons or teach them to fight; we might watch over them ourselves; we might form a posse of volunteers to protect them; or we might pool our resources to hire someone whose task it is to protect them. The last two possibilities seem the most promising, unless we have rare skills at self-defense (and other-defense). A posse system might be relatively effective in a small community, where dedicated individuals have reasons to care deeply about one another's interests (see below). If many people need to be protected, however, we will likely fare much better if we hire professionals who operate a large-scale system of protection—after all, we will not always be able to gather a posse on short notice, or be able to coordinate our actions in emergencies, or have the specialized knowledge necessary to recognize criminals.

These are things that states are supposed to do, and making a case for them would seem quite easy if they could be guaranteed to do only these. In practice, the issue is more complicated: states are never perfect, and "professional rights-protectors" can easily become "professional rights-endangerers." So our ultimate judgment about their value will have to be a relative one, which takes into account the problems to which they are prone compared to the potentially achievable alternatives. The best way to proceed, then, is to outline those alternatives and see what dangers they may hold.

Since I am concerned at the moment with states as organizations claiming exclusive rights to enforce law within a given territory, the alternatives must differ in some of their features. Two possibilities seem worth considering here. The first is to take individual choice very seriously and to allow multiple rights-protecting organizations within the same territory; the second is to create or revive vigorous communities that can protect their members without any powerful, centralized mechanisms of coercion whatsoever.[3] I will argue that neither provides a workable replacement for territorial states in ordinary circumstances. While the second ("communitarian anarchism") may remain a viable option where small and isolated communities still exist, it probably does not apply to indigenous peoples within the United States, Canada, or Australia, even if it may apply to some tribal groups in less-developed states.

II. Taking Consent Seriously

Let me consider first the possibility of multiple organizations intended to protect rights existing within the same territorial space. We could conceive of this potential alternative in two variations, one where political structures have authority over specific persons based on consent, and another (more market-oriented) where individuals contract with private "protective agencies" that provide services for a fee. While there would be important differences between these organizations in regard to those they protect (citizens versus customers), they are roughly analogous and could in principle coexist within the same geographical area. Since little has been written about purely consent-based political structures[4] while much has been said about private mechanisms for protection, I will consider them together; each promises similar kinds of benefits and faces similar difficulties.

David Friedman (1989) and other advocates of "anarcho-capitalism" argue that, absent a state, individuals could protect themselves through market mechanisms by creating "protective agencies" that deter and punish violators in return for cash payments. Similarly, one might imagine a system of purely consent-based structures, in which individuals voluntarily join nonterritorialized organizations intended to serve the same function. In either case, individuals under the protection of very different institutions could live intermingled, potentially even in the same household. Friedman (114–20) argues that private agencies would offer more effective and reliable protections than do states, and at lower cost, while also allowing individuals to decide how well and by what means they would be protected. While he has no expectations of perfection, Friedman (148) does believe such a system would be far less dangerous than states as we know them: "I am willing to accept a slightly less than optimal production of a few public goods in exchange for the security of there being no government to expand into the 95 percent of human affairs where it can do nothing but damage." Political organizations based purely on consent promise the same kinds of incentives for efficiency and effectiveness—those that fail to protect citizens well at a tolerable cost will lose potential members, and so over time cease to exist. In this system (so the argument goes), everyone will get the level of protection he or she wants, and no dangerous and expensive states will have to be imposed on anyone.

Phrased this way, these alternatives seem appealing. Unfortunately, however, there are serious reasons to doubt that the promised benefits could actually be secured. As Robert Nozick (1974) has noted, such systems may tend over time to reintroduce monopolies on coercive power within particular territories, as the strongest protective agency or consent-based political unit outcompetes others in protecting its clients or citizens. This outcome would more or less reproduce states as we know them, and while smart consumers or potential consentors would require stringent safeguards on the internal governance structures of these organizations, the lack of meaningful competition would leave these safeguards no more effective than they currently are within states.[5]

Moreover, the conflicts between these organizations seem unlikely to foster the protection of rights until monopolies are finally established. Territorial states minimize conflict by drawing clearly delimited boundaries around themselves and by largely confining their exercises of authority within these determinate limits. This is obviously an imperfect system and can never prevent all conflicts over jurisdiction, but the dangers from territorially intermixed organizations seem far higher by comparison. Profit-oriented protective agencies or consent-based organizations would often be called upon to arrest or otherwise use coercion against persons outside of their membership, and the clash of legal procedures and interests here could easily become explosive—particularly if (as John Locke warned) wronged individuals often demand immediate and excessive punishment against perceived wrongdoers.

Unsurprisingly, Friedman objects that these concerns are overstated and argues that profit-seeking agencies would choose to bargain rather than fight: "An agency which settles its disputes on the battlefield has already lost, however many battles it wins. Battles are expensive—also dangerous for clients whose front yards get turned into free-fire zones. The clients will find a less flamboyant protector" (Friedman 1989, 122–23). A similar claim might be made for consent-based organizations—if they have any options, few will join an institution that poses frequent dangers to its citizens. Friedman argues that in the long run, for-profit court systems would be constructed, so that agencies will negotiate over which court to use, rather than how particular individuals are treated, and the same might be claimed for consent-based organizations.

Yet this argument is less than persuasive given the difficulties implicit in bargaining between organizations explicitly created to deploy coercion. As international relations scholar R. Harrison Wagner (1994) has noted, negotiations involving the threat of violence are necessarily open-ended and unstructured, with outcomes highly dependent on the will and expectations of each side. Protection agencies or consent-based organizations would thus have strong motivations to threaten violence in many cases to strengthen their reputation and long-term bargaining position, and these threats would in turn provide incentives for competing organizations to develop special military forces just as states have historically done. (Alternatively, it would motivate them to create permanent institutions for solving conflicts, and thereby to re-create state-like institutions through a slightly different process.)

Both anarcho-capitalism and consent-based organizations thus seem likely either to re-create territorial monopolies on coercive power (i.e., states) or to create a system of geographically intertwined, heavily armed institutions that find it necessary to threaten and sometimes use force. These possibilities, coupled with the real-world possibilities of substantial moral disagreement and the particularly strident organizations some fringe groups might construct (cf. Nozick 1974, 131), make it doubtful that such territorially intermixed entities would really spend much time pursuing wrongdoers or protecting rights. They might even require sharp limits on the freedom of their clients or citizens to reduce conflicts with other organizations. In these circumstances, none of the nonterritorial organizations from which one could seek protection would be terribly appealing, while the creation of new structures would also be filled with dangers.

The case against either anarcho-capitalism or an exclusively consent-based political order becomes even sharper when we consider the problem of exclusion—if protective organizations serve only those who choose this affiliation, presumably they will also have rights to reject those who seem like bad risks. This kind of exclusion is an obvious problem if we have duties to aid others in protecting themselves. In the case of anarcho-capitalism, agencies will have strong incentives to refuse service to potentially problematic clients, such as those who have been charged with serious crimes in the past. Clearly one cannot say that such people always deserve this exclusion, even if we have no concerns about proportionality in crime and punishment—even in an ideal world, many innocent people will inevitably be accused and punished and will thereafter be left without protection through no fault of their own. Consent-based organizations might fare somewhat better in this regard if individuals routinely agreed to lifetime memberships, but this seems likely only to set the problem off by a generation—given expectations about environmental effects on character, the children of criminals seem likely to be regarded as bad risks.

Those who would pose a net drain on the resources of a protective agency or consent-based organization would seem more vulnerable yet. The mentally handicapped and some persons with severe physical handicaps are obvious candidates here, but more broadly anyone who cannot afford to purchase protection will be excluded in anarcho-capitalism, and this remains a more subtle problem in a consent-based system. Consent-based organizations, when they are engaged in competition with other organizations, would have good reason to exclude poor members or those without extensive training in useful fields. We are familiar with these exclusions in regard to existing states, where immigration is frequently limited to those with economically valuable skills, yet at least territorial states have few ready pretexts for ejecting those who are already their citizens. In anarcho-capitalism or a consent-based order, protective organizations would not even need pretexts—such exclusions would simply be allowed as a matter of principle.

Moreover, persons who are left without protections for even a short period of time may find themselves consigned to a permanent class of victims. Individuals interested in harming others for entertainment (for example, in creating sexual slaves) may look for those who are unprotected or who are protected by inferior agencies and take the most advantage of them that they can. If those intent on harm are prudent, they may even form their own exploitation agency so that they can present sufficient unified firepower to dissuade other agencies or consent-based organizations from interfering in their wrongdoing. If Friedman is right about the preferability of negotiation, presumably no organization will feel called upon to engage these exploitation agencies when its own citizens or clients are not involved, and so we cannot even take solace in the belief that someone will eventually put a stop to this wrongdoing (particularly since the existence of such terrifying predators will ensure that other organizations always have a ready supply of customers).

Ultimately, then, it seems unlikely that either protective agencies or consent-based organizations would fare tolerably well in protecting rights, even if these organizations did not always engage in outright war. It is not impossible that these dangers could be defused, but, pending some very clear explanation of how this could occur, such potential social orders do not seem a viable alternative to a system of territorial states. Even the best of states as we know them are far from perfect, but organizations that claim authority over everyone within a particular territory seem to generate far less violence and far less exclusion than should be expected from either for-profit protective agencies or consent-based organizations. Whatever kinds of protective organizations we have, it will be necessary to ensure that they are carefully governed and that their citizens have some say in this process. Anarcho-capitalism or consent-based organizations seem unable to remove this problem, and they would create others. Despite the promises of a better world offered by Friedman and other advocates, then, it seems unlikely that such territorially intermixed institutions could really deliver as advertised.

III. Communitarian Anarchism

The second kind of alternative to states, often referred to as "communitarian anarchism," represents a more severe departure, but also one with greater plausibility in some cases. Under this alternative, no centralized mechanisms of coercion exist at all. It has potential relevance for American Indians and other indigenous peoples, many of whom historically lived in societies with this character.

But for this to be a real possibility, the groups involved must be of a specific type. According to rational choice theorist Michael Taylor (1982, 166), "Anarchy is viable to the extent that the relations between people are those which are characteristic of community. In a community, social order can be maintained without the state." Communities of the relevant type must be relatively small, and individuals must have long-term, frequent interactions with one another. Community members must also share core values, so that they understand what norms exist to be maintained (26–29). Taylor argues that in such circumstances social order can be maintained through threats of personal retaliation, the withdrawal of cooperative relationships, and public sanctions of shame and ridicule (91). Taylor draws heavily on anthropological evidence to link his theoretical arguments to the real world; as he notes, human society existed for tens of thousands of years before states and other centralized mechanisms of coercion emerged, and likely did so without horrific levels of suffering by those involved.

Most of us, of course, no longer live in such communities, and it seems unlikely that they could be reconstructed in highly urbanized settings where individuals have few long-term interactions with one another (Morris 1998, 74–80). But that does not entirely obviate communitarian anarchism as a possibility where such communities do still exist, such as where indigenous communities have not yet been forcibly assimilated into a surrounding state. In a few parts of the world, state laws continue to have little effect on the internal lives of indigenous groups, even if these laws are often necessary to protect such groups from external enemies (such as for Amazonian tribes). If there were groups that did not need this outside protection at all, would they still be morally required to put themselves under the authority of a state, if not doing so created no serious consequences for those outside the community? It is not obvious that they would.

But are such communities structurally capable of offering the right sorts of protections to their members? Small communities clearly manage to sustain a sort of law and order within their boundaries. The question is whether it can be the right kind of law and order. According to Taylor, one common method of protecting individuals in small communities is the threat of personal retribution by those who are harmed or by their relatives. This raises concerns about neutrality, but perhaps, where people know each other very well, it is easier than we expect to recognize those who harm others. Perhaps the tendency toward excessive punishment is also blunted if both the relatives of the victim and the accused offer roughly equal threats to one another or are bound together by complex crosscutting linkages through marriages or other means (cf. Taylor 1982, 72–75). The evidence here is far from clear, but perhaps it is worth giving communities the benefit of the doubt on this score.

Taylor also argues, however, that small communities must rely heavily on shaming and ostracism as means of social control in a broad variety of situations. Most worrisomely, these tools are often used against individuals who engage in seemingly trivial sorts of unusual behavior, because the continued existence of the community requires relatively strict conformity with complex customs and behaviors that fill multiple and overlapping roles in the community's social life (Taylor 1982, 76). Since part of what binds a community is its shared set of central values, the maintenance of these values is closely tied to its survival as a community. Whether or not shame and ostracism by themselves violate the basic moral protections all individuals should enjoy, these tools are often precursors to more serious sanctions, such as criminal punishment or the withdrawal of economic resources. According to Taylor (104–12), one of the primary methods of social control in such communities is the withdrawal of economic reciprocity from rule-breakers. In many tribal communities, individuals are expected to distribute material surpluses to fellow members, and those who violate community standards may be shut out from such redistribution. More importantly, such societies often regard ownership (or usage rights) of land and other resources as dependent upon good standing within the community, meaning that the economic consequences for violating social expectations may be very severe.[6] In such tightly knit groups, there are obvious reasons to worry about the protection of anything resembling an acceptable regime of moral protections.

Yet we must be careful here: discussions of unfamiliar social practices can easily slide into raw forms of ethnocentrism, magnifying the worrisome aspects of other societies while entirely masking those of our own (see Chapter 8). Even the best of states put significant unnecessary limits on personal liberty, enforcing as they do fixed and general laws through professionalized mechanisms of coercion. According to American Indian scholar Vine Deloria Jr. (1969, 237), indigenous communities are in fact far more tolerant of and responsive to individual desires than are states: "Tribal society does not depend upon legislative enactment. It depends heavily in most areas upon customs which fill in the superstructure of society with meaningful forms of behavior and which are constantly changing because of the demands made upon them by people." Deloria (230) argues that such communities are far more open to personal choice than outsiders believe them to be: "The primary purpose of the tribe, then and now, was to ensure as beneficial a life as possible for members of the tribe. The hunting grounds of the tribe were to be defended at all costs. Outside of that, individual freedom ran rampant."

This contrast between life within states and life in indigenous communities is a common theme of indigenous authors and those who sympathize with them, many of whom are quite familiar with the operations of real governments. For example, H. C. ("Nugget") Coombs, a nonindigenous Australian civil servant who advocated greater autonomy for Australia's native peoples, characterizes Aboriginal communities as far more natural and comfortable than the alternative and argues that "the record of social change within western society and its contemporary institutions bears witness to the colossal effort which has been required to adapt men and women to life in the industrial and post-industrial world" (Coombs 1994, 4). States and their laws are obviously among the institutions that require such adaptation—laws very rarely allow for the ongoing negotiations over collective existence that characterize life in many small indigenous communities. They far more often require simple submission to fixed rules that are applied regardless of context.

Thus, a fair comparison between some loose form of anarchism or quasi-anarchism within indigenous communities and life within law-governed states might demonstrate that both require problematic limits on individual liberty and that each allows options that the other does not, but it might ultimately show the flexibility of custom in communities to be superior in many regards (cf. Denis 1997, chap. 6).[7] While the ultimate effectiveness of such communities in protecting individual rights is a complex empirical question, it seems mistaken to claim that states organized to deploy coercion through law must necessarily fare better.[8] If this is true, then there is no moral requirement that such communities give up this kind of self-organization to live under the authority of an institution explicitly charged with enforcing laws through coercion—that is, a state.

But this argument seems to apply fully only to groups that really are small and isolated and have continued to govern themselves through such mechanisms up to the present day—limitations that simply do not describe the conditions of most indigenous peoples in the United States, Canada, and Australia. In those and most other countries, what one finds instead are more partial and limited communities that continue to govern only some aspects of their social lives through noncentralized mechanisms. The United States, Canada, and Australia all historically undertook very intensive efforts at assimilation, and in the process usually fractured previous methods of community governance where other processes (e.g., advancing markets) had not already done so. In most cases, these efforts replaced historical forms of social order with regimes of written law and eventually some form of local electoral governance.

Although these attempts at assimilation were virtually always ill-conceived and the regimes of law to which indigenous peoples were subjected were deeply flawed, it is nonetheless true that most indigenous communities no longer have the habits and skills necessary to operate a successful regime of communitarian anarchism over the full range of social issues, including criminal law. In these circumstances, those who want to return to communitarian methods of self-regulation should (and, I think, usually do) recognize the difficulty of the task ahead of them and acknowledge it as what it is—a process of reconstruction, rather than one of simply allowing preexisting mechanisms to operate unimpeded.

Moreover, most indigenous peoples are now deeply entrenched in both economic and social relationships with the surrounding nonindigenous populations, and very few communities have memberships nearly as stable as those Taylor has in mind. When individuals can come and go from the community with great ease, informal mechanisms are far more difficult to deploy because all those involved have reduced incentives to know each other well and to care about one another's opinions—they know that they can find alternative social opportunities elsewhere if the inconveniences of remaining in the community become too great. Where community boundaries are relatively permeable in this way, maintaining social order in the complete absence of professionalized methods of enforcement is likely to be impossible, while the costs of severing these kinds of larger interrelationships would also be extremely high both economically and socially.

In current circumstances, then, communitarian anarchy in any full version is probably not a real prospect for indigenous peoples within countries like United States and Canada, even if it does provide a viable alternative for isolated groups like some Amazonian tribes. (Additional concerns, both principled and pragmatic, point to the same conclusion in regard to the latter groups—see Chapter 8.) In the United States and Canada, indigenous nations may have good reasons to believe that alternative mechanisms of governance can be recreated, but for the foreseeable future this will probably have to be done within the framework of state-like forms of organization. (I hope indigenous readers will agree with this assessment; I realize that some may not, however, and will try to deal more deeply with the role of such disagreement in Chapter 8.)

I want to be clear, however, about what this conclusion does and does not entail. It does not automatically provide support for the states now ruling indigenous peoples to continue to do so. As I noted earlier, I have been concerned so far with states as a type of organization rather than with the particular states we now have, and it could be that indigenous peoples should immediately be allowed to form their own states; the criteria for evaluating these questions will be different from those appropriate in justifying states in the abstract. Demonstrating that full-blown communitarian anarchism is not a real option for most indigenous groups has important implications for evaluating types of social organization, but it does not by itself provide grounds for choosing one state or the other to secure the necessary protections. This question will have to be answered below and in chapters to come.

I should also note that nothing in Taylor's arguments about communitarian anarchism privileges indigenous groups, beyond the contingent judgment that they are more likely to have the necessary preconditions in place. Some traditionalist religious groups likely have similar social resources and may be justified in continuing to make use of them or in trying to develop them further (cf. Swaine 2001; 2006). Taylor's arguments about community say nothing about firstness or any other features entailed by the notion of "indigenous." Insofar as other groups have similar kinds of communities, they may have similar options, strange as this prospect may seem strange to those accustomed to seeing the claims of indigenous peoples as inherently different from those of all other groups.

IV. Supporting Just States

I hope this survey, while far from exhaustive, at least gives a sense of why radical alternatives are plausible only in a few limited cases. Anarcho-capitalism or a consent-based order seems likely to replicate the problems of good governance associated with states, while adding additional difficulties. Communitarian anarchism, while possible for a few groups, does not seem to be a real option in most cases. But what about the dangers posed by states?

Here it seems most plausible to argue that democratic states, at least, pose a better option for most people in most circumstances than do the alternatives. Although states as we know them can be deeply flawed, democratic states do generally treat their majority populations relatively well, and in the present day they are faring better in regard to their minorities as well. Although it is hard to be sure why this is so (see Chapter 7), states in which the rule of law is secured by elected leadership seem to be the least dangerous political structures that we know how to construct. It seems most plausible for someone concerned with the protection of rights to focus on how democratic states as we know them can be improved, rather than seek out radical and relatively untested alternatives. I do not want to underplay the dangers of democratic states, of course. I believe these states are sufficiently flawed to make procedural mechanisms for separation from them extremely attractive, as I will argue in the next chapter. I will also argue that the option of communitarian anarchism should be available if, after cautious and orderly consideration of the options, any groups really want to pursue it. But it nonetheless seems true that we will generally fare best with political structures that are relatively democratic. And where they are not, we face hard questions about how they could be made so.

Yet, perhaps strangely, I have still not answered Simmons's challenge fully in making the case for states as a type of organization claiming the exclusive right to enforce law within a given territory. (The final objection here is somewhat abstruse and will likely be of greater interest to those versed in long-standing questions of political obligation; others can likely go on to the beginning of the following section without harm.) While Simmons is convinced that state authority should ideally be based only on consent, he also seems willing to adopt a fallback position in which states ban competing organizations but allow individuals to remain free of both political protections and political duties if they wish to pursue this option (Simmons 1999, 766, quoted above). In this situation, everyone who wants political protections will have to receive them through the state operating within their territory, while those who feel no need of them will be free simply to do without them. Such people are often referred to in the philosophical literature as "independents," since they choose to take their chances outside of whatever protections the state offers.

This fallback position involves questions about exactly how our natural duties justify political authority despite our choices. At first glance, it may seem eminently reasonable; after all, no one should be forced to accept "protections" that he or she does not want. But most of the protections offered by states are already easy to escape—would-be independents can simply refuse to call the police or otherwise make use of state machinery for pursuing their interests (e.g., using courts to seek compensation after injury). It is hard to see anything wrong in such refusals. What, then, is the attraction of claiming to be an independent? The attraction is in what it putatively allows independents *not* to do: if they are not receiving state protections, why should they have to pay taxes or otherwise directly contribute to the state's maintenance?[29] The independent can say that rights are being protected tolerably well for everyone who wants such protections, so his duties to aid are fulfilled and he has no need to pay to support a state that does nothing for him.

But duties to aid require more than just noninterference with individuals who make arrangements to protect themselves. They require positive action when necessary, and those who refuse to contribute to the state's continued existence through paying taxes and contributing in other ways seem to be shirking the requirements of their duties in this regard. Even if they do not want the state's protections, they cannot easily waive other people's claims to their assistance, particularly in regard to those, such as the severely handicapped, who would be extremely vulnerable to attack without aid from others. If vulnerable people are entitled to aid, they are entitled to it not only from those who personally prefer a state's protections, but from everyone.

Yet here Simmons can make a final stand. Since our duties to aid are fully generalized, he can argue that independents can choose instead to fulfill them through a variety of alternative means. They can, for example, give money directly to charities, or pay taxes to some far-off state that seems more needy than their own—after all, our duties apply equally to all persons, not just to those with whom we happen to share a particular territory. (To avoid questions about quantities of aid, imagine that independents contribute to this other state exactly what "their" government otherwise would demand from them in taxes.) If individuals fulfill their duties in this way, then they seem to give the state in their territory no excuse to coerce additional contributions from them. States cannot simply go around coercing individuals without a clear justification, and people who freely fulfill their duties by other mechanisms do not seem to give them one.

If this argument about alternative ways of fulfilling duties is correct, it suggests that states must undertake exhaustive research to determine whether individuals have fulfilled their duties through alternative means before requiring them to pay taxes. This process would presumably be much like proving guilt in a criminal trial, since the state would seem to face the burden of proof before deploying coercion in extracting taxation. But this would be not only difficult but prohibitively expensive. Should states therefore simply take would-be independents at their word when they claim to have fulfilled their duties through other means? This seems ready-made for abuse. It would be far easier, and much less expensive, if states simply assumed that all people are prone to duty-avoidance from the beginning and insisted for that reason on receiving support from everyone within their territory. But if this is true, then would-be independents must recognize the potential problems posed by their desired political status from the very beginning and therefore tolerate a state designed specifically to prevent duty-avoidance. Would-be independents must recognize, in other words, that states must prove not only the central mechanism for *coordinating* the protection of rights, but also for *coercing* individuals into fulfilling their duties to aid. Behaving as if everyone were guilty of duty-avoidance from the start seems necessary if states are to do their jobs well.

Simmons would likely object that this presumption is unwarranted because most people will fulfill their duties freely. This seems factually unlikely, however. In practice, duties to aid seem far easier to ignore than duties to refrain from harming others directly (which are already violated in excess), since we rarely encounter the results of failures to aid directly.[10] (This is presumably why charitable organizations continually confront us with graphic images of suffering: only then will we really think seriously about the effects of our inaction.) Simply recognizing moral principles is often insufficient—we must also act on them, and we would seem to be far more likely to do so where sanctions exist to help us override our more selfish urges.[11]

Nor are there are obvious alternatives to states for coercing such aid. Even if individuals somehow had the capacity to do so, their attempts would reproduce the familiar problems of criminal punishment in the absence of a professional judicial system. (For example, how trustworthy are individuals, after their family or friends have suffered a violation of their rights, in recognizing those who have failed in their duty?) The procedural safeguards provided by states can fare much better, with the most obvious indicator of each person's contribution being that rendered through state institutions. Thus, our duties seem to require that we recognize this problem and plan accordingly by supporting states that demand mandatory support from everyone within their borders. Simmons is mistaken, then, in claiming that states can fulfill their basic moral goal well while leaving some persons free of their authority in this regard.

Still, there is no reason that an ideal state could not try to meet persons who would like to render aid through alternative means halfway. It could create procedures for them to demonstrate that they have already discharged some of their duties through other mechanisms and so should be exempted from some taxation or other forms of support. Existing states already take such considerations into account in limited ways, such as tax exemptions for charitable contributions, but the generalized character of natural duties suggests that such exemptions could be extended if this could be done without strongly undermining state capacity. In this regard, Simmons's claims about alternative ways of rendering aid do contribute to our thinking about a just state. But the burden of proof might reasonably be put on the person claiming exemption. Since states are the most obvious and direct mechanism by which we can fulfill our duties, they can legitimately require those who claim to have offered aid through other means to demonstrate this.

From the finding that states as institutions are justified in coercing us to fulfill our duties, however, it does not follow that our duties justify all of the policies that actual states pursue. As I noted above, states justified by natural duties should face careful questioning whenever their policies do not work toward protecting their citizens from violence and other forms of wrongdoing. Moreover, the character of our duties to aid suggests that we are often absolved from contributing to a state's continued existence in a way that will endanger our own lives, even if it provides moral benefits to others.[12] Our duties may require that we support just states, but they do not easily require undertaking actions that will lead to our own deaths, at least in the absence of truly overwhelming reasons. Military conscription and other forms of involuntary public service in dangerous fields, which demand that persons expose themselves to very high risks in aiding others, seem particularly problematic in this regard.[13] The limitations that natural duties put on particular types of state laws, and the ways in which individuals may legitimately defend themselves against laws that exceed these limits, are serious and difficult questions to decide (cf. Walzer 1970). While these questions cannot be explored in depth here, we cannot assume that states are justified in pursuing the full range of their familiar policies. Our duties thus seem to require that we work to change the unjust policies of democratic states while continuing to support the continued existence of such political institutions. As I will argue below and in the next chapter, this can be consistent with political separation—but separation of an orderly, procedural type.

What about nondemocratic states, or states where democracy has not yet been fully established? Here matters are highly dependent on the quality of state policies, which can vary far more wildly than those of democratic states, and our response to the system of governance as a whole will often have to be far more tactical. Mildly unjust states almost certainly deserve our support for the benefits they provide that cannot be secured in any other way, but they also deserve our nonviolent political action to change their dangerous policies. At some point, difficult to define in principle but often obvious in practice, pervasively unjust states cease to provide more moral benefits than dangers. At this point, their "citizens" have good grounds for revolt, and even duties to assist attempted overthrows when this will not put their own lives at serious risk. Natural duties suggest only that states that help to protect rights deserve our support, and these will generally be democratic states rather than some other type. Our duties themselves provide no justification for states that choose instead to abuse those they rule.

V. Boundaries, Duties, and Rights

If states are justified by their role in protecting individuals from violence and other forms of wrongdoing, what does this tell us about their jurisdiction over particular populations and territories, especially indigenous populations? If, as I have just argued, democratic states deserve our continued support, this may seem to slam the door on the political aspirations of indigenous peoples in the United States, Canada, and Australia—they are, after all, clearly ensconced within stable democracies. Yet there is a difference between supporting the continued existence of political institutions that are governed through democratic means and supporting the particular set of democratic states that now exist. The question of *which* democratic state should govern a certain geographical area and a certain population must be answered on somewhat different grounds. The difficulties implicit in broad-scale political reorganizations are the basic reason for supporting the array of states we now have. But, as I will argue, these difficulties can be largely mitigated through careful procedural design.

The negative conclusions of natural-duty arguments are perhaps the most important, both for indigenous peoples and for the states now ruling them: political organizations do not derive their authority from ownership or historical transfers of sovereignty and so cannot claim absolute rights to territorial integrity or (in the case of indigenous peoples) rights to a separate status stemming from past independence. Because political units that help to protect rights are extremely valuable, they deserve our support, but they do not have an inherent right to their current configurations. What they have is a contingent right based on the function they serve (Wellman 1995); the primary reasons for valuing existing states are pragmatic, and any rights political organizations have must be justified accordingly.

Indeed, if there were no difficulties involved in changing political boundaries or predicting the outcome of different kinds of changes, a natural-duty justification of state authority might suggest that many existing boundaries should be greatly altered. To see what standards natural duties would supply for evaluating political boundaries in the abstract and why these standards are difficult to apply directly, imagine that you have been commissioned to reconfigure all of the world's countries from scratch. Imagine also that there are absolutely no transition costs in moving from the existing world to the one you are about to design. In these strange circumstances, you would have two standards: political boundaries should be constructed to maximize the protections individuals enjoy and to minimize the costs of our duties. (If we were really starting from scratch, we might want to design a global federation or something similar instead of sovereign states, but pursuing this option would obviate the illustrative purpose of this thought experiment.) How much change would you ultimately choose to bring about, and how easy would your decisions be?

More difficult than one might think. The first criterion requires maximizing the protections from violence and other forms of wrongdoing, a criterion that would apply to everyone in the world. (Remember that duties are generalized to all people equally.) For the sake of argument, imagine that we know exactly what natural rights individuals should have and that we also have full information about how every way of structuring political boundaries would affect each person in the world. Would constructing ideal boundaries according to this criterion be straightforward? Probably not. Even if we knew what natural rights everyone had, how would we recognize what maximizing their protection might entail? Would we, for example, want to maximize the average level of protection that people enjoy, or maximize the condition of the worst off, or pursue some intermediate position? If trade-offs between specific rights (or elements of those rights) became necessary, which ones would have first ranking? Imagine that very small states are unusually effective at protecting rights to life but that increasing the number of political boundaries reduces free movement and so hampers rights to liberty—should we create such small political units or not?

Even in a world of full information, then, such judgments would not be easy, even if we could often recognize arrangements that would be particularly ineffective. And our world is manifestly not one with full information. In practical terms, it is difficult to predict the effects of particular borders or of multiple trade-offs. It seems likely, for example, that jurisdictions that reflect natural geographical features like mountains or rivers are easier to administer, but so might be states that include fewer language groups. Borders that match large-scale economic patterns seem beneficial for some elements of governance, but so do those that reflect major ecological zones. In these circumstances, should we try to ensure that as many good characteristics as possible overlap, or should we focus instead on one feature (such as language) over all others? Although important things could almost certainly be said about each of these factors and about what they imply in combination, it will be difficult to know whether any particular set of boundaries will have the effects we impute to it, and we will often be uncertain what the trade-offs we are making really consist in.

We face another set of uncertainties when we consider the degree to which real people disagree about the character of the moral rights individuals have, about how these should be balanced against each other, and about the ideal conditions necessary for their protection. These disagreements are especially challenging because viewpoints are unlikely to be distributed randomly across populations and geographical space; instead, some groups will have differing judgments based on their history or cultural values (cf. Ivison 2002, 50–54) or on the idiosyncratic directions of their current political debates. What role should these disagreements play for an ideal boundary constructor? Should boundaries by drawn around like-minded groups, or drawn to ignore or even dilute these kinds of patterns of disagreement?

While choosing an ideal set of boundaries for the entire world might not be impossible, then, it would clearly be no simple matter. Moreover, natural duties also imply a second standard for evaluating political boundaries—the degree of costs they impose on those who must support them. If the costs of our duties matter, as it seems they must (see Chapter 5), then states must try to minimize them whenever possible.[14] Even if protecting rights should generally have priority, costs can never be entirely irrelevant—surely some increases in the protection of rights are so minuscule as to not be required by our duties to aid.[15] These concerns may seem irrelevant if we believe that most existing property holdings are indefensible (see Chapters 3 and 4), since individuals will not have strong claims against particular regimes of taxation. But this impression is mistaken. There will always be a point at which marginal increases in the protection of rights are no longer worth the costs, since this protection will use up funds that could otherwise be used differently (e.g., redistributed directly to the poor).

Given these complex considerations, even if there were no political barriers or transaction costs, it would not be easy to redesign the world's existing political boundaries to improve their effectiveness. In light of these uncertainties, it does not seem unreasonable simply to conclude that many kinds of boundaries are equally acceptable (insofar as we are able to recognize determinate differences at all) and that the issue of interest should be the quality of a state's governance rather than which territories or populations it rules. Indeed, it seems accurate to conclude that the most severe political problems in our world come not (or not primarily) from the geographic shapes of particular states, but from governments that fail to treat some or even all of their citizens well. As I noted above, some states have well-designed governing institutions and use them effectively, while others do not, but even the best-governed usually fail persistently in regard to some elements of their population. Given the realities of imperfect governance, why not focus on improving the structures of government and remediating particular policies rather than on imagining uncertain benefits from redrafting the boundaries between states as they now exist?[16]

This conclusion, coupled with the real-world difficulties of trying to reconstruct political boundaries in even the best of circumstances, suggests that we should generally support the continued jurisdiction of existing states over the territories and populations they now rule. Nonetheless, we should be wary of concluding too much, as there are almost certainly some cases where this presumption should be overridden. Because some governments, even those of democratic states, can fail over and over again in their treatment of particular groups, many people have suggested that mistreated groups should have remedial rights to political separation (e.g., Buchanan 1997; 2004; cf. Philpott 1995). Given the logic of our natural duties, this looks like a reasonable position—states that fail so egregiously destroy their moral claims to rule those so mistreated and give these groups moral rights to pursue a separate future if they are able to do so. By extension, natural duties allow or even require outsiders to aid them in this struggle.

What would this remedial standard say about the claims of American Indians and other indigenous peoples to full independence? The answer depends on one's judgments about how badly indigenous peoples are now being treated and about what the future is likely to hold. Most of those who invoke a remedial standard have very severe levels of mistreatment in mind, in which governments are systematically oppressing or failing to protect a particular portion of their citizenry. Historically, there can be no doubt that the United States, Canada, and other states mistreated their indigenous populations severely enough to justify independence on these grounds. (Obviously these states should not have engaged in conquest and fraud in the first place, either.) But for a natural-duty conception of political authority, past mistreatment matters only insofar as it is predictive of the present and future. How bad is the treatment of indigenous peoples in the present day? Clearly the United States, Canada, and other democratic states are doing far better than they once did: indigenous citizens now receive equal legal rights, and a variety of social programs intended to improve the status of indigenous communities are in place. These states do continue to fail in important ways, but are these failings severe enough to dissolve their claims to authority over the indigenous populations now within their borders and give those populations remedial rights to separation? A full judgment in this regard may depend in part on questions about historical ownership as outlined in Chapters 3 and 4, but many nonindigenous observers will nonetheless seem likely to conclude that the answer is no. And at least some indigenous populations will likely disagree.

This brings us to the crux of the issue for a remedial-rights theory of separation: who has the right to decide whether a state is doing its job well enough? If indigenous peoples or other groups believe they are being misgoverned, do the states now ruling them have rights to reject these claims, or does the final decision lie with the dissatisfied populations themselves? While we might try to specify exhaustively the grievances that are legitimate and those that are not, at some point a final judgment about the quality of a state's protections will have to be made—but by whom?

I believe the most reliable judges of a government's character are those ruled by it and that it should matter a great deal when a population rejects an existing state strongly enough to seek separation from it. Even if consent is an unachievable standard, that does not mean the wishes of dissatisfied populations should be treated simply as a failure of their own judgment. In the next chapter, I will argue for a democratic right of self-determination, in which virtually any large population has a right to seek separation if it can pass a carefully defined set of referenda. As I will try to show, referenda structured in this way can reduce the dangers of such changes, in particular by fostering democratic deliberation throughout, and in these circumstances independence seems likely to be chosen only when there really are substantial causes for populations to feel aggrieved. Indeed, I will argue that allowing groups to pursue this kind of self-determination will often have beneficial effects on the political performance of the states facing such claims, even if no referenda are ever passed.

The default position, if the arguments of the next chapter are rejected, is probably to continue to insist on some version of a remedial-rights theory while trying to specify some alternative conception of the conditions under which these rights might be exercised, or else simply to insist that all borders remain fixed, no matter what. Both seem to me distinctly inferior options, but the readers themselves will have to be the judges of the arguments in the next chapter.

VI. Partial Separation

Throughout this chapter, I have focused on binary oppositions, either between states and statelessness or (where self-determination is concerned) between one state and another. But I could reasonably be accused of misunderstanding the claims made by most indigenous peoples (if not by Ward Churchill [1999] and a few other writers at the extremes), which are often not for full statehood but for increased control over their own affairs within the overarching structures of existing states (see, e.g., Tully 1995; Niezen 2003, 202–7). Isn't such a partial status, grounded as it often is in treaties and other historical relationships, something rather different?

The answer within a natural-duty theory of authority is no. As I have tried to show throughout the book so far, a natural-duty justification of political authority is uninterested in history; its concern is with the sorts of protections states *now* offer. Authority over particular populations and territories does not derive from historical transfers or consent, as I tried to show in Chapter 4, and for this reason contemporary structures of authority seem bound by historical transactions only as these affect their future activities. The strongest arguments for honoring historical agreements in these circumstances are pragmatic and conservative, having to do with the degree to which well-functioning political arrangements currently have entrenched historical agreements within successful policies. Thus, an independent or quasi-independent historical status has no force on its own terms, but the general presumption in favor of the status quo suggests that contemporary cases of quasi-sovereignty should be maintained unless they are failing in obvious ways. Matters are more ambiguous when historical relationships are entrenched into law but are being breached in practice. In these cases, the answer seems to depend on the quality of existing arrangements and the magnitude of the change implied.[17]

But this suggests that we are back to the same problem once again—who has the right to decide when present arrangements are working acceptably well, even when they entail only partial separation rather than full? As this uncertainty should make clear, the questions for partially separate relationships are the same as those surrounding full separation and must be solved, so far as possible, on the same grounds. To evaluate such claims fully, then, we need to look more intensively at what self-determination might consist in. That is the topic of the last two chapters.

SEVEN

DELIBERATION AND SELF-DETERMINATION

The previous two chapters have probably not been the most comfortable ground for indigenous readers, and many may view my presumption in favor of the status quo as absurd on a number of grounds. It is, after all, very easy for me to say that stable democratic states are relatively effective in protecting their citizens—I am not indigenous and have not lived under extreme forms of political failure. Here we come to a central question: who has the right to judge when a political system is tolerably effective?

In this chapter and the next, I will examine the notion of self-determination in two variations. In this chapter, I will consider whether populations that reject the state now ruling them should have rights to pursue separation based on this rejection alone. In Chapter 8, I will consider whether such rejection is especially important when the population involved shares special features, such as culture or a sense of nationalism. My argument in the present chapter will be that a natural-duty justification of authority should allow groups to separate if they are able to meet some careful procedural safeguards in the process, but that this kind of right may not encompass most indigenous peoples, given their extremely small populations and limited territories. (The Navajo Nation, in the American Southwest, is the most promising exception to this pattern.) This suggests that any claims to separation will have to be at least partially based on different criteria, involving cultural difference. I will consider these in Chapter 8.

In most of this chapter, I will focus primarily on the question of full separation, in part to see the limits of its acceptability but also because arguments for more partial arrangements rest on the same kinds of foundations. Toward the end of the chapter, I will outline the ways that this argument might apply to cases of partial separation—as I will show, movements toward partial separation may paradoxically be subject to some greater limitations and will always be harder to negotiate.

I. Separation and Preferences

As I noted in the previous chapter, most theorists seem willing to accept separation in cases of severe mistreatment, although their arguments leave persistent questions about how such mistreatment can be recognized outside of the most extreme cases. I will now consider whether we should allow groups to choose separation even in the absence of such unambiguous oppression. There are at least three reasons why separation might be permitted in these cases. The first is that allowing it minimizes elements of the costs of our natural duties; the second is that separation is appropriate in cases of mild disagreement about balances in the moral protections individuals should enjoy; the third and, I will argue, the strongest is that allowing such separation provides the most reliable mechanism for ensuring that states treat all members of their populations tolerably well even in ambiguous cases.

The first potential reason involves the costs of our natural duties. As I noted in the previous chapter, the costs of our duties are a relevant consideration in evaluating particular regimes of authority. But what exactly is entailed in the notion of cost in this context? The meaning is clearest where our duties require some relatively determinate kind of action from us, such as physically assisting someone in need. If it takes ten minutes to assist one person and twenty to assist a second, the exercise of our duty is correspondingly more burdensome in the second case (even if both are equally mandatory). Similar markers are easy to find where our political duties are concerned—states always need assistance from their citizens in terms of taxation and personal contributions of time and energy (e.g., for jury service), and these can easily be recognized and compared. A state that provides a high level of protection with minimal contributions from its citizens is preferable to one that accomplishes the same while requiring more; generally we will not find it beneficial on balance to reconstruct borders with this in mind, but the aspiration toward keeping down the costs of our duties is clear enough.

Yet there is another set of costs that might provide some limited justification for allowing groups to separate from existing states even where no overt mistreatment is involved: the psychological costs associated with living under a state one dislikes. An initial reaction might be to say that these costs simply cannot count, particularly within an argument that rejects a central role for consent—if our duties require us to live within states in the first place, how can this requirement be considered among the costs? After all, we are familiar with many cases in ordinary life where people must learn to overcome or ignore their desires if they are to live a moral life; consider someone who has a pervasive desire to dominate others through violence and who must consistently resist such feelings to remain a moral person. We might want to conclude the same in regard to political preferences—why not simply say that we must override these preferences entirely and simply support the states that protect rights most effectively in objective terms?

Yet this conclusion, however natural it seems, is too strong. Although it is exceedingly difficult to see how the limits of our duties might be determined in a principled way, similar difficulties inhere in the rights that individuals are posited to have as well, and virtually all of us accept that for psychological reasons, some violations of rights are more severe than others. Indeed, some violations of rights may be violations only *because* of their psychological effects. Putting a gun to someone's head and threatening to kill him, for example, will probably strike most people as a violation of one right or another, but why? It does no physical harm until the trigger is actually pulled, yet most of us would find this profoundly wrong even if the gun was never loaded. What seems important is the terror of the person threatened and the lingering psychological effects that may be created. Thus, concerns about psychological states are not always irrelevant to moral evaluation, and the psychological costs of living under a state one rejects may also matter to at least some degree.

Cases can occur in which the psychological costs of living under a state one dislikes are truly substantial and fully understandable. Consider the case when the state was responsible for horrific injustices to one's ancestors, even if it has now reformed itself so that it no longer offers such threats. Although the state may now fully protect all of its members, its very claims to authority may be a continuing reminder of the horrors and humiliation it formerly produced. (These concerns are obviously relevant where indigenous peoples are concerned, but many populations worldwide likely share similar misgivings about the states they live under.) If these costs matter in calculating the weight of our duties, they seem to provide some impetus for allowing groups to separate even in the absence of serious ongoing mistreatment. Even if the weight given to these psychological states must be relatively limited—or else they would threaten to swamp our duties themselves—they might still provide some force in favor of reshaping boundaries around the wishes of as many people as possible. Since the only way to find out what people really want in this way is by allowing them to express a preference, this concern with psychological costs suggests that populations should have the option of separation simply because they vote in favor of this—all else being equal.

In practice, of course, all else rarely is equal, and at the end of the day this argument must probably have limited force. While it is hard to know how much changes to existing boundaries might reduce these costs, it is certain that such changes will be difficult and expensive where the more familiar kinds of costs are concerned. Indeed, such changes could easily create states that are less efficient in their operations and could thereby increase the costs for citizens over the long term (e.g., as memories of historical injustices fade with time). So this kind of concern with reducing costs, while relevant, leaves a great deal of ambiguity about its implications and can probably provide no more than a supporting argument for allowing populations to separate in the absence of unambiguous forms of mistreatment.

A second and somewhat stronger argument for allowing populations to separate if they so choose focuses on the uncertainties implicit in the balance between rights and duties, as well as in the balance among rights themselves. We do not need to have a commitment to a strong notion of moral pluralism to believe that such balances are difficult to make in a fully principled way and that there is room for reasonable disagreement about what the most appropriate balances are. Because different ways of valuing (say) liberty in comparison to safety are likely to be distributed in part according to different historical and cultural experiences or different social characteristics (e.g., primarily rural societies versus primarily urban), it seems plausible that such disparate rankings should also, where possible, be reflected in structures of political authority. This suggests another reason to allow groups to separate if they wish: to give them opportunities to fine-tune this balance in ways that will seem more appropriate to most people within a particular territory. Since there is no way to ensure that any state has exactly the right balance, this step permits mild moral disagreements to be worked out in slightly different formulations. It does not, however, invoke more substantial forms of moral disagreement—it holds that all states should protect rights, but that they can do so in slightly different ways.

But once again, this argument will not take us very far in justifying rights to procedural separation. Like the argument from psychological costs, it is mostly an all-else-being-equal argument. It suggests that where separation holds no substantial costs or dangers, it should likely be allowed. But it would probably be hard to find anyone who would deny this. Instead, most opponents of easy separation would likely have a different response—that changing political boundaries is dangerous business; there are few guarantees that the new states will end up as effective as those we have now, while the costs and difficulties of such change are guaranteed. On this view, stable and effective states are a substantial political accomplishment and are potentially fragile—they might fall into bad kinds of political behavior, or even into utter ruin, if their authority is not given a fundamental moral status. The challenge facing a theory of self-determination, then, is to show that this concern is misplaced, which would open up greater room for the two arguments outlined above. Even more strongly, we might show that a principle of self-determination is actually beneficial to ensuring state effectiveness and is therefore unambiguously required by our natural duties. I believe that this latter position is in fact correct and that rights to self-determination are not only morally permissible but morally required.

II. Democracy and Judgment

In the previous chapter, I argued that our duties require us to support existing democratic states, since other forms of political organization seem far less reliable over the long run. But the argument there was simply factual and said nothing about why democratic states might have such features. To evaluate a principle of self-determination, we need a better idea of the reasons why democratic states might be more reliable, and whether these reasons are consistent with allowing populations to separate through procedural mechanisms.

Perhaps the most important thing to notice is that existing "democratic" states are actually extremely complex as political constructions; indeed, they are more accurately described as "representative republics." These states are in fact governed by representatives rather than the people themselves, and the representatives are usually limited by a variety of constitutional checks and by competing branches of government. The states have massive bureaucracies that make and enforce a variety of rules of their own, and most have multiple kinds of federalist subunits that are responsible for numerous elements of local governance. While the states generally have relatively clear lines of authority, so that elected leaders in the central government can shape virtually all aspects of policy when they choose to do so, in practice the exercise of this authority is piecemeal and haphazard, with policies often determined by legal inertia or political neglect. The citizens of these countries rarely encounter instances in which their votes will create entirely determinate political outcomes, and their ability to influence specific policies is indirect at best—democratic populations are usually capable of voting out leaders they dislike, but they rarely have extensive choices in who replaces them or what the new leader's specific policies will be.

Of course, some people believe it is exactly such complexity and governance by elites that allows such states to be relatively successful. On the strongest version of this view, existing representative republics are fragile achievements, akin to an extremely important house of cards, where myriad and fractious social forces are balanced against one another in ways that could easily collapse if this political framework were perturbed too much. Thus, one might see it as necessary that such states be governed largely by elites, since only these people have the specialized skills necessary to manage such a complex social project, while multiple interest groups competing for their attention will ensure that the elites continue to receive new knowledge as it becomes necessary. On an optimistic version of this view, these elites are generally better motivated than those they rule, so that elections are necessary primarily to generate acceptance for their decisions. On a slightly more pessimistic version, elections, while necessary to ensure that the experts do not fall into truly egregious misuses of power, contribute nothing particularly positive because citizens in general lack the knowledge to evaluate any policies and will only pursue their self-interest anyway.

If we accept such a view of representative republics, it may seem reasonable to hold that separation should be permitted only in cases where a population is being mistreated in truly spectacular ways, so that the extremely high risks of such change may be worth the benefits. (Who decides this is another matter.) Indeed, this view may also suggest that states are morally prohibited from allowing *consensual* secession, in which the government of the existing state willingly allows such exit—after all, doing so may upend this careful balancing act, drag ignorant and vicious passions to the forefront of political life, and in general be too dangerous to consider.

I am probably caricaturing such views slightly here, but fears like this do seem to play a central role in many arguments against separation. The expectation sometimes seem to be that any population wishing to separate must either have bad intentions or not really understand the consequences of what it is doing, so that in either case its desires should be ignored as long as the consequence is not outright civil war. I think that this view is profoundly mistaken, however, and underestimates the role that ordinary citizens already play in the political stability of democratic states. It also, I believe, sharply overestimates the possibility of expertise in evaluating the quality of governance as a whole—and, not coincidentally, leaves unanswered the question of who should judge when a state is failing in sufficiently serious ways.

Because there is more than one way to interpret the argument I am advancing, I want first to outline what I do *not* mean, but in doing so to give a general idea of the plausibility of the position I am arguing for. According to an understanding of democracy that many people hold in some form and is most clearly articulated by deliberative democrats like Jürgen Habermas (1996), the goal of ensuring that individuals are well protected by their states can be met only if citizens are given greater control of their common political life than they now have. For Habermas and other deliberative democrats, states must initially protect a set of rights so that individuals will have a safe space from which to debate moral and political questions, but this regime of rights must itself be subject to revision by those who live within it. If this tentative regime of rights is valuable, those who live under it will choose to leave it intact; if it is not, they will revise it in ways that seem more appropriate to them. On this argument, if we really want to create a satisfactory set of legal protections, they must be ones that everyone who lives under them can accept, and the only way to determine whether they meet this standard is by allowing citizens to debate and decide political questions for themselves. Any regime of legal protections is thus fundamentally and necessarily self-correcting (Habermas 2001; cf. Ferrara 2001)—those conceptions of rights that still seem valid after extensive social deliberation deserve to be taken seriously, while those that fail to be accepted were never as good as they once seemed.

For many deliberative democrats, the goal of listing a set of freestanding "natural" rights is essentially a fantasy of stepping outside of political processes and real political life; it does not really describe the role of philosophical argument in a democratic society. Within the framework of deliberative democracy, philosophers and others are free to suggest improvements to existing political life, but they should recognize that these suggestions will be accepted only if they actually convince others. Those who would claim expert knowledge must take their chances in discussion like everyone else, and any society that hampers this free flow of discussion cannot claim to know whether it is really protecting an acceptable regime of rights or not. While various kinds of political obfuscation can impede effective deliberation, and while power can sometimes force conversations to stop, these cannot contribute anything positive to realizing an ideal regime of rights. That can come only from the decisions of citizens who are allowed free access to information and resources for deliberation and who know that their political judgments will be taken seriously in creating political outcomes. Thus, fearing greater democratic involvement in the name of protecting rights is fundamentally paradoxical—it purports to defend a set of principles that are theoretically justifiable to all people, without ensuring that they are actually tested against people's choices.

Although the deliberative account is flawed in important ways, it does have a number of extremely positive features, some of which will be central to my arguments below. Perhaps most importantly, it reminds us of the degree to which moral and political debate is fundamentally a social activity rather than one best pursued by a few experts in isolation. As Michael Walzer (1981) has noted, moral philosophers are frequently tempted to treat themselves as heroic figures almost magically capable of seeing truth while others remain mired in illusion. The arguments of deliberative democrats rightly remind us that such fantasies do not describe the socially anchored way in which real debates take place. Forgetting that argumentation is fundamentally a large-scale social project can often leave philosophical arguments disconnected from real-world problems and lead to positions that few people could ever really accept.

Perhaps most importantly for the present discussion, recognizing moral and political debates as socially anchored makes it easier to see the degree to which ordinary people already participate in the political life of democratic states and how firmly successful states rest on the beliefs of those who are ruled. Arguments about rights, for example, have the broad resonance they do because most people already understand and accept the basic concept, and most have considerable skill in arguing intelligently about why rights may be justified or where their limits might lie. It is probably true that ordinary citizens are ill-informed about who their representatives in government are or how specific laws are worded. But life in a democratic society is permeated by experience with the effects of generalized types of policies and with various moral and political arguments; ignorance about specific political facts is not the same as ignorance about ways of organizing social life. Indeed, without this broad familiarity and acceptance, political leaders would have few ideals to appeal to publicly (whether seriously or cynically), and political life would be far more self-serving and unstable than it now is. So deliberative democrats are absolutely right to call our attention to what argumentation has already achieved within democratic states, and they seem to be on plausible ground in believing that it can achieve still more when given chances to do so.

Where I differ from the deliberative account is in its central ambiguity about the status of real disagreement. Given their focus on justifying moral and political principles to all involved, deliberative accounts sometimes seem to suggest that the *only* criterion of moral rightness is actual agreement, and this causes problems in real-world cases. If everyone really did agree, of course, this tendency would raise no problems—we could remain agnostic on whether principles were right because everyone agreed with them, or whether everyone agreed with them because they were right. Since we will never have any issue on which all people agree, however, we can be in a bind when faced with real disagreement—are the principles *most* people accept necessarily valid, or are all of them equally dubious until everyone actually comes to agree on them? The first seems to make the will of large populations correct by definition, while the second seems to leave us unable to say anything at all. In instances of real disagreement, those on both sides will usually say that all right-thinking people will believe as they do. But this leaves us no way to decide without engaging the claims involved on their own merits. While the agreement of other people is very important in some ways, then, it cannot be the sole or even primary criterion of rightness, and we should avoid any implication that it is.

Therefore, I want to avoid any appearance of making the decisions of democratic populations morally right by definition. I have argued throughout this book that some moral principles seem better than others, and while I am clearly aiming to convince, it is the *reasons* others can offer in response that matter, rather than simply their acceptance or rejection of these principles. Democratic populations can and do make grievous mistakes, and we should not pretend otherwise.[1] The real question, once we accept this, is whether democratic populations should be trusted more often than supposed experts, and if so, whether the reasons involved here will also provide grounds for a principle of self-determination.

Here the deliberative account's reminder of how deeply democratic populations already participate in political and moral debates is extremely helpful. While I do not deny that people can become very expert in regard to particular policy fields, in the processes of government, or in particular moral questions, it is hard to see how anyone could become expert in evaluating the quality of governance as a whole. Doing so would require not only a wide array of types of knowledge, but also the making of a number of interlinked and complex moral judgments about issues that no single expert can claim to understand in depth. Where the quality of governance is concerned, most experts, for all but a few areas of political life, share with nonexperts a kind of generalized experiential knowledge about what it "feels like" to live under a particular regime of law.[2] While experts are probably the best judges of specific policies, then, and thus essential for the functioning of actual governments, whatever success democratic states have had seems to rest ultimately with the ability of the larger population to discriminate between directions worth pursuing. Just as the best judge of a shoe's fit is the person who wears it, so the same might be said for laws—those who live under them know best where they pinch.

But if it is true that existing democratic states fare as well as they do because their citizens are competent judges of the protections they offer, then we also have reasons to take matters very seriously when a territorially concentrated population is sufficiently dissatisfied to seek separation. While we could require that they demonstrate mistreatment, the question is, to what authority should they demonstrate it? And what happens if that supposed authority disagrees that there has been mistreatment? (There are other problems with attempts to demonstrate mistreatment as well, as I will outline below.) This suggests that we need to give real consideration to how a principle of self-determination might work. This principle will have to be carefully designed because groups can be wrong in their evaluations, just as the full populations of existing states can make myriad mistakes. What we need is a principle explicitly designed for the imperfect world we live in, where both allowing self-determination and preventing it can have negative outcomes.

The recognition that both sides in any separatist debate can be wrong means that to settle the issue, it is not enough simply to note the kinds of problems to which secessionists may be prone. One might, for example, argue that secessionists are virtually always in the grip of a nationalist ideology and thus precisely the worst judges of their current circumstances. After all, nationalism always contains elements of mythologizing and exclusivism (cf. Miller 1995, chap. 2; Levy 2000, chap. 3), and it seems wise to avoid giving in to these. But in fact we will never face the case of a status quo ruled by a perfectly objective population in comparison to an unthinking nationalist minority, for majority nationalisms have the same features and involve the same kinds of self-mythologizing. Both, then, are at risk of bad judgment, and this fact cannot be used to argue either in favor of the status quo or against it.[3]

So while the fear that secessionists will ultimately be ill-motivated is reasonable, it must be balanced against the ways that states can fail large parts of their population. The best solution in the face of such permanent uncertainty, I think, is to allow the population within separatist territories to make the final decision, but to create procedures that foster democratic deliberation, ensuring that this population actually understands the change it is about to undertake and allowing it significant opportunities to rethink its decisions. If separatists only have to vote once, on a future that is still relatively indeterminate, we may have important reasons to doubt their judgment in the heat of the moment, with so much yet unknown. The solution, therefore, is to make the decision facing them as clear as possible and to ensure that they have thoroughly debated it before any change actually occurs (cf. Chambers 2002, 248–52).

On this strategy, groups would have to pass at least two and perhaps three referenda, each separated by a period for debate, and would have to draw up the central features of a draft constitution for their proposed country before the final vote. Instead of a single vote to decide whether to remain with their present country or reject it in favor of an uncertain alternative, at each step the decisions involved should be formulated clearly as possible, the costs and benefits discussed clearly, and those involved given opportunities to change their minds. The first vote in this process would simply be an indicator of whether a group really wanted to think systematically about separation or not, to provide an initial sense of seriousness. (Voting of a sort may also be necessary for specifying exact boundaries—see below.) The second referendum would be separated by some years from the first, at a minimum three but ideally five or more.[4] The goal would be to foster widespread social deliberation about what the costs and benefits of this change might be, and presumably for those involved on both sides (assuming that citizens of the current state oppose this separation) to offer reasons for favoring one outcome or the other.

Either between the first referendum and the second or between the second and a third, the leaders of the separatist movement would be expected to present to the government of their current state a comprehensive document describing the dangers to that state from separation, the likely resources of the new country and the challenges it may face, and, perhaps most importantly, a detailed provisional constitution. This document would then be made publicly available so that it could become a central topic for social debate. If the present state believed that the proposed secession would be excessively dangerous to its own survival as a protector of rights, it would be responsible at this stage for stating clearly what these dangers might be, and again for making these reasons fully public and allowing them to be rebutted.

In practice, I suspect very few groups would actually be willing or able to pass all of the relevant votes. In many instances, would-be secessionist leaders would find their claims to a wide constituency within a territory disproved in the very first referendum. While they would be free to call for another vote at a later time, this vote would also be considered the first of a sequence—those involved would have to approve the separation at least twice in sequence, rather than simply voting twice. In other cases, the phase of constitution drafting would end the process—those involved would realize that they had been pursuing separation for very different reasons, many of them imagining an alternative to the status quo that is in fact unlikely to result. But secessionist leaders could not easily turn a refusal to write a constitution to political advantage, either—once the issue is raised, those involved will want to know what to expect, and can scarcely begrudge the state now ruling them fears of chaos on its doorstep.

These referenda should not be regarded simply as procedural hurdles. Rather, they are intended to create serious debate about what the real changes involved might consist in, what the results of such changes might be, and how they are related to quality of governance. They make it difficult for groups to secede on a momentary whim or in response to particular short-term grievances and for political leaders to maintain artificially heightened passions throughout the full process, and they allow groups to determine exactly what their real concerns are. In most cases, groups will recognize that there are other ways of resolving their concerns, or that these concerns cannot be resolved by separation at all. As Will Kymlicka (2001, 116) has noted, "while secessionist parties have been competing freely and actively in several Western democracies for decades, they have never received a democratic mandate for secession, and no referendum on secession has succeeded." It seems unlikely that such mandates would emerge much more often even where states acknowledge their possibility more readily (Weinstock 2001, 188–89). Where votes for separation do actually occur, on the other hand, they will have been as thoroughly debated as seems possible in political life, giving us very good reasons for taking them seriously.

Indeed, the common concern that secessionist leaders would merely use separatist demands as a way of blackmailing central governments would also be generally limited. In most cases, secessionist leaders will be exposed as more skilled in rhetoric than in designing an actual constitution for the proposed state and will be turned into a more garden-variety kind of politician in the process. Moreover, states will have few reasons to worry about the real prospects for separation until the first vote occurs, and then there will be substantial time to offer reasons for remaining or to remediate the policies of most concern to ordinary voters in the potentially secessionist territory—or to decide that separation would not be so bad after all. Of course, such procedural safeguards would not blunt the political leverage gained from secessionist claims entirely, but then no policy can do that—even states that have no legal provisions for secession can face such claims (Weinstock 2001), and this kind of procedure at least prevents them from looming larger than they really are.

This focus on democratic deliberation also makes it clear why requiring separatist groups to claim serious grievances can be counterproductive, even though improvements in the protection of citizens' basic moral interests remain the fundamental justification for my argument. If secessionists have to outline a strong set of grievances to make their case, it will be tempting for leaders to find or imagine incidents of victimization even when these are relatively few, and strong assertions of blame are less conducive to useful deliberation than other kinds of arguments. If secessionist leaders have to make a generalized case that separation will be worthwhile for those within their territory, they will be able to appeal to many kinds of reasons, including, most promisingly, those about different balances in the protection of rights or different social goals that governments might pursue. Doubtless many separatist leaders would choose to invoke notions of victimization anyway (and in fact serious victimization may exist in some cases), but where these are not central, discussion can more easily turn to the possible constitutional nature of their new state and thereby to more constructive dialogue.

What about the protection of cultural or national minorities within the potentially separatist territory? It is hard to imagine that any group would admit to plans for mistreating minorities within its boundaries, not least because it will probably want their votes to ensure success. Indeed, it seems likely that separatist groups would, in claiming the moral high ground, draw an explicit contrast with the government of the present state by endorsing strong protections for their own potentially endangered groups. And if separatist leaders must have at least a provisional constitution constructed before the final vote, they will not be able simply to give lip service to such concerns—it would certainly be noticed by opponents of separation if these promises were not given institutional form. Once protections are written into constitutions, both legal and public expectations will become built up around them, making it difficult to remove them. Thus, such commitments during the process of separation will usually be substantially carried over into the new state. As the best of possibilities, the prospect of procedural secession might even lead to a virtuous cycle, in which both states and separatist leaders try to outdo one another as exemplars of justice toward their minority populations.

So even where few secessions ever occurred, allowing the possibility of them would foster debate about what makes a state worth supporting, would spur states to take seriously the interests of their minority populations, and would provide incentives for dissatisfied groups to think seriously about how real or escapable their grievances may be. Allowing the possibility of exit might thus paradoxically make both the desire and need for it more rare, while allowing clear and orderly mechanisms through which groups can escape when they truly feel it necessary. I do not claim that allowing for the possibility of procedural secession would never create dangers, but then we live in a world where political dangers can never be avoided entirely. We can only minimize them, and I believe that taking the judgments of the ruled seriously whenever possible does that. We often say that democratic states are worthy of support because they provide valuable benefits. Why not allow that claim to be tested by the decisions of those who actually must live under their laws?

III. "Recursive" Territorial Boundaries

If this generalized case for self-determination is plausible, then we need to think seriously about a number of further questions, including how boundaries should be drawn for the relevant units, what limitations should exist on state size and enclave status, and how this kind of self-determination might apply both to indigenous nations and to the design of federalist arrangements. Let me consider first the question of boundaries.

Most of us probably envision separation as involving the largest subunits of a current country, whether these be provinces, states, or other entities. There are natural reasons for this: such subdivisions already have many elements of self-government, have determinate boundaries, and are relatively few in number. However, the existing boundaries will not always be the most appropriate for a potential new state. Consider, for example, a province where preferences for one allegiance or another are sharply divided along geographical lines, so that it could easily be divided once again. With such instances in mind, Harry Beran (1984, 29) has argued (on somewhat different grounds than I have here) that the option to pursue secession should be "recursive," with minorities having the right to secede from the newly independent country themselves.

While I think Beran has the right idea, his apparent mechanism for dealing with these adjustments seems needlessly complex. Beran seems to have in mind a sequence of changes, in which separatist territories achieve full independence and then subunits (e.g., counties or districts) go through a similar process, either to choose independence themselves or to join another state (including potentially that which the larger territory originally left). This seems needlessly awkward, particularly if each incident of separation must take as long as I have suggested it should. It seems more efficient and transparent simply to gather geographical information about preferences within potentially secessionist territories before any official votes are taken, so that boundaries can be more properly tailored to what people want. If the population in an existing subdivision is divided according to geography, why not take that into account in the first place?

Indeed, it would seem necessary to do so if voters are really to have much certainty of what they are voting on. Voters' judgments about the relative plausibility of separation will depend on what the proposed state will be like, and to evaluate this they will need to know what its size, shape, and population will be, in the same way that a provisional constitution will give them a better sense of how such a unit may be governed. Even if groups could still in principle choose to secede from this new unit, in practice this could be made very unlikely by taking such preferences into account from the very beginning—most potential changes will already have been taken care of in the initial stage of boundary construction.

But allowing the reshaping of boundaries does pose some challenges. While we could, for example, start from the level of counties or townships and work up, this would almost certainly reveal that populations with shared preferences are distributed in strongly noncontiguous ways. A majority within a checkerboard of counties might favor secession, while an interspersed minority might prefer the status quo, and another minority might favor joining another state.[5] The more exactly we try to reflect preferences on the ground, then, the more intermingled those preferences may turn out to be and the more difficult it becomes to say why new boundaries should be drawn in one place rather than another. Moreover, it would not do for my argument here simply to pose a set of abstract standards for drawing such new lines. Any solution must be one that states and secessionist leaders can actually apply and that can be understood by observing citizens.

As with everything else surrounding self-determination (and political life in general), there is no perfect solution here that avoids all dangers and gives everyone what they want. The best approach, however, is probably to begin at the level of the subunit(s) over which separatist leaders are making claims, gather information about preferences sorted by whatever subdivisions form the next level down, and use this information to fine-tune the borders. (For reasons of privacy, it would be mistaken to gather information down to the level of individual property holdings—doing so would make votes no longer secret, and so less likely to reflect honest judgments.) State and secessionist leaders could then begin a set of negotiations about specific boundaries—to be publicized as the process continued—in which areas were subtracted from or added to the edges of the original territory as seemed to fit the initial preferences of those involved.

In these negotiations, both sides would paradoxically have motivations not to claim too much territory. Separatist leaders, knowing that they would have to pass at least two referenda, would seek to limit their claims to areas where they expected to have a clear majority, while states, if they hoped for the referenda to be defeated, would proceed cautiously in dealing with secessionists. Even so, it would make sense to require some limits on the ways in which these negotiations could occur and on the language used in them. They should, as I have said, be made fully public, and since the basic function of a state lies in protecting rights, it also seems reasonable to hold that official arguments from either side must be directed toward creating boundaries that will ensure state effectiveness. On this score, the basic presumption would be that the relevant territories must be contiguous rather than divided and that they should follow natural boundaries or patterns of social interaction where possible (e.g., with a focus on population centers).

This would still leave multiple possibilities for the final arrangement, but beginning with existing subunits and requiring arguments for changes from them would ensure that the changes made were as transparent as possible. It would also make clear that a *better* fit with everyone's preferences was being sought, not a *perfect* fit, which has never been a real possibility short of returning to consent-based authority and all of its dangers. Throughout, the emphasis would be on political process and orderly deliberation, to make sure that everyone understands the changes being considered, their rationale, and their likely outcome. It would be too strong to pretend that such negotiations would always occur without rancor, but the possibility of self-determination in any form will always lead to charges that exact boundaries could be better constructed. The only way to avoid this would be to reject the possibility of procedural change entirely, thereby leaving populations without effective remedy even when they deeply reject the status quo. If all of those in the marginal territories where lines could have been drawn in multiple ways understand what the process has been and why one line rather than another has selected, they will have reason to regard the process as the least arbitrary available.

In most cases, the stage of information-gathering and negotiation over boundaries would probably once again dampen enthusiasm for separation. Such a process means that separatist leaders would not be able to predict in advance the exact shape of their final state (if they are ultimately successful), and gathering geographical information on judgments about secession would probably show that feelings are far more mixed and diverse than secessionist leaders might want to claim. Not only would this suggest that electoral victory may be less certain than secessionist leaders might hope, but it would also lead those involved to wonder whether separation would result in the kind of state they envisioned once the process has concluded. It would, in other words, reemphasize that potential political futures need to be evaluated seriously and not remain wide-open fantasies with whatever result one most desires. Some attempts at secession would doubtless continue anyway, and these would likely be the ones that deserve to be taken most seriously.

Because early information gathered about the geographical distribution of preferences for purposes of boundary construction would be rather indeterminate in its full implications (with the final territories as yet undefined), this initial solicitation of preferences could not legitimately count as a round of voting on secession itself. Successful secessions, then, will have to include at a minimum three instances in which individual judgments are solicited, with only the second and third taken as determinate judgments on the question of secession itself. From start to finish, the process of separation could thus reasonably take something like ten years or more once all of the relevant votes are carried out.

This may seem at first glance like a somewhat extended time line, but given the importance of the potential changes it involves, it makes sense to ensure that those involved really have chances to talk about what they are planning to do and to seek other options for whatever dissatisfactions they may have. When changes really do occur—and they will probably be very rare—we will have very good reason to take them seriously as the profound rejection of an existing political order, a rejection that surely deserves our moral respect.

IV. Enclaves and Size

The next set of questions, about the viability of enclaves and of extremely small states, is of central importance in evaluating the potential for separation by indigenous peoples. Both apply to most indigenous peoples and raise some serious concerns about separation; whether these concerns are sufficient to render full independence implausible is a harder question. (I should note that neither of these concerns inevitably arises in considering self-determination for indigenous peoples. Not all indigenous peoples would form enclaves; some might petition for and receive the option of annexing themselves to a state other than that presently ruling them.)

Consider first the question of whether territories can separate when they would become enclaves, that is, remain entirely surrounded by the country presently ruling them. Beran (1984, 30–31), in listing the conditions that might make secession illegitimate, suggests that enclaves are problematic but need not always be disqualified. The basic fear concerning enclaves is that because they are necessarily too dependent on the state surrounding them, they cannot control their own fate sufficiently to claim sovereignty. If that state chooses to cut off commerce with them, how will they survive? Perhaps some potential enclaves might be large enough to grow their own food and otherwise produce most of what they need, but most will not. Can such a territory really regard itself as independent?

But this may not be the right way to think of independence in the modern world. As American Indian scholar Vine Deloria Jr. (1974, 171–73) has noted, few states try to remain economically independent in this way anymore, and those that do are staggeringly poor. Most states now recognize not only the value of such interrelationships, but also the moral legitimacy of them, and it seems extremely unlikely that states would prohibit businesses within their territory from involvement with an enclave. As Deloria (172) notes, although large and powerful states could easily use military force to conquer small and weak states, they rarely do this in the present day. In the same way, crushing economic sanctions are generally recognized as illegitimate, their deployment permissible only when states are mistreating portions of their own populations very badly (and then such attempts are usually counterproductive). Therefore, this kind of extreme scenario is probably not likely where potential enclaves are concerned, particularly if there is substantial time before the political transition occurs for tempers to cool and business plans to be made.

Still, I do not want to deny the generalized political vulnerability of enclaves and the difficulties of clearly establishing full independence when so much depends on a single surrounding state. But I believe the decision about these risks is best left to those within the potential enclave, who will have obvious reasons for caution in seeking separation, since their practical (rather than legal) independence will be reduced and in separating they will lose whatever political influence and legal rights they had under their former government. They will, for example, be giving up their ability to solve disputes through a shared court system, their ability to rely on assistance from a much larger population in cases of economic downturn, their easy right of travel throughout the larger area, and their ability to choose representatives for the surrounding state, which will continue to affect their political prospects. They will also certainly recognize that the loss of their legal relationships might prompt the surrounding state to be rougher with them politically in a number of ways, even if it does not engage in a wholesale economic blockade. If, after a long process of deliberation, a majority within this territory chooses independence despite a detailed awareness and full discussion of these problems, it seems wrong to regard them as fools or dupes who simply do not understand the consequences of their actions. So I see no reason for a ban on the formation of enclaves within existing democratic states. It is hard to imagine that they would be formed very often, and presumably only by populations who felt they had been mistreated over a very long period—who else would feel compelled to attempt such an incomplete kind of separation?

Another concern that leads many people to believe that the promise of full independence for indigenous peoples is a counterproductive myth (e.g., Cairns 2000, 4–10) is the extremely small size of most indigenous populations. A recurrent and serious fear is that without outside assistance, indigenous populations simply could not manage the governing institutions necessary for them to operate. In most states, government programs are administered by professional bureaucrats, and there are significant reasons for this: such persons can develop the specialized knowledge to carry out these programs over time and can master the complex legal environments in which these programs are emplaced. For some administrative and policy roles, such as environmental regulation, extensive scientific education is necessary, and often teams of experts are necessary to analyze particular problems. (Remember, my assumption above was that populations are generally good at evaluating the *overall* quality of governance; this did not challenge the importance of expert knowledge for shaping particular policies.)

But there are reasons to question how disqualifying this concern really is. Certainly, various kinds of expertise are needed for resolving policy questions, but many people with such expertise are available for hire from private businesses. Why wouldn't we expect minuscule states to make such arrangements whenever they need such knowledge? Moreover, tiny states do not need to solve all problems for themselves; they can also adopt policies as templates from other countries if these seem appropriate. And, perhaps most importantly, very small states do not need the massive bureaucracies found in larger states. These are designed for an anonymous population, where persons from myriad circumstances find themselves affected by a single policy. In smaller states, laws and policies do not need to be designed for such a wide range of circumstances. They can instead be designed for the real problems at hand, with knowledge of the actual circumstances to which these policies will be applied, and thus can at least potentially be targeted far more effectively (see, e.g., Kershell 1992). These costs and benefits seem to be, then, of a kind that those within the relevant territory can reasonably judge for themselves—when the costs are too high, we would expect groups simply to reject such separation.

There are other concerns about the efficacy of extremely small states as well, such as the risk that their governing institutions will be captured by some element of the population or that they will be excessively vulnerable to economic downturns (cf. Armstrong and Read 2000), but these concerns likewise seem best dealt with through the choices of those involved. Anyone contemplating an attempt at separation by a tiny enclave would be extremely aware of the dangers involved and of the sharply reduced room for real political maneuvering, and in most instances it is hard to imagine groups really choosing to attempt this. But it nonetheless seems premature simply to say that small populations cannot protect their own members without extensive involvement from a larger state's legal mechanisms—why should we believe that a small population cannot solve its correspondingly limited challenges for itself? Why shouldn't we allow populations to choose this for themselves if they wish to do so?

V. States and Social Order

The most serious concern about indigenous states as potentially minuscule enclaves, I suspect, lies not in the inherent incapacity of such units to protect their own populations well, but in the implicit possibility of radical fragmentation. In other words, "What if everyone did it?" In the last chapter, I argued against consent on the ground that it could lead to a bewildering array of territorially intermingled political units, where recognizing the limits of political jurisdiction would be extremely difficult and quite chaotic. Allowing tiny groups to form states might seem to imply such chaos as well. While in the present day there are three independent states with populations of twenty thousand or less (Tuvalu, Nauru, and Palau), would it really be a good idea to allow such states as a matter of general principle? I have been arguing so far for rights to separation that can in principle apply to virtually any group, but doesn't there have to be a lower limit on the size of independent political units to avoid a descent into political chaos?

Perhaps, although whether such states should be prohibited on principled grounds depends in part on how many groups would actually choose this. In practice, few of them are likely to demand full separation, and even fewer are likely ever to vote on it. (Remember that I have been talking about procedural separation from stable democratic states, where there are generally powerful reasons to remain in a strong relationship with the larger state.) But this is doubtless too convenient an answer.

If we want a generalized lower limit on the population size of self-determining groups, what should it be? There is no perfectly principled way to decide this, since it will depend partially on the relative risks to political order. Setting it at a population of one million, for example, would in theory allow the United States to be divided into three hundred different countries, but no one, I take it, really has any expectation of that happening. Consider the Navajo Nation in the American Southwest, however, which has easily the largest indigenous population on contiguous lands in the United States, Canada, or Australia. The current land area of the Navajo reservation is about the size of the American state of West Virginia and substantially larger than Denmark or Switzerland (Deloria 1974, 166)—surely this must be a "state-sized" entity in territorial terms. The reservation's population of one hundred and eighty thousand is considerably less state-sized but is comparable to that of independent island countries such as Samoa and Vanuatu and is not far behind that of Belize (Pirotta et al. 2001, 160–61). At a minimum, the prospect of independence for this territory is more difficult to dispose of out of hand. So while, to prevent jurisdictional chaos, we probably do need some lower limit on the size of fully independent states, it is not entirely clear how this should be determined. (In practice, there is nothing to suggest that many Navajos are interested in separation anyway, so this example is mostly hypothetical, but also indicative of the success democratic states can have even with populations who might be expected to reject them.)

But wherever we draw the limit, there may be reasons to allow smaller groups to exit if we can provide reasons why. When discussing the bases of political authority, we faced an all-or-nothing decision: either states could have authority only through consent or the authority would have to be based on something less voluntaristic. Natural duties, however, can allow for greater subtlety in deciding which arrangements deserve our support. Moreover, there is no assumption in natural duties that each person's preferences will be equally reflected in structures of governance. Those who are dissatisfied with an existing state, for example, and happen to live in a territory where many others feel the same will have good chances to live in a state fitting their preferences; persons with similar preferences living elsewhere will not. Thus, if we can show reasons for including some groups rather than others within the relevant categories, there is nothing illegitimate in allowing some groups political options that are not available to all to all people. Simply because we cannot allow *all* small groups to escape the states now ruling them does not entail that no groups should *ever* have claims to do so.

Consider as an example ten people on board an airplane about to crash that has only three parachutes. None of us, I take it, would find it objectionable that three people should use the parachutes to survive while the rest should perish, even if there were no morally relevant differences between them. We would want, if possible, some clear method for choosing among the candidates—those on board might choose three people randomly, for example, or might give rights of first acquisition to those who found the parachutes hidden in a storage area. If there were some hope that the crash will be survivable, on the other hand, we might want to assign parachutes to give everyone an equal chance—we might, for example, give the parachutes to those who were least healthy or who were for other reasons ill-suited for surviving a crash (e.g., if they were very large and therefore likely to receive less protection from the airplane's extraordinarily protective seats). Perhaps most interestingly, we also might want to give the parachutes to certain people if it were especially important that they survive for extrinsic reasons (e.g., if they were doctors on their way to cure a plague).

The point, then, is that if we can show some compelling reason, there is nothing illegitimate in allowing some very small states to exist without allowing everyone to pursue this option. In the next chapter, I will consider whether indigenous peoples might be relevantly different and thus entitled to more extensive rights to political exit than ordinary populations. As I will argue, the case for doing this is not as obvious as indigenous arguments sometimes suggest (particularly since it can have nothing to do with first arrival in a particular territory), but this kind of specialized right is not as absurd as skeptics about indigenous rights might contend, either. The potential for such rights hinges on whether a substantive case can be made that shows that indigenous groups either (a) are more liable to mistreatment than other kinds of groups or (b) have special resources to offer that deserve to be protected for extrinsic reasons. I will argue that there may be reasons to believe both to be true.

VI. Partial Separation

To this point, I have been focusing on the question of full separation, but given the small size and political vulnerability of most indigenous populations, it also seems essential to consider how the argument for self-determination might apply to more intermediate kinds of separation, especially since most indigenous peoples seem more interested in such arrangements than they do in full separation.

There are good reasons why groups might want to avoid full separation. A group that chooses to entirely sever legal relationships with the state now ruling it is embarking on an uncertain venture, one that is even more uncertain when the group is extremely small and relatively poor. Moreover, having legal control over the group's own affairs (subject only to the limitations of international law and basic morality) does not always translate into greater substantive control. While achieving independence allows a group to shape the laws it wishes for itself, it also subtracts most of the legal protections the group previously enjoyed from its original country and leaves it with few certain mechanisms for ensuring that other states live up to whatever agreements they reach with it. This is of particular concern to very small groups, but it is something that any population seeking separation will have to consider seriously. The uncertain benefits will usually persuade most populations, particularly very small ones, that the risks are not worth taking. Thus, in most cases groups may want something short of full separation but less than full inclusion; they will want opportunities to control those aspects of their political life that seem most important to them, while leaving others under the legal control of the larger state.

There is a wide range of intensity in the relationships that groups might seek with their current state. American Indian scholar Vine Deloria Jr. (1974, 176–83), for example, has argued that many Indian nations might do best to strive for a protectorate status, with the United States continuing responsibilities for defense (something quite easy in the case of enclaves) and perhaps some other international matters, and Indian nations enjoying full self-rule over their own territories, along with a limited international status for some purposes. This status would clearly allow far more room for self-rule than these nations now have, since it would allow them to control all aspects of lawmaking within their own borders and might allow some direct representation in international forums. Deloria seems to have in mind that each group would negotiate its relationship through treaties or something similar, with some retaining far closer ties to the United States than others.

In the case of protectorates, Indian nations would generally not have citizenship in the United States and would therefore not have votes in choosing its leadership. However, there are also a variety of more closely integrated forms of partial separation. Groups could, for example, seek a form of association in which they have extensive self-rule but also limited representation in the governing structures of a surrounding state, so that those in a territory are citizens for some purposes but not others. We might conceive the relationship between the United States and Puerto Rico in this way (cf. Deloria 1974, 182). We can also imagine a range of cases where separation is less sharp and the kinds of self-rule are thereby reduced. Federalist arrangements are most tightly integrated in this way—all populations within federalist subunits tend to have the same kinds of citizenship rights and theoretically equal opportunities to influence the central government, but these subunits themselves have limited authority over a variety of issues that are primarily of local interest.

Groups interested in a very attenuated relationship, such as protectorate status, may be able to sever their legal ties entirely and draft their relationships anew after secession. Most kinds of partial separation will not have this quality, however. They will instead require that the group maintain a very substantial legal relationship with the state now ruling it. For that reason, a group's hopes for customized protections will have to be quite sensitive to the future of interactions with the state now ruling it. Partial separation is always a balancing act and requires delicate care in deciding how to constitutionalize whatever autonomy groups are seeking. In some cases, groups will be able to adopt a legal template that other groups already use, as happens when new groups are recognized as Indian tribes in the United States. But groups that seek to extend existing protections or to create new types of autonomous areas will always have difficulty determining what kinds of legal relationships they really want and will always face disagreement about whether what they want is appropriate.

These negotiations are made doubly difficult by the reasonable concerns central governments can have about such partial relationships. One concern lies in the potential for purely strategic behavior, where groups seek increased self-rule simply to pursue self-interested political goals. But if the procedures for seeking increased self-rule are as demanding as those for full separation, this kind of behavior is probably less likely; groups will often find it easier to make threats than to carry changes out, and, unless they believe they have real grievances, will generally see the costs of such activity as outweighing the benefits. (Once again, it will not do simply to note that such groups might have bad motivations—so might majority groups.) The more persistent concern lies in striking the correct balance between inclusion and exclusion so that the group is tolerably satisfied and the rest of the state can continue to govern common issues well. The biggest worry here is political paralysis, but another is the creation of a situation in which one side or the other ends up exercising undue influence. As Will Kymlicka (2001, 108) has noted, in an ideal world the representatives of groups with self-rule on some issues would be required to recuse themselves when those policy fields came up for vote in the central government, so that they would not play a role in choosing policies that did not apply to them. But, as Kymlicka notes, this kind of separation between policy fields is never easy to achieve and can pose some puzzles in deciding whether groups are being represented fairly.[6] This is less of a problem for small groups such as indigenous peoples, who are usually unable to influence government substantially through electoral means anyway, but striking the correct balance remains a real concern.

How, then, should these concerns be defused? It should be obvious that groups seeking to change their status will have to pursue it through the same deliberation-intensive processes used for full separation, since we will need mechanisms for recognizing whether they really desire the change, what territorial boundaries the change might apply to, and so on. The best method, I think, would be to have groups go through multiple phases of voting in the same way for partial separation as for full, but to require that they produce a qualitatively different kind of public document. Rather than constructing a constitution for an independent state, they should be responsible for listing in careful detail the kinds of self-rule they are seeking, their reasons for doing so, and the constitutional revisions that might be necessary. They would have both a mandate and a motivation to propose revisions that were consistent with what already existed; the odds of their proposals being accepted would thus increase. The central state would then be responsible for responding carefully to their claims for a separate status in a public way, considering the viability of the proposed self-rule, the appropriateness of their constitutional proposals, and so on.

But at this point we face a difficulty: can there be a binding vote, and if so, who would be involved? In instances of full separation, those seeking independence will have to establish clear boundaries with their former state, but they will not have to maintain an intensive legal relationship over the long term, in which representatives will decide common issues and shape at least some laws together. In instances of partial separation, however, allowing the group seeking self-rule to make a final and binding choice seems to give it a very large degree of power in this shared state, particularly if it is able to choose the way in which its protections will be constitutionalized as well. While it is hard to imagine that a group would be too abrasive in its demands when it planned to continue interacting with the rest of the state, it is nonetheless possible that some groups would behave badly even after a long and focused public debate about the changes they were seeking. But if we refuse them the right to make the choice, the whole process may seem underwhelming—what good will it do for groups to vote on anything, if they will not ultimately have the legal right to decide? What makes partial separation a necessarily awkward arrangement is that groups are seeking to become the final authority for some purposes and not for others.

As with much of political life, there is no perfect way to escape this difficulty. Any legal regime we can design always has the capacity to leave groups in disagreement about what relationship is appropriate, and this cannot always be resolved in a determinate way so long as they wish to remain together. And yet there are good reasons to want groups to find a middle ground whenever possible—not only is separation always uncertain, but groups that use claims for full separation as a mere bargaining chip in pursuing something short of it will face deliberative barriers in expressing honestly and clearly what they really want. Moreover, not all groups will be able to use such a threat effectively or desire to do so, and it seems unwise to say that due to their political weakness they must remain with the status quo.

So what should be done? For partial separation, the strongest that can be achieved is to allow groups to go through a series of referenda and to develop a clear and public plan for a partially separate existence, and then to have an honest chance to receive this if they vote for it. Although there is no unambiguous way to give them a legal right to achieve this status, it seems reasonable to hold that states should allow groups to pursue this kind of process and should take the results seriously as creating a mandate for negotiation. If groups are willing to continue long and systematic discussions in search of self-rule even in the absence of determinate legal tools for ensuring that they receive it, then, by the arguments in this chapter, states should make every effort to provide them with what they seek, even if not always through exactly the constitutional provisions they suggest. In many cases, such a systematic attempt to outline goals, coupled with multiple positive votes in favor a change in status, would persuade the population of the encompassing state that the change should in fact be permitted, while in others it would persuade those seeking partial separation that this would not achieve their desired goals after all. In still other cases, it would lead to a standoff, in which a central government refused to acknowledge the judgment of a large population believing that the state has failed. But this would be nothing new, since most groups that pursue the full process will have been expressing similar desires before it began anyway.

This is an instance, then, in which the deliberative democrat's faith in the power of argument will have to play a central role. The power of ideas and arguments never seems as decisive as that of unambiguous laws or political leverage, but it is the primary tool at the disposal of many groups. It is always dissatisfying to say that states should negotiate "in good faith" with such groups, since states do not always do this and there is no way to ensure that they do. But many states will in fact negotiate if the case can be made to their citizens in compelling terms, and this kind of exhortation (included in legal standards whenever possible) will have to be the best option available. If necessary, however, truly dissatisfied groups will have a final option available to them, if they wish to exercise it: separation, and the chance to pursue their own future alone or in conjunction with any other groups that may wish to join them.

Would an expectation that groups seeking self-rule be given the benefit of the doubt sometimes lead to strategic behavior or foolish decisions or constitutional difficulties? Yes—but then so will the expectation that an existing state will behave wisely and fairly. As I have tried to argue throughout this chapter, we cannot live in a political world with no dangers, where all governments are magically administered by the wise and just. The best we can achieve is an imperfect government of humans, and in doing this we will have to trust to human judgment, with all its potential for failure. Judging the impact of laws is a difficult and demanding thing—why not, whenever possible, leave that decision to the population living under them?

But does this room for self-rule extend down to small groups like indigenous peoples? Here again we face the question of small populations, and whether some populations should find an easier road to protections than others. That, then, is the topic of the next chapter: do cultural differences matter, and if so, how should they be reflected in political arrangements?

EIGHT

CULTURE AND MORAL DISAGREEMENT

To this point in the book, I have generally been working within Western philosophical viewpoints, and my close focus on the nature of political authority and mechanisms by which virtually any group can pursue separation may have seemed to miss many of the issues relevant to indigenous peoples. In this chapter, I will try to show why this is not so, and will try to determine whether there is something special about indigenous peoples that entitles them to protections other groups lack.

As I noted in the last chapter, if we can show compelling reasons, it seems plausible to allow some small groups opportunities for full or partial separation that cannot be allowed to all groups. In this chapter, I will argue that, at least within wealthy democratic countries like the United States and Canada, claims to cultural difference should be taken more seriously when made by indigenous peoples than by other groups. In doing so, I will have to disentangle some of the complex and ambiguous linkages between nationalist self-conceptions, cultural practices, and moral disagreement. Ultimately, I will argue that judgments about real degrees of cultural difference are persistently difficult to make and that existing states will fare best if they begin from a presumption that indigenous groups remain different in relevant ways. I will close by outlining what I take to be some broad patterns of indigenous difference and by suggesting that indigenous peoples might provide sources of creative intellectual tension for surrounding settler populations, particularly if they are allowed greater space to put their social conceptions into political practice.

I. Nation, Culture, and Moral Disagreement

What does it mean to talk about cultural difference, and how should we recognize populations that are different in important ways? There are many interpretations of what a "culture" might be; some authors (e.g., Kymlicka 1995, 11; cf. Kymlicka 1989, 179–80n2) treat the term as synonymous with "nation." I believe this interpretation confuses what is really at stake, however. While most national groups believe themselves to be culturally different, this is not always accurate—groups can often perceive themselves to be more different than they really are, and there will rarely be anyone in a position to judge whether these perceptions are correct. Even where groups really are different, recognizing them as such will usually be difficult, and we will frequently have to use a variety of proxies to navigate the challenges of judgment involved.

To make the relevant distinctions as clear as possible, let me begin by outlining what I take to be the basic character of a "nation." Reduced to its core, the concept of a nation need not reflect any fundamental attachment to a particular notion of culture, even if in practice it tends to do so. A sense of national membership, as I understand it, entails a feeling of attachment to some relatively determinate population that is believed to be of special political relevance. This attachment can be conceptualized in a variety of ways (cf. Levy 2000, chap. 3). While most involve culture, they can also involve race or descent, shared religion, or something else. To be a member of a nation in this sense is to see oneself as part of a much larger collective entity that extends both backward and forward in time and that somehow naturally fits together as a social actor for many purposes, particularly political ones. In many ways, nations imagine themselves as families writ large, with a kind of naturalistic and long-standing character to them, in which persons generally become members by birth or background rather than by choice. While people can sometimes choose to join a nation (in the same way that families can adopt children), the converse is more difficult, with people subject to being treated as traitors even by nations that they never identified with personally (see, e.g., Levy 2000, 72–81).

This way of imagining oneself as a member of an often-anonymous but strangely naturalistic group with a political character seems to be a pervasive feature of human life in the present circumstances, whether we want it to be or not (cf. Miller 1995; Yack 2001). But it has no necessary relationship with cultural difference, not only because nations can be imagined in slightly different terms (e.g., by descent) but because a sense of connectedness is qualitatively distinct from culture (see below).

Where should feelings of nationalism, taken in their pure form as imagined connections to other people, fit within the conception of political authority that I have been developing throughout this book? There seems to be little need to give them a central place, because once rights to carefully regulated procedural separation have been acknowledged, then mechanisms already exist allowing for boundaries to be readjusted around these perceptions (in a slow and orderly way). New boundaries, when they are created, will often reflect these perceptions of connectedness, although they will also reshape them in important ways as groups come to realize that they are united by less or more than they believe. While one might be tempted to suggest, as I noted in the last chapter, that groups seeking separation are more likely to be under the spell of blindly nationalist ideologies, this seems an implausibly convenient view, since it implies that majority populations are inherently more tolerant and enlightened (see, e.g., Denis 1997, chap. 1). The fact is that both majority and minority populations can engage in bad behavior because of their perceived connections to some people rather than others, and there is no obvious way to ensure that only the truly virtuous will get their way in any real political system. The best we can do is to allow groups to separate when they wish to do so, but subject to careful procedural guidelines that foster as much debate as possible about the issues involved.[1]

Even if the idea of a national identity is not inescapably linked to a notion of cultural difference, however, many individuals will nonetheless believe their nation to be different in important ways, and in practice many patterns of national identification have grown out of historical divergences. When called upon to say why certain people belong together and not others, people will often say that their common nationality lies in shared social practices or values—that, for example, "we" believe in liberty while others do not, or that "we" believe in charity to our fellows, and so on. And even if the purely imagined attachments characteristic of national self-conceptions should play no independent role in determining the character of self-determination, it may be that cultural difference should play a more substantial role—perhaps even a role that is mediated through nationalist perceptions in some cases.

What, then, is cultural difference, and how much should it matter? Even with questions of nationality left aside, there are multiple ways of conceptualizing what is at stake here. For initial purposes, we can define a culture as a set of persons who are engaged in a common set of social practices, about which they at least potentially share a set of beliefs. Given this definition, we can attempt to distinguish one culture from another primarily by contrast. The relevance of the contrast will vary according to the context with which we are concerned; groups that seem culturally different from one perspective may appear very similar when viewed in comparison to those with even more divergent practices (such as for "indigenous peoples" as a category). For the moment, I will leave aside the difficulties involved in recognizing when one culture ends and another begins.

Do shared social practices entail shared beliefs about the values and reasons for those practices? As I will argue, this is often difficult to say, but so that we can see more clearly what is at stake in different conceptions of cultural difference, I will assume initially that practices really are based on substantial agreement within the group. Broadly speaking, there are two types, or levels, of cultural difference, each of which has a very different political status and calls for a different political response. The first, the "neutral" level, calls for the protection of individual rights but can provide additional impetus for rights to self-determination as I outlined them in the last chapter. The second, the "deep" level, raises more difficult issues and takes us into more uncertain political terrain.

I call the first level "neutral" because it involves issues that are morally indifferent from the standpoint of protecting rights. Any group recognizable as a culture will by definition share a variety of social practices (albeit with varying levels of intensity and commonality), but many of these practices will not deal with deep questions about the protections that individuals should enjoy. Cultural groups usually show at least some patterns of commonality on a variety of everyday matters, such as preferences for patterns of dress, styles of art, standards of politeness, and so on. For any given person, many of these preferences can be impeded without great distress, and this makes it tempting to see them as unimportant. However, while this may be true of each small piece, the whole is usually of great importance. These small things play a fundamental role in shaping who we are, allowing us to feel at home in the world and to understand what a happy human life looks like (see, e.g., Kymlicka 1995, 82–84). Failing to take our preferences seriously means failing to take us seriously as human beings.

This might seem too obvious to need mentioning, since the basic justification for rights in the first place comes from the differences between the kinds of projects individuals have. Unfortunately, such "neutral" differences can too often become seen as political problems to be changed by coercive means. This is often true in regard to minority cultures, and especially indigenous peoples.

Colonial states, once they gained control over indigenous groups, often spent vast time and energy giving them new names, forcing them to wear new styles of clothing and live in new kinds of dwellings, and so on. While one might argue that democratic states have outgrown such policies, it seems hard to say this too confidently. While matters in this regard may be improving over time, there remains a persistent tendency in all of us to see our own cultural features as natural and to legislate accordingly. Given this tendency, we can see additional force in the argument that groups should be able to escape a state that seems deeply misguided to them; they will in many cases be escaping a state that, in "merely" interfering with their cultural practices, was persistently failing to treat them as persons worthy of respect.

Perhaps more importantly, Will Kymlicka (1995) has rightly noted that many state policies cannot be constructed to be neutral among different cultural practices and symbols, even if majority populations could be counted on to pursue this goal. Kymlicka (108–13) argues that the notion of "benign neglect," in which states simply stay out of cultural matters (e.g., Waldron 1995), simply is not a real option where laws must be drafted in one language or another, where any set of state holidays or public uniforms will reflect the traditions of some cultures better than others, and so on. States can do a better or worse job of reducing their impact in this way, but states that do not reflect any particular set of cultural idioms and practices are nonetheless not social possibilities in the real world, and no amount of exhortation can make them so.

Kymlicka argues that, given these realities, minority groups should receive particularized protections to counterbalance these disadvantages. He argues that these protections should be seen not as competitors to individual rights, but as additional protections designed to offset the dangers posed by the legal system itself. Given the far greater vulnerability of indigenous peoples to this kind of disadvantage, it seems reasonable to give them relatively more extensive protections. For similar reasons, it seems plausible to give indigenous groups precedence when concerns of public order require that options to full or partial separation be limited to some groups rather than all (see the last chapter). Of course, one might object that indigenous groups are really not different in the relevant way anymore. For the moment I will set this objection aside; below I will address why I think it is mistaken. If these groups really are different in some substantial way, then Kymlicka seems to be right in holding that particularized protections will be appropriate for them—at least where they are willing to protect the rights of their members.

And this brings us to what is in many ways the central question where cultural difference is concerned. I have so far been discussing "neutral" forms of difference—those that are easily consistent with the protection of individual rights.[2] In practice, cultural difference can often run much deeper, and indeed many groups may want to choose a separate status precisely because they (or some of their dominant members) feel that the value put on rights within existing states is in error or that these rights are better protected through some alternative forms of political organization. In many cases, groups are quite willing to protect rights as they are usually understood and to use means of electoral governance. This is not always true, however, and we should not let the analytic distinction between neutral and deep forms of cultural difference blind us to the existence of the latter.

II. Traditions of Moral Argument

How, then, should we conceptualize "deep" cultural difference? To understand it as a form of difference that necessarily *endangers* rights would be misleading—it is, rather, any form of difference that posits a conception of the moral world that either rejects formulating moral protections for individuals as "rights" or rejects particular features of democratic governance that I have asserted to be essential to the protection of such rights.

Since the terminology of cultural difference could mean many things in this context, let me try to clarify further. I do not mean to suggest that cultures are holistic entities in which a single moral viewpoint is shared by all members in some monolithic sense. Some people, particularly those influenced by classical anthropology, continue to hold views of a world neatly divided into self-contained and internally unified "cultures," but this no longer seems a tenable view. John Cook (1999, chap. 7) argues that this conception of cultures arose from a methodological choice by early anthropologists, intended to limit the amount of bias the observer himself brought to the task. The reasons for it were plausible: if an observer expected to see commonality between his own normative viewpoint and the viewpoints of the group studied, he could easily fail to probe deeply enough to learn what they believed they were doing. This was coupled with an additional methodological assumption that could be called the principle of "probable consistency"—if the reasons for some practices were not obvious or seemed to clash with the reasons for other practices, it made sense to assume that there was actually a coherent system underlying the way of life as a whole. If observers had, by contrast, simply assumed that the practices were incoherent, they would have been likely to give up before discovering anything new.[3]

While these methodological choices seem to have been reasonable when they were adopted, they unfortunately made it easy for those who came after—particularly in nonanthropological fields—to continue to envision cultures as entirely unified wholes and to assume that different worldviews are fully distinct and basically incommensurable. On this view, some groups believe certain things and some believe others, and meaningful arguments across boundaries are impossible because the normative presumptions involved simply do not allow real commonality. In popular debates in the present day, this clean distinctiveness is sometimes taken to imply a generalized cultural relativism, in which moral and other kinds of arguments cannot proceed across these different borders; more reasonably, it can be taken to imply a straightforward cultural tolerance, in which every different group should be left alone to live according to the view of the world that all members apparently share.

It now seems clear that this view of distinctive and utterly separate cultural wholes is descriptively implausible. Anthropologists now recognize that patterns of cultural belief and practice are more complex and transient than this view allows, and that many people "within" the same putative culture often have very different conceptions of whether their social practices are justified, and why. Women, for example, will often have very different perceptions of what a set of cultural practices entails than do men within the same group (e.g., Moody-Adams 1997, 48–49; Okin 1999) and may therefore share more with similarly placed persons in other groups than they do with those they interact with daily. In many cases, members of a "culture" will continuously contest dominant practices as unjust, incoherent, or based on factually implausible beliefs, and all of these complicate any simple view of cultural groups as riveted together by a unitary set of beliefs about what they are really doing. Michele Moody-Adams (1997) argues that our experience of moral disagreement within "our own" cultures should make us unavoidably aware of this fact—social practices, whoever's they may be, are always subject to challenge and revision through time because the individuals living within them are constantly testing their worth and evaluating them. Indeed, it would be surprising and strange if the beliefs of different cultures were really so incommensurable in this way; all societies are made up of human beings with similar physical and (more roughly) psychological needs, and all have to solve many similar problems (cf. Walzer 1994, 8)

We should not, however, move too swiftly to the opposite conclusion that all people actually value the same things and that the source of divergent cultural practices lies in the bad faith of those who have social power (cf. Moody-Adams 1994) or in the sheer weight of bad traditions. Even if cultures are complex and internally divided and have substantial overlap across them, it does not follow that real and deep divisions do not exist between the practices accepted by most members of one cultural tradition and those accepted by most members of another. Nor does a belief that some moral principles are better than others mean that we can easily recognize which are most defensible. Even if the problem is not one of mutually incommensurable cultures facing one another across a divide where only power can decide the issue, nothing in the fact of cultural complexity suggests that arguing across different cultural and moral traditions will necessarily be easy. People from different normative traditions or frameworks can usually argue with one another in mutually comprehensible and even persuasive ways, but doing so is not a simple matter when they bring very different preconceptions to the table (Mehta 2000; Hendrix 2007; cf. Waldron 2000).

We cannot, in other words, jump directly from the fact that cultural practices are always contested in profound ways to the conclusion that our own frameworks are therefore validated by default. Nor can our sense that oppression is bad lead us automatically to some endorsement of liberalism or natural rights, despite the ease with which that conclusion may suggest itself. As Claude Denis (1997, 152) has noted, "Liberal ideology is, in some sense, the West at its best—the West as it likes to dream itself. . . . But liberal ideology is not, by any means, an accurate description of life anywhere on this planet." Denis's point is not (or not only) that liberal societies engage in bad behaviors in practice—it is, rather, that liberal arguments can create the illusion that barriers to individual autonomy will disappear once and for all in the right kind of society. In fact, however, any social system will inevitably put a variety of relatively arbitrary limitations on the choices and behaviors available to those within it. The problem, then, is that it is extremely easy to compare our own idealized conception of ourselves to the most visibly repugnant behaviors of others and to conclude that we are civilized and they are barbarians in need of social change, by force if necessary. It is tempting to believe that we could not possibly have a mistaken view of what a good social order looks like, because we feel so sure of ourselves, but we should remember that the people who created disastrous programs of assimilation in the past usually believed in the value of what they were doing as well (cf. Sparrow 2000, 357–58). It is perhaps comforting to believe that such people were always acting in bad faith, but it is historically wrong—some of those who fought most fiercely to abolish slavery in the United States, for example, played central roles in crafting deeply misguided policies (e.g., allotment) toward American Indians. Confidence or sincerity is thus no protection against profound moral error: even well meaning people can be led deeply astray by illusions about their own wise judgment.

Since we ourselves are unalterably anchored within a set of historically constituted debates about what a good social order consists in, the simple fact is that we have no certain way of knowing whether other normative traditions represent a legacy of error and bad faith, or whether they are in fact superior to our own. Nor can we be certain that we will judge more reliably if we bear down and apply our full reasoning capacities over an extended period of time, given the limits on the knowledge we have available to us and the limits of human cognitive capacities (cf. Hendrix 2007). Since we cannot debate everything at once, we will always have to rely on a large set of assumptions and preconceptions about the moral world that are likely to be mistaken, incomplete, or incoherent in their own right (Mehta 2000). It would be helpful, of course, if we could design experiments as scientists do so that we could at least winnow out a wide range of bad ideas, but in practice such experiments occur only where human societies choose to engage in them, and the lessons learned are rarely unambiguous.

If we think too deeply about the historical failures of well-meaning people very like ourselves, the complexity of moral questions, and the unavoidable incompleteness of all argumentative traditions, it is easy to fall into a moral paralysis. (Alternatively, we can fall into ethnocentric arrogance and decide that since moral argument will not help anyway, we can act in whatever way we prefer.) If we know that all normative traditions, including our own, are incomplete in various ways, then we must admit that we have no certain way of knowing whether any action we take will cause or allow moral atrocities to occur. Seen in this light, the tendency to treat all cultures as relatively equal becomes understandable. (Cook [1999, 28] calls this "moral recusal" rather than simply toleration.) But utter nonaction will not rescue us either. Not only is it impossible, since we will affect the world in one way or another if we are to live at all, but the internal diversity of other cultural traditions makes it likely that our inaction will help to facilitate multiple horrific wrongs. Nor will it help much to say that we are merely allowing the wrong, not doing it ourselves. This may be true, but, as I noted in discussing natural duties, we are not thereby absolved of all culpability.

Thus, whether we reshape a set of social practices or leave them alone, we can never really be sure whether we are acting rightly, although (given a basic knowledge of the past) we can be sure that we are getting things wrong at least some of the time. While we may have greater confidence if we have exposed our ideas to argumentation as widely as possible, this again is no guarantee, particularly given the relatively limited audiences we are likely to interact with. It might help our confidence if we could gain the agreement of members from alternative normative traditions, since this would demonstrate that our conclusions can be reached from different starting points (cf. Mohanty 1997, 234–51). But we will not always receive such comforts, and at any rate agreement among the purported spokesmen for diverse traditions will not always indicate moral rightness; it may simply demonstrate that multiple traditions share the same kinds of errors, as has generally been true in regard to the status of women (cf. Pollit 1999).

It is thus easy to see why thinking too deeply about these issues may result in moral nihilism or a blind adherence to our inherited moral frameworks, but giving up on reasoning and argumentation is ultimately no kind of cure. We will, after all, have to do something in the world, and reason and argument seem to be the only tools we have for deciding on the quality of our choices. So my point here is not that we should simply stop making arguments—indeed, that would be a strange thing to say at this point in the book! It is, rather, to say that we should be wary of excessive confidence in our own viewpoints, particularly where something as complex as the correct organization of a society is concerned. The best that we can do, given the need to act and the limits of our cognitive capacities, is to open up some room for the possibility that we are on the wrong side of the argument in fundamental ways and to try to find productive methods of dealing with the uncertainties that we cannot avoid. One way to do this is to continually expose our arguments, in the clearest form possible, for rebuttal, ideally by those from other moral traditions, and to try to take seriously the productive possibilities of moral disagreement where it exists. In the remainder of the chapter, I will try to specify the range of the uncertainty in the cases of interest for this project, and to suggest the value that allowing the continued existence of independent or quasi-independent indigenous nations may have for those both inside and outside those nations.

In previous chapters, I argued that democratic states generally fare the best in the protection of natural rights because they allow the input of the populations ruled and are likely to be most effective when they are able to foster extensive deliberation about what policies they should pursue. One might, however, contest the importance I have given to both rights and democratic states. If the objection is only that existing states do not in practice protect rights well, then the cure will be procedural change, as outlined in the last chapter. If it is that no states can protect rights well, however, then we have a factual disagreement about the structures necessary to achieve this, one that likely cannot be resolved by revisiting the arguments of Chapter 6. More deeply, one might concede that democratic states tend to provide substantial legal protections for "individual rights," while objecting that protections formulated in this way are not as helpful as I have been assuming. If this objection meant simply that people should receive no protections whatsoever, it would be easily disposed of, but the objection can also be given a more plausible form: that formulating these protections as "rights" as they are commonly understood is an egregious error.

All of us can acknowledge, I think, that the language of rights can seem to neglect the importance of interpersonal relationships and may in some cases stand in the way of acknowledging the foundational duties to aid that I have argued must exist. Some other potential formulations of the limits on the ways that individuals should treat one another may be more conducive to a satisfactory human society, particularly where community resources still exist to make them possible (even if this requires some reconstruction of these resources along the way). These alternatives may or may not provide a realistic template for structuring human social life given the conditions in which we now live (my own doubts should be clear by now), but they at least deserve a fair chance of being attempted by those who hold such views and have the best chances of making them work. We should take seriously the procedures by which indigenous groups might choose to pursue the development or reconstitution of unfamiliar political and social structures; indeed, where most of their population desires it, indigenous nations might provide important sources of experimentation.[4]

III. Deep Disagreement and Procedural Separation

How, then, should existing states proceed in regard to groups that seem to be culturally different in such nonneutral ways? The relevant questions involve institutional diversity: should groups be permitted to attempt nonstate methods of organization if they wish to do so, and should they be allowed to attempt to protect their citizens through alternatives to individual rights?

As I argued in Chapters 6 and 7, there seem to be reasons to believe that democratic states will fare the best at protecting rights over the long term. While very small populations with intensive community bonds may represent an exception in some cases, I argued that even here there are reasons for skepticism. Any changes in such alternative directions would have to be made through the kind of deliberation-intensive processes outlined in the last chapter, so that they occur only after extensive discussion of the options. But even at that point, some groups may still want to pursue options of this sort. Should democratic states permit them to do so?[5]

Movements in this direction would raise few concerns if the population was unanimous in its desire for this outcome. Even if it was in error about its own interests, preventing change would seem mistaken if everyone involved really did believe it was for the best. Consider, as an example, persons who willingly join a monastic community that requires them to do without food or shelter in many cases, either as punishment or as a way of building character, but that also allows members to exit whenever they want. Even if this group's ideas seem to outsiders extremely strange and irrational, it would be deeply mistaken to say that such persons should be "liberated" from this way of life if they do not want to leave, and it would be extremely arrogant and unjust to tear them away from it. And if this is so, then it would also clearly be wrong to prevent people from forming such communities in the first place (Swaine 2001; 2006). There may be limits here, of course. One might, for example, be wary of allowing even voluntary groups authority over life and death, although it is not immediately obvious why such groups should have fewer rights in this regard than *non*voluntary states. But there would nonetheless have to be a very high threshold on such interference.

If other kinds of social groups had complete unity in their beliefs, it would seem illegitimate for existing states to prevent them from attempting whatever kind of government seemed most plausible to them. Indeed, there would be few reasons for me to say much about the bases of authority in the first place—each group would have its own view, and the only relevant issue would lie in negotiating the relationships between these inherently self-contained units. But no real society is like this, which means that we need to be sensitive to the ways in which some people (or even most people) might suffer from attempting alternative political forms. Where disagreement within the group exists, matters are more ambiguous; given the ways in which real states can fail, those within a group who seem most vulnerable may not always want outside interference, but in other cases they may want it very badly.

One alternative would be to hold that *any* disagreement with a proposed change, even by a single person or a handful of people, should be sufficient to block change. This solution takes the case for the protection of rights to be absolute and indefeasible except where unanimity exists. Another solution would be to exhibit greater deference toward the desires of majorities within particular areas and to allow groups to pursue any option for governance and social organization that can succeed through the procedures for change, unless it will result in some truly extreme outcome like genocide or slavery (cf. Walzer 1992, chap. 6). But this seems to swing too strongly to the other extreme. What we need is some middle position that takes seriously the fact that attempts at nondemocratic or non-rights-based governance could have damaging effects, falling short of full atrocities, on certain portions of the population, but that also allows these alternative arrangements to be attempted in some situations.

In many cases, those who have concerns about their potential treatment will be able to make them heard during the deliberation phase of the process, when they will garner either sufficient attention to derail the process or some substantive guarantees about their future. It would be too convenient, however, to take refuge in this hope. In circumstances where some members of the population look likely to suffer heavily under the proposed alternative political regime, it seems essential that the state consult with them. But states must be extremely specific about what they are asking in these circumstances. Even if those who are worst off in a particular situation resent this status immensely, it does not follow that they would prefer action by the state instead (cf. Phillips 2005). This caution about intervention seems particularly prudent where the state has a history of ignoring cultural traditions or behaving in extremely opportunistic or incompetent ways (Kymlicka 1995, 165–70; cf. Carens 2000, 188–93).

The best approach of states to alternative institutional forms or alternative conceptions of the protections people deserve, then, lies in discovering how those likely to be made worst off feel about the proposed change in comparison to their present circumstances. If women within the relevant population seem likely to be endangered, for example, the state should actively seek out their opinions and listen carefully and systematically to their concerns (as Canada's Royal Commission on Aboriginal Peoples did—see Canada 1996, vol. 4, chap. 2). This extra voice will provide additional reasons for group leaders to offer revised proposals that allay their concerns, and in some cases this may be sufficient. But in other cases, if most of those within the apparently endangered group seem unwilling to go along, it may become necessary for states to exercise a veto. States would seem to have a right to continue to exercise this veto until most members of the relevant group seemed satisfied, at which point they would lose that right. (There would obviously be room for strategizing by both states and "vulnerable" groups here, but there is no way to avoid this possibility, short of stopping all change whatsoever.)

Some group leaders might claim that the voices of the apparently endangered members of the group are not relevant, because the traditional methods of governance among the group do not take them into account. But, as I have said, given the internal complexity of all purported groups, we must draw the line somewhere. If, however, leaders can secure the approval of those who seem mostly likely to be disadvantaged, there is no reason that a system could not be attempted in which, for example, only men, only women, or only elders had the right to govern. Again, I think such systems would probably be a bad idea, but many indigenous groups traditionally governed themselves by such mechanisms, often tolerably well, and there is no obvious reason why they should be prohibited from making the attempt where the apparently worst off are willing to accept this.

I recognize that agreeing on a suitable procedure is an awkward balancing act, and some readers will doubtless feel that the presumptions should lie more fully on one side or the other. It is made more awkward yet by the contradictory goals involved: I have argued that alternative kinds of social orders are likely to be in error, while also suggesting that indigenous forms of political organizations may provide alternatives from which we can learn. But whether I have struck the exact procedural balance here or not, it does have to be struck somewhere, and not simply avoided. Moral confidence and moral uncertainty are both necessary and are often in tension, and the best we can do is strike a balance that seems appropriate for the circumstances. Even if the procedural strategy I have proposed could be improved upon, something resembling it seems necessary if we are not to swing too far to one side or the other.

Thus, though the role that deep cultural difference plays in the theory of authority I am outlining here is secondary, it is still important. Groups that can make a convincing case for change to their own membership will have the right to engage in the process of change even when outsiders see it as extremely risky or counterproductive. The result may be the construction of alternative forms of governance, possibly including movements toward communitarian anarchism, as suggested in Chapter 6. Although my own sense is that such attempts will generally be unwise and that those who engage in them will come to regret their decision, it may be that small groups will succeed in rebuilding community-based methods of self-government, and perhaps will even showcase different ways of organizing social life that are best both for group members and for outsiders. Democratic states and legally protected individual rights as we know them may not be the absolute last word in the construction of a morally defensible human society; there are reasons to hope that better alternatives can be found. The best approach seems to be to allow groups to pursue other options if their most vulnerable members are willing to go along, in the hope of improving the lives of not only their people but perhaps everyone else over the long term.

In this section, I have generally been talking about culturally different groups that are entrenched within the legal structures of stable democratic states and are seeking an escape from this status. As I noted in Chapter 6, there are also indigenous groups in some parts of the world that have not yet become strongly integrated into the states now surrounding them (although these states are usually not terribly democratic, either, and so tend to be outside of this book's inquiry). Insofar as the concerns about counterproductive intervention discussed here are correct, there are good reasons to believe that such states should exercise serious caution in bringing these people fully under their legal structures too quickly, because they are likely to do far more damage than good in the short run. As the populations around such groups increase, movements toward more state-based methods of protection will almost certainly have to occur, but there are good reasons for states to proceed very carefully, and only with intensive consultation with those in the relevant population. Even the best of states have a tendency to behave roughly toward small and divergent groups, and the results are rarely successful even when state goals are admirable—as they often, unfortunately, are not.

IV. Culture, Identity, and Change

In the remainder of this chapter, I want to say a bit more about alternatives that American Indians and other indigenous peoples might want to pursue, and also to show why I believe that the viewpoints of indigenous peoples may be valuable to the settler populations now surrounding them. Perhaps more importantly, this discussion should help readers to understand in more detail my perception of what cultural difference looks like in the relevant cases, and should in particular help indigenous readers to better determine the sources of my errors.

One reasonable question is whether at the present day there really are deep cultural differences involved. In practice, cultural differences between indigenous peoples and the majority populations of the surrounding states may be less substantial than either group is comfortable admitting. As I noted above when discussing national identities, groups can often regard themselves as more different than they actually are, and this seems particularly true when these identities are closely linked to deep differences in the past and to historical injustices. Those who consider themselves members of a particular nation will need criteria for deciding whom the bonds of membership reasonably link them to. Usually these criteria include cultural ones (though not always—see, e.g., Shelby 2003), which can create a variety of feedback effects between identities and cultural practices. Those who feels themselves to be members of a particular nation (or any other group, for that matter) will often want to behave in ways purportedly typical of such members, not only to demonstrate to others that they belong, but also because these seem appropriate for the kind of people they believe themselves to be (see, e.g., Appiah 2005, 62–69). Where differences in cultural practice are central to a group's identity, individuals have reason to focus on what makes them different rather than what makes them similar.

By itself, this tendency to focus on what divides us can raise questions about the match between perceived differences and actual differences, and other forces operating on cultural practices can enhance these worries. Cultural practices usually originate as ways of solving social problems, determining how people will interact so that each person knows what to expect from others. As the social challenges facing populations shift, many cultural practices have to shift along with them. This process is particularly acute when technologies change, since many things that were formerly central to a way of life (e.g., making tools by hand or farming) may become far less so, goods that never existed before will suddenly become plentiful or possible, and certain kinds of knowledge will no longer confer substantial benefits. For example, the hunting and gathering that many indigenous peoples historically engaged in has become largely unnecessary in an era when food is extremely plentiful, and for that reason much of the knowledge, skills, and cultural practices associated with that lifestyle has become abandoned. (Indeed, this process of losing formerly important skills can happen very quickly—see, e.g., Richter 2001, 50–51). Such change can often lead people to hold onto those markers of their culture, such as artistic styles or forms of dress, that are least inconvenient to maintain, even as they reshape other practices to match the needs of their daily life. Thus, nearby groups operating within the same technological and economic context can swiftly become similar, even if that was never their intention or, indeed, is distasteful to them.

All cultures change through time, then, and there is little that can be done to stop this process, even though certain features can be given the appearance of permanence with some effort. Consider the case of indigenous peoples within wealthy and stable democracies like the United States and Canada. Given how long indigenous peoples have been interacting with these states and the degree to which they are now linked socially and economically to the populations that encompass them, it would be very strange if there were not a great deal of overlap between the practices of the indigenous and nonindigenous peoples.

Moreover, these interactions have historically been far from peaceful or consensual, and indigenous peoples have often suffered horrifically from heavy-handed attempts to assimilate them into the colonial culture, while rarely receiving opportunities to integrate smoothly. They have been forced onto reservations, prohibited from speaking their traditional languages and practicing their traditional religions, forced to dress like their colonial masters and use their standards of etiquette, banned from meeting obligations of reciprocity with their extended families, and many other things besides. While these kinds of policies often spurred indigenous peoples to hold on to particularly central cultural practices as strongly they were able, doing so in the face of such pervasive coercion was anything but simple. This history of injustice thus makes it doubly likely that indigenous peoples will see themselves as more different than they really are—not only have traditional cultural practices been attacked through force, but the anger and distrust generated by these attacks make it uncomfortable or even odious for many present-day indigenous populations to accept that such policies often largely succeeded in their assimilationist goals.

As indigenous readers will likely know better than nonindigenous ones do, I am not making a new claim in suggesting that contemporary indigenous identities have these tensions built deeply into them. Vine Deloria Jr., for example, who was an eloquent advocate for the value of traditional American Indian religions and worldviews throughout his life (e.g., Deloria 2003), wrote the following in his contribution to a volume on American Indian philosophical thought:

> When we speak of American Indian philosophy today, we are probably talking about several generations of Indian people who have popular notions of what Indian philosophy might have been or might have become within the Western philosophical enterprise.

> Conditions in Indian communities have radically changed in the past generation so that the experiences and memories of most people today refer back to the communities that existed in 1960 when the many Poverty programs began to bring modern Western civilization to the reservations. Elders of the 1960's might well have known some of the old beliefs and ceremonies, but more likely they would have remembered the boarding school days of the 1920's. They would probably have expressed regrets that they had been taken away from their relatives during their childhood years when they could have learned something from their elders. Thus we have a body of people wanting to be Indians but badly handicapped by the rush toward assimilation that we have seen in the last 40 years. An elder today, at age 75, would probably remember the Great Depression of the 1930's and the revival of ceremonies in the 1950's but would know little else of any importance (Deloria 2004, 4).

Deloria goes on to suggest that nonindigenous colonial writings from the periods when Indian peoples remained politically and socially independent may provide a valuable guide for reclaiming some of these lost or damaged views of the world. Many other indigenous authors have expressed a similar need to reconstruct historical indigenous viewpoints for use in reinterpreting the present (e.g., Williams 1997), while admitting the difficulties of doing so (e.g., Alfred 1999, 24–30). Such reconstruction is clearly a different kind of project than maintaining or further developing a set of traditions that has not been interrupted.

Perhaps surprisingly, there are also reasons for the nonindigenous citizens of surrounding states to envision indigenous peoples as more different than they actually are. As Elizabeth Povinelli (2002, 17–29) and others (e.g., Denis 1997, chap. 1) have noted, surrounding states now have multiple interests in indigenous peoples remaining "different" in clearly recognizable but also nonthreatening ways. Povinelli notes, for example, that Aborigines are central to Australia's campaign to attract tourists, and in the United States the prevalence of the "cowboys-and-Indians" motif means that many nonindigenous Americans conceive of semiautonomous and culturally different Indian nations as somehow necessary to their own national identity (albeit in a relatively decorative way). Showing that indigenous groups continue to retain important elements of their historical culture is also a way for states to pretend that the mistreatments of the past were not really so bad after all, and encouraging groups to promulgate particular cultural and artistic styles can provide a method for those concerned about alienation in indigenous communities to demonstrate a commitment to inclusion. (To believe that these attempts help to foster an artificial sense among the majority population about indigenous difference, one need not assume that they are cynical or based in ulterior motives, or even that they are counterproductive on balance.) What makes these perceptions dangerous is that political and legal support can come to depend on whether groups can make a display of being sufficiently "authentic" to fit them (Povinelli 2002, chaps. 5–6)—if they cannot, they risk being regarded as "fake Indians" and losing the legal protections upon which their communities rely.

There are thus multiple reasons to be wary of making claims about the degree to which contemporary indigenous populations are different in deep ways from the populations surrounding them. But we must also be careful about leaping to the converse conclusion that no such difference exists anymore. All sides can be mistaken about the depth of difference, and it is hard to imagine how any person or set of persons could be perfectly placed to judge these issues. One could try study in extremely detailed ways what the differences are by creating a long list of social practices within indigenous groups and within the surrounding populations, but this would not tell us, for example, how much most members of either group value a particular set of practices, or what they would be willing to give up to preserve them. Groups can change over time without converging on fundamental issues, so no mechanical comparison is likely to be especially reliable—although it would provide states and majority populations with ready pretexts whenever indigenous claims began to seem tiresome.

Ultimately, we will probably do best to take a common-sense approach that recognizes that questions about "real" cultural difference cannot be answered in any very satisfactory way, while holding that the clear historical differences between indigenous peoples and majority populations make it reasonable to believe that substantial cultural differences will occur here if they occur anywhere. If rights to full or partial separation must be limited to some small populations rather than all (see the last chapter), then it seems to make the most sense to allow this option to indigenous peoples, who unambiguously began from very different starting points, were historically mistreated in severe ways, and in many cases continue to feel themselves to be different. Given the range of contemporary circumstances and social practices among indigenous groups, some groups probably really will be different in fundamental ways while others will not, but we do not live in a world in which all uncertainties of this type can be avoided. Thus, it seems most reasonable to begin with a generalized presumption that indigenous peoples retain at least some cultural differences of the relevant kind. Once this generalized approach is acknowledged, the best practical gauge of real difference will probably be what these groups choose to do with the options allowed to them—if they choose to pursue no wholesale revision of existing relationships, this will be a likely indicator that they do not believe anything truly fundamental to be at stake. If they choose, after careful deliberation, to pursue alternative ways of protecting their members, this will suggest that on some greatly important matters they remain fundamentally at odds with the practices of the states now ruling them. Again, this is not a perfect gauge—but no such gauge exists in our world, and it will not help to pretend that one does.

Moreover, beginning with this presumption in favor of indigenous difference would spare these groups the task of trying to reinvent traditions that have fallen out of use. If we begin with a general presumption that indigenous groups have rights to a separate status if any small groups do, then indigenous populations will feel less threatened and have less need to rely on theatrical demonstrations of "authenticity" to retain the self-government necessary to protect less obvious forms of cultural difference. Some groups would, of course, choose to undertake various reinventions of "tradition" anyway (see, e.g., Alfred 1995), but it is hard to see why this should be much of a concern. Majority populations find it convenient to reinvent their social practices at many points, and they find nothing odd about looking back to the ideas of Jefferson or Lincoln (or Aristotle or Pericles) in trying to decide how best to proceed. Why should looking toward the ideals of Deganawidah or Handsome Lake (e.g., Alfred 1999, 24–30) be stranger or less valuable in comparison? Insofar as these alternative traditions contain different ways of understanding and valuing the world, there are probably in fact reasons to value attempts at reinventing or reinvigorating them as ways of seeking alternative methods of living in the modern world. In most cases, those attempts will not succeed if they are deeply out of step with day-to-day practices, and where they do succeed it is likely that they have substantial arguments on their side. In other words, opening up this kind of space allows indigenous peoples both to remain different *and* to change if they feel this is most appropriate.

One cannot simply say, then, that indigenous peoples are no longer sufficiently different in relevant ways. They may generally not be as different as many on either side might prefer to think, but that is far from the end of the matter. If any groups within stable democracies like the United States,

Canada, and Australia will have substantial degrees of cultural difference, it will likely be indigenous peoples, and the best solution is not to lock them into conditions in which they must continue to demonstrate this in some theatrical way to majority populations, but to let them decide for themselves what the future will hold. If in some cases, after careful procedural and deliberative barriers and with the consent of their apparently vulnerable members, they choose to pursue alternative forms of political organization, it is hard to see why they should be prevented from doing so.

Indeed, insofar as cultural practices are really about ideas and ways of valuing the world, there may be positive reasons for surrounding states to value the space for choice thereby opened up to indigenous peoples: it might ultimately result in better ways of living or understanding the world for everyone. As I have tried to make clear, states as we know them are not perfect and can never be made so, but perhaps they can be improved or some alternative that performs better can be found. If indigenous peoples wish to undertake these kinds of controlled social experiments, and are the most likely of any present populations to succeed in them, it seems to make sense for surrounding states to allow them the political breathing room to do so by recognizing their rights to full or partial separation. If majority populations are concerned with living in the best achievable social structures, they should take seriously the intellectual engagements that will be possible with indigenous peoples who are allowed to pursue their own conceptions of a just political order free from interference.

V. Indigenous Alternatives

I do not want to oversell this last point, which might suggest that the case for allowing indigenous peoples a separate status hinges entirely on the benefits that this might provide to nonindigenous populations. Nor do I want to caricature indigenous peoples as "noble savages" or anything of the sort. Indigenous peoples are under no obligation to try to impart sacred wisdom to the surrounding populations, nor is there any guarantee that indigenous viewpoints really do have something to teach; as I have tried to make clear, anyone can fall into moral error, and some views of the world may be better than others, even if we lack any certain metric by which we can compare their relative merits and failings. But there are nonetheless reasons to believe that processes of interaction and conversation can themselves be extremely valuable, and if majority populations can secure the noncoerced agreement of indigenous peoples for particular policies or ways of organizing their society, they will have more solid reasons to believe in the value of their own practices. When they fail to secure such agreement, on the other hand, they will have good reason to probe more deeply into whether their own ideas might ultimately be justified.

So if indigenous peoples might provide a source of creative tension and revised ideas for the nonindigenous populations that will continue to surround them whether they seek legal separation or not, which kinds of ideas might be involved here? This is not easy to say, and there are multiple dangers in my making too many specific claims in this regard. One barrier is simply that the great variety among indigenous groups makes any general statements likely to be mistaken in multiple ways, with potentially limiting consequences for any groups that do not comfortably fit the template. To suggest that groups as diverse as the Hopis, Onondagas, and Tlingits all somehow share the same views would simply confuse matters in many ways—as would conflating these groups with the Yolngu or Pintupi of Australia. The general category of "indigenous" arose only by contrast with colonial societies, and one must be careful not to ask more of it than it can bear. (Thus, my arguments in, say, Chapter 6 about communitarian anarchism and indigenous nations need to be treated with caution as partial representations at best.) Generalized claims about what majority populations could learn from indigenous peoples are certain to shortchange the variety of indigenous worldviews, which are often deeply divergent. Moreover, I am myself not the product of any indigenous tradition and so cannot claim to have anything more than secondhand knowledge of indigenous worldviews. I am a Western-oriented, academic political theorist with natural-rights leanings and secondary sympathies with deliberative democracy, and to pretend otherwise would be deceptive. Even if the internal complexity of groups and cultures always makes the notion of being "authorized" to speak for a particular way of life problematic, the basic point is that both my history and my identification leave me fundamentally an outsider to indigenous conversations.

Still, I would like to outline my general sense of how indigenous viewpoints might be contrasted with Western or liberal viewpoints, realizing that I will have to stereotype both sides somewhat to do so. (The clean division between the two sides is itself a nontrivial kind of caricature.) Indeed, given my invocations of "indigenous views" in multiple places throughout the book, it would be bad faith for me to back out of such an attempt at description now.

My point is rather to make clear that my discussion will be broadly generalized, will inevitably involve caricature, and will probably be simply wrong in regard to most (or even all) cases. But it has informed my claims so far about indigenous peoples, and it deserves to be outlined both so that my errors can be recognized and so that some sense of (what seems to me) the value of indigenous worldviews might come through. If I am generally wrong in my portrayals here, I do not think that the broader case for indigenous rights to a separate political status will be thereby disrupted in powerful ways, but that is something others will have to decide for themselves.

My approach to questions about the character of indigenous cultures throughout the book has been to take some of the writers who claim to speak for indigenous peoples at their word, while recognizing that this can be problematic in all of the ways noted above. I hope it will seem less problematic if we keep in mind that divergent normative traditions are fundamentally about ideas, assumptions, and valuations rather than simply about practices that are followed blindly. If many indigenous populations seem to accept a characterization of their views by an indigenous academic or activist as tolerably accurate, there is no one in a position to say they are in error. Even if some of the views of contemporary indigenous spokespeople involve composites of multiple indigenous traditions or combinations with nonindigenous traditions, this does not meant that their arguments are somehow inauthentic or that they do not offer real and coherent alternatives to dominant worldviews. So what I will say here should be taken as extremely tentative, and certainly not as a standard of authenticity, but nonetheless as a real attempt to say something generally about the areas in which nonindigenous populations might ultimately learn from indigenous peoples. When it goes wrong, I hope indigenous readers will recognize this swiftly and thereby be better able to refute the errors to which it leads.

Among many indigenous writers, there seems to be a rough consensus on some central points of disagreement between most indigenous peoples and surrounding populations. Three broad points of difference from dominant Western conceptions seem important in this context, each of which I have already suggested at various points throughout the book. The first and most overtly political is a commitment to a noncoercive kind of political life; the second and somewhat more diffuse politically is a focus on the value of community and the importance of relationships rather than rights; the third and most theological involves the place of humans in the larger order of the world and universe. Each of these will sound relatively sterile and familiar in generalized terms, since it is the particular ways they can be instantiated that can make all of the difference. Nonindigenous readers are encouraged to seek out indigenous writers themselves to get a far richer sense of the argumentative field (see, e.g., Borrows 2002; Turner 2006; Alfred 1999; Deloria 2003). (Nonindigenous readers should likewise remember that our conceptions of rights, deliberation, democratic governance, and so on are themselves quite thin without the much deeper set of practical experiences and particularized referents to give them their full complexity [Tully 1995]—a complexity that we take for granted where our own traditions are involved, but too often forget when we consider those of others.)

The first broad point of agreement among indigenous traditions seems to be a commitment to noncoercive or noncentralized forms of social organization. Although most Indian nations in the United States are currently governed by electoral institutions similar to state subdivisions of similar size (e.g., townships or counties), many have tried to retain historical elements of direct democracy and consensual politics as well (along with, in some cases, religious governance). The belief that such consensual forms of governance can be strengthened and extended seems to be a recurring one for many indigenous scholars. Taiaiake Alfred (1999, 25), for example, argues that "In choosing between revitalizing indigenous forms of government and maintaining the European forms imposed on them, Native communities have a choice between two radically different kinds of social organization: one based on conscience and the authority of the good, the other on coercion and authoritarianism." He continues: "A crucial feature of the indigenous concept of governance is its respect for individual autonomy. This respect precludes the notion of 'sovereignty'—the idea that there can be a permanent transference of power or authority from the individual to an abstraction of the collective called the 'government'" (25). As I noted in Chapter 6, other indigenous advocates have made similar claims about the ways in which indigenous communities can govern themselves without the heavy hand of state institutions.

As should be clear by this point, I suspect that substantial attempts to move further in this direction will probably fail for all groups but the most isolated and self-contained, and that most indigenous groups will ultimately choose to reverse any such attempts. But these options nonetheless have a powerful appeal, and there are reasons to hope that exploring them might in fact lead to improvements in the quality of governance within indigenous communities, and perhaps ultimately, by example, within the colonial states that surround them. While I have argued that there are good justifications for the nonvoluntary coercion exercised by states, I have also noted that political authority has implicit moral limits that are rarely respected perfectly. Alfred is not wrong to invoke a contrast between consent and coercive authority. Even if democratic methods of governance can lessen these tensions somewhat, that authority does act without the agreement of everyone involved, and this is always cause for discomfort. Given the multiplicity of historical traditions of governance among indigenous peoples, it seems possible that better ways of doing things can be found or are already known, in partial reversions to community-based methods of protection if not in entire ones. There are thus plausible reasons to believe that indigenous peoples might eventually have a great deal to demonstrate about the best ways of organizing political and social life, but this will never come to light unless they are allowed the space to follow their choices. As Robert Williams Jr. (1997) has tried to show, colonial populations had this opportunity to learn once and failed to do so. It would be unwise to refuse this offer were it made a second time.

The second broad pattern of indigenous difference lies in the character of the basic moral protections individuals are believed to have. I have proceeded throughout the book on the belief that the basic protections individuals deserve are best formulated as rights, because doing so allows each person a protected space in which to pursue the kind of life that person deems best. But this formulation can create the appearance of far greater social distance between individuals than in fact exists, while the legal regimes necessary to secure such protections can put greater limitations on individual action than the abstract notion of rights leads us to believe. Most arguments for rights acknowledge that we will develop a variety of obligations in the course of our lives, but they often give these only a secondary status, thus downplaying both the importance of interpersonal linkages and the way that those linkages help to constitute our real range of choice.

Vine Deloria Jr. (2004, 10) argues that indigenous viewpoints are able to provide a more realistic conception of what human life is like by shifting the focus directly onto the interpersonal relationships themselves: "In contrast to the West, where 'rights' reign supreme, the tribal peoples through family, clan, and societies created a climate in which 'responsibility' would be the chief virtue. One had all manner of duties toward others and could expect to reap the benefit of one's loyalty in fulfilling these responsibilities by receiving in return the blessings created when others fulfilled their responsibilities reciprocally." In their basic form, these obligations were not primarily about enforcing strict rules, but about maintaining relationships over the long term. Can these networks of relatedness satisfactorily protect their members in contemporary circumstances?

My own sense is that such obligations cannot be entrenched into law in any tolerable way, so that the case for them hinges partially on the possibility of living without coercive forms of governance. But we should admit that this focus on responsibilities and reciprocity is not in fact as distant from what we actually do in social practice as we might like to pretend. Even in liberal societies, people are required to adhere to all kinds of rules made for them by others, and indigenous approaches at least have the virtue of making this interconnectedness more explicit. Insofar as questions remain open about the balance between rights, responsibilities, and interpersonal connections, there once again may be much that surrounding populations can learn—but only (once again) if indigenous peoples are allowed to attempt to put their ideas into practice.

The final point of apparent agreement lies more in the theological or metaphysical realm and can be given broad or narrow readings. Many traditional indigenous spiritual beliefs involve sentient, nonhuman beings that are attached to particular geographical spaces, or other kinds of intensive linkages to particular spaces that involve responsibilities of care. Where these nonhuman sentient beings are believed to exist, they are often conceptualized as part of the web of noncoercive, reciprocal relationships in which humans also take part (see, e.g., Deloria 2003). On this view, humans have responsibilities toward the world around them that require care in the actions they undertake and a need to keep in mind the interests of animals and other kinds of beings.

While I am extremely skeptical about the empirical accuracy of these views (see Hendrix 2005a), it should be obvious that they have important implications if they are correct. Insofar as nonindigenous populations are failing to maintain these relationships with sentient nonhumans, they are failing to exhibit due care toward other moral beings who do not deserve to have their purposes frustrated in such ways. But even if these views are utterly wrong in their factual assertions, they nonetheless provide alternative ways to conceive of the human place in the natural world (cf. Denis 1997), and thereby an alternative set of tools for rethinking the ways we will choose to live. This is particularly relevant since even our putatively secular views usually end up influenced by religious preconceptions in a variety of ways (see, e.g., Deloria 2003.) I noted in Chapter 3 that alternative arguments might be provided from within a distinctively indigenous framework for the return of historical lands. This broader conception of the human place in the natural world can help to support such claims—if nonindigenous populations simply cannot be trusted to behave in appropriate ways, then indigenous peoples deserve to regain many lands so that they can do so in regard to them, and can thereby provide examples of what treating the land well would look like in practice.

Taken as a whole, this unavoidably stereotyped outline is, I hope, enough to suggest at least the generalized contours of an "indigenous alternative," in which noncoercive (or less coercive) relationships with other humans and the natural world play a much larger role in shaping the character of human social relations. This is, I think, an appealing conception of what human life could be like, and while I have my doubts about its achievability, if such forms of social organization are practicable anywhere, then indigenous societies seem to have both the size and cultural resources to attempt or re-create them. I realize that in this swift outline I have failed to do anything approaching justice to the richness of particularized indigenous traditions, but I hope I have at least suggested that there are real issues involved here, which indigenous peoples may play a valuable role in resolving in ways that are beneficial to everyone in the long term. But they will be far more likely to achieve this if they can engage with nonindigenous populations without fear of their capacity to govern their own members being suddenly torn away, and if they have space to put these alternatives into concrete social practice. Once that space is provided, the elements of indigenous conceptions can be presented to surrounding populations in much deeper detail, and the dialogic interactions can take new and unexpected turns; alternatively, if we partisans of individual rights and democratic governance are correct, we can receive some validation of our views by groups who had meaningful options and potential reasons to choose something else, and abstained from doing so. My own sense is that after groups have engaged in careful deliberation about their options, we will see far more of the latter than the former, but that, as I have tried to make clear in this chapter and the last, is not my decision, or that of majority populations within existing states.

I should also note, before concluding this chapter, the rather obvious fact that I could be wrong about everything I have said in the book up to this point, although just as obviously I do not think this is true. It is not absurd to believe that some indigenous account of how social and political life should be ordered may ultimately prove much different from what I have said here, and superior to it. The traditions of argument I have adopted here are not without historical taint, and it would not do to mask this fact. For some indigenous authors, any satisfactory theory of our social relationships will have to make a more fundamental break. According to Taiaiake Alfred (1999, 21), "At their core, European states and their colonial offspring still embody the same destructive and disrespectful impulses that they did 500 years ago. For that reason, questions of justice—social, political, and environmental—are best considered outside the frameworks of classical European thought and legal traditions." If this is true, then one can make another kind of case for indigenous separation as a way of preserving a livable human society for at least some people, and claims for the return of land as a way of regaining territories on which such a life can be lived. I have tried to make clear why I think states similar to those we know will be the best option for most people in most circumstances, and I have argued that those states are not so inherently vicious as they are sometimes thought to be, but I have no illusions that my argument is perfect. This book is intended as a contribution to these larger debates; at least I have tried to make clear why indigenous peoples deserve the space from which to pursue these kinds of alternatives, whether only for their own good or ultimately for that of wider populations as well.

VI. Separation and Small Groups

I argued in the last chapter that full or partial separation for very small groups seems appropriate if one can show reasons why some groups should be allowed such options while others are not. To be included, groups would have to be especially vulnerable or have special resources that might render their status valuable to everyone. In this chapter, I have tried to make the case for why, if any groups are to have these options, indigenous peoples should. They are more likely to suffer because of their cultural differences, and, at least potentially, they have special resources that may allow them to pursue unusual kinds of political order that may provide benefits more broadly over the long run. Such alternative normative resources seem especially important for settler societies like the United States and Canada, where widespread immigration has created cultures that largely share common conceptions of the moral world and where, therefore, relatively limited prospects exist for the kind of creative disagreement that can lead to fundamental rethinking of social and political matters. Countries like these should thus put a positive value on opportunities for indigenous peoples to choose a partially or fully separate existence, rather than seeing this choice as an impediment to their power.

But what if, as seems likely, states refuse to offer indigenous groups these opportunities? These groups may be forced to behave more strategically and take advantages where they can find them. They may also have to behave more contentiously in defending their own interests. I will take these matters up in the book's final chapter.

NINE

ENDING COLONIALISM

Throughout this book, I have tried to evaluate the moral case for claims to a fully or partially separate status by American Indians and other indigenous peoples now lodged within stable democratic countries like the United States, Canada, and Australia. As I have tried to show, to justify claims to some sort of independent status, one need not attribute a foundational role to the mechanisms by which these groups came under the control of the states now ruling them. I have argued that political authority is most plausibly justified by our duties to aid others in protecting themselves from violence and other forms of wrongdoing, and that while this argument contingently supports democratic states where they now exist, it does not provide a warrant for them to continue forever in their present political shape. Since populations themselves tend to be the best judges of how well they are being ruled, I have argued that large groups should generally have the right to choose a fully or partially separate status if they can pass a carefully designed series of referenda, and have also argued that small groups should have similar opportunities if we can show why some groups should have such chances even when all cannot. Indigenous peoples seem to have the clearest claims in that regard—they are culturally different, have been unambiguously mistreated in the past, and may have the resources to attempt innovative forms of political order that may prove to be better social alternatives for everyone. In these circumstances, it is hard to see why present states should still have rights to rule these groups if they would prefer an alternative status after careful deliberation about what their real options might be.

In Chapters 3 and 4, I also tried to make a case for the return of substantial lands to indigenous peoples where sufficient public lands exist to allow this without displacing current nonindigenous residents. Even where no such public lands exist, states seem bound to provide funds so that indigenous groups (who remain on average relatively poor) can buy back lands as they come on the market. While this case hinges in important ways on historical ownership, it does not assume that such ownership continues down unchanged to the present day, nor that property rights must take precedence over all other kinds of moral considerations. Unyielding property rights are not necessary to make the case; more limited kinds of rights that can sometimes expire but do not automatically do so seem sufficient. If this is true, indigenous peoples seem entitled to the return of a substantial land base, and thereafter to the opportunity to control politically the lands regained in this way. Importantly, however, the case for indigenous rights to a separate status does not hinge on whether they retain such rights to land or not—it rests on a separate foundation and can go forward even if claims for the return of some historical lands are ultimately rejected.

In combination, the return of some historical lands and the allowance of options for indigenous peoples to pursue increased political separation might change the political landscapes of existing democratic states in important ways, but it is impossible to say in advance how substantial these changes might be. Granting (or recognizing) rights to pursue this status does not entail that many groups would really find it in their interests to exercise such an option, nor that if they did, they would choose to try to rebuild historical forms of governance. Indeed, if the general case in favor of democratic governance and individual rights that I have laid out here is correct, indigenous groups seem likely to recognize, after substantial deliberation, that they do not really want any radical changes. In the meantime, existing states would have increased reasons to offer them motivations for staying—something most easily done by demonstrating a commitment to treat them well in the future. Ultimately, a few groups might choose to pursue full separation (see, e.g., Alfred 1995; 2005), while a few others would pursue increased distance without fully severing ties, but in broad terms none of this should be particularly threatening to countries like the United States and Canada. It might be annoying to them, but disruption of self-satisfied conceptions about the acceptability of existing political arrangements is far from a bad thing. A North America with three large countries (or possibly four, depending on the future of Quebec) dotted by a few extremely small ones is hardly something to be terrified by, nor a raw political chaos from which there can be no return. Indeed, if it looks like anything, it looks like the end (or at least reduction) of colonialism on the continent, and this is difficult to see as a negative outcome.

I began in Chapter 1 by asking whether the historical injustices by which the United States and other countries acquired control over their current territories called into question their claims to authority in the present day. In a strict sense, the answer of this book is no—indigenous groups do not have claims to a separate status simply because their ancestors happened to live in those territories first, or because their status as sovereign nations was lost through violence and fraud. The natural duties that justify political authority leave little direct role for these sorts of historically based considerations. But if the arguments I have made here are correct, there is another kind of case for rights to a separate status to be found in the combination of dissatisfaction and cultural difference, which may make it plausible for existing states to behave as if indigenous peoples still retained original sovereignty for many purposes. In these circumstances, the language of retained sovereignty might be regarded as a valuable shorthand—it can remind existing states that they should take seriously the dissatisfaction of the indigenous populations they now rule and should acknowledge the rights of such groups to pursue something different if they so choose. In most cases, those who have such rights acknowledged will not choose to go very far anyway (cf. Weinstock 2001), but in the meantime they will have the breathing space to consider what they really want over the longer term.

There is another set of reasons to retain legal categories based on original sovereignty where they already exist. As I noted in Chapter 7, incidents of partial separation are always difficult to negotiate, and the balances involved are never easy to strike. States that have already recognized rights to indigenous self-government have thereby provided at least a template for striking these balances, something determinate against which groups can react and argue. The fact that the extent and legal status of these rights is usually somewhat ambiguous might thus be seen as a kind of strength (cf. Kymlicka 2001, 110–12). The details can be filled in as the process of negotiation continues, and states have space to extend different treatment to different groups without having to change many existing laws. Claims about historically grounded rights thus do not have to be taken literally to be important; they can be valued instead for the spaces they provide to indigenous choices in the present and future.

But all that I have said here could be subjected to an extremely important objection: that the options I have outlined are simply not going to be offered. While I argued in Chapter 7 that democratic populations generally play a far greater role in maintaining the moral successes of democratic states than they are sometimes credited with playing, I also acknowledged that majority populations (like everyone else) can make severe errors and can be blinded by nationalistic self-conceptions. One might easily, and perhaps rightly, object that majority populations are simply unable to conceive of truly self-governing indigenous political units, or of disruptions to their territorial integrity by groups too small to demand exit unilaterally (in contrast to, say, the Québécois). The American map as most citizens have learned to see it does not have "holes" in it representing areas of indigenous self-rule, even if, in many places, something resembling self-rule does exist. The history of democratically elected governments of the United States toward indigenous peoples is not a very happy one, and it would be disingenuous to pretend that a few good arguments can change this rapidly. (If my arguments are not good ones, of course, then this is another matter entirely.) If this is true, is the entire argument moot?

As should be obvious from my undertaking this book in the first place, I think it clearly is not. I have argued in other places (e.g., Hendrix 2005b) that many kinds of strategic behaviors may be necessary and justified when the pursuit of justice requires them. In these circumstances, the question of how American Indians and other indigenous peoples should go about pursuing the acknowledgment of such claims to separate status is very much an open one. One approach is to try to develop extremely powerful appeals that can lead mainstream populations to reconceptualize matters in a fundamental way. While this approach has often failed in the past, it has had successes too, particularly when it could be coupled with nonviolent social activism to force attention to the moral arguments. Martin Luther King Jr.'s successes in the American Civil Rights Movement (however incomplete) are the paradigm case, and the American Indian Movement–organized Trail of Broken Treaties is a similarly instructive example.

But this is not the only strategy available to indigenous peoples, and probably not the only one they are justified in using. Violence cannot be part of the equation, since, as I have tried to make clear, the problematic kinds of treatment now received by indigenous peoples fall far short of anything sufficient to justify it. Thankfully, violent strategies have little appeal to indigenous groups anyway (and not merely because of their self-defeating consequences). Armed resistance in a defensive way, say at the borders of a reservation, has a more ambiguous status and probably depends a great deal on the details of the case and whether violence is really likely to result. Whether such strategies can be effective is also open to doubt. Even without these incendiary kinds of actions, however, a variety of nonviolent forms of contention seem fully legitimate (see, e.g., Alfred 1999; 2005), as does a much wider and more familiar set of strategies involving the pursuit and exploitation of legal, political, and economic leverage, along with attempts at various forms of propaganda or something similar.

This is not the place to explore the weaknesses and merits of different strategies, particularly since some are likely to fare better than others while others will be mutually contradictory in combination. I would, of course, like to think that moral argument or innovative moral reimaginings coupled with straightforward kinds of activism would be sufficient to achieve what is necessary (see Hendrix 2005a), particularly given the troubling quality of strategic action for those of us with sympathies toward deliberative democracy. In practice, however, these wishes must probably remain unfulfilled. I have argued elsewhere that strategic action can often be both effective and morally justified (Hendrix 2005b), and it would be too late to retreat from this position now. In the long term, strategy by itself probably cannot succeed in the absence of compelling moral arguments, but it can nonetheless serve as a valuable supplement to them. If surrounding settler populations are troubled by this kind of strategizing by indigenous peoples, they have an obvious solution—they can allow indigenous groups greater opportunities to choose their own futures and thereby put the responsibility on them to decide what their real goals might be.

Before proceeding to some considerations about the global limits of the arguments I have made here, it is worth reemphasizing some caveats about the project itself. I am under no illusions that I have captured everything of importance involved in indigenous arguments, nor that I have done anything approaching justice to indigenous conceptions of these issues. The questions I have considered here in regard to political authority do not say much directly about existing legal rights shaped in regard to historical treaties (cf. Thompson 2002), although, as I noted in Chapter 6, there seems to be a general presumption in favor of existing arrangements where they are working tolerably well. Nor have I said much, aside from a few references in Chapter 8, about the arguments that might be made for various kinds of cultural rights while not challenging the claimed authority of existing states (see, e.g., Kymlicka 1995). Not all existing indigenous rights may be derivable from the account I have provided here, and some, even some with good reasons behind them, may ultimately be in conflict with it. But dreams of perfection in moral argument are probably misplaced in any case, and I hope the arguments of this book have at least shown why indigenous calls for rights to separation are important matters indeed.

I should also reaffirm that I do not in any way speak for indigenous peoples. The arguments here are my own, and if they fail to capture the full character of indigenous arguments (as they almost certainly do), the responsibility is my own. Indigenous peoples are not now under some sort of obligation to rebut my arguments where they are in error, or anything of the sort, and nonindigenous readers should not use anything I have said here as a weapon. This book is intended only as a contribution to much more widespread debates about the future of indigenous peoples currently within stable democracies like the United States and Canada, and if it provides those involved in these debates with some new tools for argument, it will have achieved its central goal.

I. International Law in a Complex World

Throughout this book, I have focused on claims for increased separation from stable, mostly successful democratic states where partial or full exit can occur by peaceful means. As I noted in Chapter 1, moral petitions for exit from stable democratic states involve very different issues from those surrounding less effective kinds of states, where more severe forms of violence or oppression are a likely danger. The question arises now of what degree the arguments I have made here can be exported to different circumstances.

The short answer is that they cannot be exported without caution. Many readers will know that a substantial globalized movement of indigenous peoples exists that is attempting to foster increased protections for indigenous peoples in international law, generally framing these claims under the rubric of "self-determination." As Ronald Niezen (2003, 69–86; Kingsbury 1998) has noted, however, the groups claiming to be indigenous in this regard have far less in common than the word might suggest, often having very different histories with surrounding populations (e.g., as in Africa or Asia), as well as very different goals (e.g., ending recurrent massacres rather than gaining self-rule). Perhaps more importantly, many of the states these groups now inhabit are fragile and prone to much more severe forms of oppression and violence than can be found in countries like the United States and Canada. The procedures I have outlined for allowing groups to separate are demanding in many ways and require that most of those on all sides be committed to peaceful solutions, if not uncontentious ones. In societies where there is not already substantial trust in the value of the rule of law and democratic governance, the consequences of recommending procedural rights to separate status are likely to be explosive unless powerful outside parties (that is, First World states) are willing to see that they are followed through without violence. Unfortunately, this seems unlikely in practice.

Therefore, as I have said, my arguments apply most fully to stable democratic states in which moral debates about authority have their best chance of shaping outcomes in peaceful ways. This does not mean that the arguments here could not be extended to different circumstances through careful alterations to context, but it does mean that they cannot be transferred whole-cloth without sensitivity to their impacts in different situations. Is it unfair to suggest that groups regarding themselves as indigenous in some parts of the world should have opportunities that other groups in different circumstances do not? Not at all. If there is not enough food for everyone to eat, no sane person would say that everyone must starve; similarly, there is nothing unfair in saying that indigenous peoples within stable democratic states should have such options where similar groups elsewhere cannot, or cannot have them in the same way. It is unfortunate that we do not live in a world where all similarly placed groups can have such opportunities. But it is not unjust to respond as best we can to the world that exists.

Yet this concern with uneven world conditions does point to an important question for the theory I have outlined here—that is, to decide how, with the fewest collateral effects, these asymmetries of possibility can be reflected in international legal structures. As my discussion of international law in Chapter 2 should have made clear, legal principles can make some kinds of actions easier to justify publicly than others, and while they cannot directly cause bad behavior, they can sometimes provide pretexts for it (see Hendrix 2001; Kohen 2001; Murphy 2001). Indeed, the relative lack of enforcement and adjudication mechanisms within international law means that opportunistic uses of ambiguous principles are easier than usual in this arena, and we must be wary both of providing challengers to existing states with additional pretexts for violence and of providing states with pretexts for oppression.

The easiest way to defuse dangerous signals to actors in nondemocratic states would be for stable democracies to acknowledge rights to full or partial separation within their own legal structures, so that any changes become framed as consensual "domestic" transactions with no direct implications for international practice. (Much the same should be said about the procedural options for larger groups defended in Chapter 7 as well—cf. Buchanan 1997; 2004, 338.) But if democratic states refuse to do this, it nonetheless seems essential that the indigenous peoples within these states and other groups dissatisfied with their current political status (e.g., Québécois) exercise caution in their rhetoric in international forums, particularly on the question of full independence—as in fact they generally do (see, e.g., Niezen 2003, 202–7). It also seems important that indigenous peoples and others focus on the peaceful nature of their claims for change (as in fact they do) and on what I have argued should be the well-regulated, procedural character of legitimate alterations to existing arrangements. If they are carefully framed in this way, it is hard to see that there could become anything particularly disruptive about the principles I have outlined here, particularly in contrast to some of the more absolutist conceptions of self-determination that currently circulate in international debates (see Chapter 2).

At any rate, the arguments of this book should not be transferred without care into existing international law, or recommended as appropriate solutions for circumstances very different from those existing in regard to stable democratic countries like the United States, Canada, and Australia. Existing international law in this regard may already be in its best achievable form (cf. Kohen 2001), or it may be in need of serious kinds of reconstruction; this question will have to be answered on some other grounds that those I have outlined, although I hope what I have said will be indirectly helpful. Ultimately, many of our judgments will depend on how we believe powerful states will choose to act in the future and what sort of order or lack thereof they will create. In the meantime, it seems unfair to hold the futures of indigenous peoples now lodged within these states hostage to the more profound political disorders found elsewhere on the globe.

II. Transcending the State?

If the geographical scope of the arguments I have made is limited, what about their temporal range? One objection that might be made to my arguments is that I am emphasizing the importance of political boundaries at the very time when global flows of capital and culture are rendering them essentially irrelevant. In an age of transnational corporations, high-speed information flows, and perpetually hybridizing cultural products, can a few more boundaries here or there really make any difference? Are the issues I have been considering therefore already expired, musings on a world already gone?

Not by any means. If political boundaries really are weakening radically, then there is not really much at stake in indigenous claims for separate status anyway, and therefore no reason for states to be particularly opposed to such claims; if everyone's authority is fading, then there cannot be anything at stake that would make it worthwhile to stifle indigenous aspirations. These aspirations might ultimately be meaningless and delusional, but that seems neither here nor there—in these kinds of scenarios, virtually any valuation of political authority seems to have the same erroneous quality.

I think, however, that strong claims about the disappearing importance of political boundaries and structures of authority are primarily imaginings of a world that may eventually emerge but has not yet done so. It remains vitally important to most individuals to know which government has legal authority over them, what its procedures for changing and appealing laws or decisions might be, where the boundaries of its authority might lie, how its leaders will be chosen, and so on (see, e.g., Rabkin 2005). For those who are satisfied with present arrangements, these protections seem as natural and easily accessible as the air itself. The experience of indigenous peoples is often much different: the law ruling them often seems arbitrary, distant, and virtually uncontrollable. Given these circumstances, we must not let our sense of how fast the world is changing blind us to how fundamentally some parts remain the same. It may be that indigenous peoples will ultimately find too few options open to them to make the pursuit of full or even increased partial separation worth the costs and dangers, but the pretense that nothing is at stake should not be used as a mechanism for barring this attempt in the first place.

There is also a second and somewhat different objection to my arguments. This would be to argue that they are too conservative in their vision because circumstances are changing sufficiently to open up new social possibilities if we can provide compelling normative portraits of them. Since the state system as we know it can foster substantial violence and injustice, and since political boundaries are often used as pretexts to ignore our natural duties toward all other humans (O'Neill 1994), it does not seem unreasonable to consider whether changing circumstances may make something broader in scope both possible and desirable.

By now, everyone realizes that the idea of a single world-state is unworkable in practice and threatening in principle (see, e.g., Teson 1998; Laberge 1998), but many scholars see in the birth of the European Union possibilities that might be deepened and eventually extended elsewhere. Some of these alternative models assume the growth of multiple, overlapping structures with no central locus of authority. Onora O'Neill (1994, 72), for example, has argued that "The evident link between territoriality and some task of government does not then provide clear reasons for establishing or maintaining a plurality of sovereign states, which will circumscribe all the functions of government at a single set of territorial boundaries. Would it not make more sense to start with functional rather than territorial divisions of the tasks of government? And if we did so, would not the optimal territorial arrangements probably differ for different types of government function?" What is needed, on this view, is a complex set of authority structures, some of them global for world-level problems, others smaller for more local challenges. However one imagines the exact details (see, e.g., George 1998; Held 1991; Pogge 1992), the intention is to remove the dangers of territorial sovereignty while ensuring that political structures can actually govern the fields of human activity they are intended to control.

In abstract terms, there is nothing particularly menacing about this picture, and given the degree to which many social problems have become globalized, it does not seem absurd to consider how we might create a better match between given social challenges and the governmental structures available to deal with them. But, as the experience of the European Union has shown, no one yet knows how to achieve this in a truly satisfactory way, even among states that have willingly undertaken the task, and there are serious reasons to wonder about the capacity of more radical arrangements to allow for democratic control over outcomes in the long term (see, e.g., Dahl 1994). Although we cannot be certain, serious attempts to move swiftly in this direction might result only in an unbreakable technocracy leaving far too little room for innovation or cultural difference (cf. Walzer 2000). It may be that movements in this direction will happen nonetheless, or that political life will evolve spontaneously in this direction, but it is hard to see any obvious cure for the challenges faced by indigenous peoples in this system if they cannot gain substantial rights over their own fate first. Even within such a system of overlapping jurisdictions, groups would need mechanisms for at least partial escape when they are dissatisfied, and for that reason the principles of exit I have outlined here would remain important even in this very different kind of world.

But such a world is far off, if it is coming at all. In the meantime, there seem to be important reasons for stable democratic states like the United States and Canada to take much more seriously the dissatisfactions of the indigenous populations they continue—for the time being—to rule. Such states often claim that they have no colonized groups within their borders. Perhaps it is time that these claims be put to the test by the choices of indigenous peoples themselves.

NOTES

Chapter 2

1. It is no accident that treaties of cession were often signed by minority factions or were deceptively worded. Lindley (1926, 169–75) provides an excellent and lucid analysis of colonizing practices in this regard. Colonizing powers often relied on the political weaknesses created by the complex nature of "undeveloped" political structures to support certain local groups with whom they could then bargain for territories to create the illusion of consensual transfers of authority.
2. Thus, Brownlie (1998, 152) describes title to territory as "based upon the better right to possess, as opposed to a unititular system, in which title must be traced directly to the original title holder." See also Musgrave (1997, chap. 10), Kaikobad (1996), and Chen (2000, 125–26).
3. Steven Ratner (1996) is highly critical of the principle of *uti possidetis*. Elements of this chapter owe a considerable debt to his clear thinking, which helped me to restate some of my earlier objections (Hendrix 2001) with greater focus.
4. Implications for particular kinds of lands would not always be clear in Canada, however, where many indigenous groups hold a variety of rights acknowledged in contemporary treaties. Similar problems would exist in Australia; Arnhem Land would be an obvious candidate, but other lands returned under more recent Aboriginal title legislation would have a less certain status since they currently lack substantial rights to self-government. Because "existing administrative boundaries" has usually been interpreted narrowly, the most legalistic understanding would probably also be the most limited, particularly given the degree to which this interpretation of international law is uninterested in particular kinds of borders in preference to others.
5. See, e.g., the difficulties the International Court of Justice notes regarding a possible "Mauritanian entity" in *Western Sahara* (1975, 60–65).
6. I made stronger claims about the dangers of these legal principles in Hendrix (2001); I now suspect, as Kohen (2001) warned in that exchange, that existing international law deserves more deference in its natural venue.

Chapter 3

1. Taiaiake Alfred (1999, 120) adopts some of the strongest language in this regard, which seems worth reproducing here: "Those who do not accept the idea that indigenous peoples own all of their traditional territory unless it was surrendered by treaty are either ignorant of historical reality or racists who ignore that reality in order to impose a hierarchy of rights based on 'conquest.'" I hope the arguments of this chapter will demonstrate the unfairness of this position toward those who oppose such claims. It may be that the reasons outlined here are ultimately mistaken, but they are reasons nonetheless rather than mere ignorance or racism.
2. This also reflects in part the reasonable view that the past cannot be changed and that we should therefore focus on the present and future (e.g., Waldron 1992, 4–5), although giving a central role to this concern threatens to beg the fundamental question involved—after all, if historical ownership somehow maintains present relevance, failing to return properties is a contemporary wrongdoing rather than a historical one.

3. He does seem willing, however, to make an exception for sacred lands and other areas with special cultural significance. See Waldron (1992, 19). See also later in this chapter, and further discussion of this point in Chapter 8.
4. I am not sure how well this strategic argument fits with the argument that indigenous peoples should focus on seeking common moral ground that I recently made with an American Indian audience in mind (Hendrix 2005a), but I like to think that it is simply a matter of adopting different strategies depending on the opportunities available. For further discussion of this point, see Chapter 9.
5. That such rights exist does not mean that they are always protected in practice, but surprisingly this remains a source of confusion. We often hear arguments from otherwise-careful scholars that property rights cannot be natural because they depend on states for their enforcement. Would they argue that rights against rape are similarly mere political creations, since women can rarely be secured against it without political assistance? Surely not. Mechanisms of enforcement have no intrinsic relation to fundamental moral claims (cf. Lomasky 1987, 101–5), despite the tendency of some philosophers to pretend that they do. See Chapter 5 for further discussion of this issue.
6. This way of bracketing many of the foundational issues in moral philosophy will doubtless be dissatisfying to some readers, but beginning at any more fundamental level would make it very hard to say much that is new or interesting about the authority of political structures over particular persons and territories. My starting in the middle is not an underhanded tactic that is somehow necessary to defending natural property rights; the Rousseauian approach to property, if it is to say anything determinate whatsoever, also has to assume that certain basic moral claims are common to everyone.
7. One possibility, which Nozick (1974, 30–35; cf. Steiner 1994) often seems to intend, is that any regime of basic rights must be designed so that no conflicts between them will be possible. Otherwise we will have to weight different people's rights against one another, which will inevitably lead to some people being treated as less valuable than others. While developing a regime of rights in which conflicts can never occur is a noble goal, it is probably an unattainable one, since conflicts can occur in a variety of situations that can never be entirely predicted and resolved in advance and where solutions often depend on debatable factual judgments about what the situation really is. In such situations, we will often need to ask what basic goals particular kinds of rights are intended to protect, so that we have some sense of which should usually give way before the other (e.g., whether rights to life always, usually, or never come before rights to liberty). Moreover, it is not clear that a regime of private property is really necessary to ensuring that such conflicts never occur—why couldn't we simply hold that all goods shall be held forever in common, with, say, lottery mechanisms to decide who will use particular things when more than one person at a time claims to need them? Trying to formulate rights that will never conflict thus cannot take the place of asking deeper questions about these moral protections.
8. This focus on individual agency rather than instrumental maximization of other goals across multiple persons is obvious in cases like promising. While it is morally permissible to make all sorts of promises (so long as they violate no moral duties to others), it is difficult to conceive of moral arguments demonstrating that one should (be required to) make a specific set of promises, or that we as hypothetical contractors should compare various regimes of promise-making on their relative social value. Instead, promise-making is usually justified as expression of natural liberty. Often I will make commitments that do not maximize the aggregate good of society (e.g., I will promise something to a vicious person in a way that fails to change that person's behavior), but it seems odd to claim that these promises are not binding. It would be far odder to treat promises as somehow subject to redistribution. Doing so would destroy what promises are—free choices that both express and help constitute who a person is. Similarly, entitlement theory suggests that the acquisition of property is both an expression of and necessary for human liberty and so not subject to the Rousseauian considerations that "rational contractors" might apply. For further discussion of this point, see Simmons (1994).

9. Those who are familiar with these objections will recognize them as anything but trivial, but it also might be possible to deal with them within a suitably revised theory of natural property rights. Since I am primarily interested in historical claims here, I do not want to engage the intensive question of whether these objections are fatal to the theory. For present purposes, it seems more useful to discover what a theory of natural rights might imply if carried to its logical conclusions.
10. Although Nozick's entitlement conception of ownership has often been used as a foil for those who critique historical theories of property rights, what he actually says about rectifying historical injustices is extremely limited, and the principles involved are very tentatively suggested (Nozick 1974, 152–53). As usual, he offers more questions than answers, wonders about how far back historical injustices should be pursued, and then suggests that widespread redistribution may necessary if specific injustices cannot be sorted out (230–31).
11. In some cases, there are reasons to be concerned about the purported moral innocence of those who receive stolen property if they know its history, even if this occurred a long time ago. This is particularly so in long-standing democracies like the United States, Canada, and Australia, where generations have understood the processes by which indigenous lands were expropriated (at least in outline, if not in detail) and where political action to repair these wrongs and the damage caused by them would have been possible for most people for a very long time (see Hendrix 2005a). Still, it would probably be hard to make a case that they are sufficiently culpable to bear full moral responsibility for these original wrongs. Therefore, this concern probably justifies at best more limited kinds of compensation. At any rate, complicating factors like this might be seen as only tangential to the question of historical ownership itself—we can always look for a case in which clearly nonculpable persons have come to occupy lands historically owned by someone else (say for one indigenous group forcibly displaced onto the historic lands of another), and thus the fundamental question of why property rights might maintain moral force over time would remain unanswered.
12. Do rights that fade in this way deserve to be called "natural rights," given the kind of definition of them I have provided? I think they do, but they could also be reframed under a certain kind of Rousseauian view, so long as it took account of history in a serious way.
13. I am simplifying here. As Waldron (1979, 326–28) notes, Locke also acknowledged duties of charity to those in need, but adding this complication would make an already more complex argument even more so, and such a duty is probably not required within a theory of natural property rights.
14. David Armitage (2004) argues that Locke was developing his views on property at exactly the time that he was drafting a governing document for the colony of Carolina, and surely much of the resonance that Locke's arguments about labor had after their publication stemmed from their capacity to justify what many colonialists sought to do in self-interest (see, e.g., Williams 1990, chaps. 6–7; Kolers 2000; Tully 1994). (Locke was also financially involved in the slave trade.) Locke also had a number of less repugnant reasons for his position, however, including a theological belief that God had commanded humans to labor, an intense interest in the capacity of labor to create wealth, and presumably a conceptual commitment to the literal idea of mixing labor that I have rejected here. To my knowledge, there is no evidence that Locke was *merely* being opportunistic in outlining a justification for property that allowed the expropriation of indigenous land—his mistake was probably the more insidious one of allowing self-interest to render certain conclusions easier to reach than others.
15. Edward Feser, speaking of Locke's theory of acquisition through labor, argues that there is no definitive way of drawing these limits: "What we have here is just one more example of the sort of vagueness classically illustrated by the paradox of the sand heap. A million grains of sand constitute a heap of sand, and ten grains do not, but at what precise point in removing grains from a heap are we no longer left with a heap? There is no principled way to answer this question, but that fact casts no doubt on the existence of heaps of sand. . . . That there are intermediate cases where it is unclear how to apply the labor-mixing principle does not cast doubt on the principle itself" (Feser 2005, 64–65). This also holds for the uses-of-liberty argument I have made here.

16. Not everyone agrees that Locke intended this as a limit on ownership in this way; see, e.g., Waldron 1979. Nor does everyone agree that such a limitation on ownership is really necessary; see Feser 2005.
17. Except insofar as the natural resources within these kinds of goods are in short supply. In a market system, providing individuals with something equivalent to their share of the value of natural resources would take this into account (cf. Steiner 1977; 1994). In the absence of such a system, it might require some direct redistribution when particular kinds of minerals became both very important and very scarce.
18. This simplified way of framing the proviso's requirements will doubtless be annoying to those who are deeply immersed in philosophical discussions of the topic, but my description seems to me largely consistent with what even the most redistributivist interpretations of the proviso suggest, with the exception that I am accepting here strong rights to inheritance that Steiner (1994), Otsuka (1998), and other so-called Left libertarians usually reject. For the purposes of this argument, of course, taking this approach would simply cut off any reason for considering natural property rights, and indeed getting rid of rights to inherit seem to me to strip away much of what is interesting and challenging about Nozick-style arguments for strong ownership rights. (Without inheritance, the kinds of arguments that Steiner, Otsuka, and others want to pursue become very difficult to distinguish in any practical sense from most other kinds of egalitarianism, and given the complexity they entail, we may be better off simply focusing on what makes egalitarian standards succeed or fail in practice—cf. Otsuka 1998, 92). But, as should be clear from my discussion of residual indigenous property rights, I believe that any easy rejection of inheritance generally proceeds far too swiftly.
19. Nozick (1974, 175–82) seems to argue that a baseline income is what matters, with individuals receiving "enough and as good" if they are able to stay above this baseline by laboring for others (see, e.g., Arthur 1987; Cohen 1995, chap. 3; cf. Christman 1986, 175). Only those who fall below this baseline despite their labor would then be entitled to transfers of property from others as necessary to reach this minimum (Sarkar 1982, 49–53). But this seems to me a confusion on Nozick's part; it seems to conflate wealth created through labor with the value of resources acquired from nature. A more logically rigorous way of treating people equally would be to provide them with an initial endowment of unearned funds equal to their per capita share of the total value of natural resources (Steiner 1977; 1994), and then to let them rise to wealth or fall into poverty according to their own actions and decisions. This is the interpretation of the proviso implicit in the text from which this note comes, but I am not committed to arguing for one possibility over the other.
20. I am not entirely sure how Waldron intends his arguments about changes under the Lockean proviso to fit with the earlier argument about how property rights can fade with new styles of usage. At points he seems to suggest that they are simply different justifications for the same conclusions, but by their logic they have different implications, as I have tried to show here.

Chapter 4

1. The quotation from Chief Justice John Marshall with which the book began is especially revealing in this regard. It invokes the "rights" that the United States inherited from Great Britain, while at the same time claiming that the rights of outside political units are necessarily irrelevant from a legal point of view.
2. Locke (1980, § 97) actually uses the term "original compact," which is frequently rephrased today as "original contract." To maintain continuity with this contemporary usage, I have used the latter term throughout.
3. While consent is often conceptualized simply as a transfer of rights over one's own life to a state, it is probably easier to conceptualize the transfer as involving control over property as well. That is, individuals who consent to a political authority give up some of their liberty and allow their

lives to be occasionally put in danger (e.g., in conscription) by the new government they create, but also transfer partial rights over their property on the kind of terms Beitz attributes to Locke. States are, after all, territorial, and simply focusing on the transfer of nonproperty rights might make this difficult to understand.

4. It may also have dubious value, since children are taught to recite the words from habit long before they are able to understand their content, an unappealing practice that cheapens the value of these words as an expression of real allegiance.

5. Consider also volunteering for military service, where one specifically undertakes risks in the service of given country (cf. Simmons 1993, 219). Does this unambiguously indicate consent? Probably not—American Indians have been heavily represented in the military, particularly in wartime, but Indian soldiers have often included many who would have preferred to re-create political units separate from the United States if given the option (e.g., Iroquois soldiers whose nations had declared war on Germany in parallel with the American government—see, e.g., Howard 2003, 68). Simply defending a particular country against terrifying enemies does not always entail that one prefers that country over all potentially achievable political orders; it only entails that one prefers that country to another far worse, which is not the same thing at all. Even in the case of military service, then, it is reasonable to assume that most people who volunteer for it intend to express their consent to a particular political order, but difficult to be sure that any specific person has really offered consent.

6. It probably is fair to say that *many* of those who choose to remain on reservations or other legally acknowledged indigenous lands in the present day do intend to express something by this, since the relative poverty of most indigenous communities often creates strong economic inducements to leave and since exit is usually very easy politically. Nonetheless, it seems difficult to conclude that *everyone* who remains in indigenous-controlled territories intends thereby to consent to this unit's political authority. Many may remain because they are too impoverished to leave or fearful of the racism and cultural barriers they may face if they do leave. In these instances, the proviso seems to come into effect, with all its complications for collective property holdings.

7. When consent fails, some authors seek to ground political obligations in fairness. According to fairness arguments, individuals must obey the state if they receive desirable benefits that can be provided only when other citizens do likewise (Klosko 1992; cf. Simmons 1999, 753). Since individuals usually want national defense or the rule of law, for example, fairness demands that they bear their share in funding those goods and abiding by the necessary laws. Unfortunately, however, fairness theory requires clear indications that individuals regard the benefits received as worth the costs of their provision (Simmons 1979, 136–42). In daily life, you cannot obligate me by providing something valuable unless I willingly accept that benefit, understanding the costs that accompany it. Similarly, you cannot extort my acceptance by barring others from offering the same benefit at a lower price. Thus, fairness theory seems to reduce to a type of consent, where the central question is whether I have accepted benefits freely or not (Simmons 1979; 1993), and so cannot provide an alternative argument here.

8. This kind of careful limitation clearly does not describe contemporary circumstances in the United States, where eminent domain is used in a variety of ways that are both frivolous and pernicious.

9. If states can permissibly acquire such properties, potentially they can also exploit some of them for profit, or to defray the long-term costs of protecting rights. They might then use these profits to acquire other properties, much as the early United States acquired lands from American Indians that were then sold piecemeal to citizens to fund further expansion. If we are also willing to make some concessions to the indeterminate number of consentors in real states (for whom higher levels of taxation may be tolerable), then permissible state holdings seem likewise increased. Strict proponents of natural rights will likely reject "indirectly conducive" lands, of course, and likely concessions to consentors as well, and their core impulse here

seems reasonable—public lands are easiest to justify when they are strictly necessary or acquired through market mechanisms, even if they deserve at least some moral respect when they cross the bounds of strict necessity.

10. Does this imply, then, that whenever indigenous political organizations can be shown to hold excessive amounts of land in a public way, the states now claiming authority over them should force a reduction of holdings? Not at all; simply because another political unit holds more land than can be strictly justified by its role does not mean that outsiders have an automatic right to reshape its laws through force. The reason, at least in part, is that such interventions will rarely be worth the damage they cause. Indeed, it is hard to see how American Indians could produce a regime of property rights less effective than that under which many now live, courtesy of U.S. policies in the 1880s. On reservations where lands were historically allotted to individuals, many contemporary persons have inherited radically fractionalized shares in particular plots of land, rendering many of these properties virtually useless (see, e.g., Wilkins 2002, 162–64; cf. Rosser 2005). David Wilkins (2002, 162) cites one reservation on which a typical parcel of land has 196 individuals holding shares in it, and notes one instance in which it cost seventeen times more to administer a property each year than that property generated in revenue.

11. If boundaries were changed in this way, some public lands would have to be included both to maintain contiguity and to ensure a fair distribution of resources. Insofar as these lands were necessary for the protection of rights, they would raise few interesting issues—if they were necessary to protect rights in one state, they will likely be equally necessary in another, and seemingly no one will have any complaints when they are transferred one way or the other. Nonessential public lands are more complex, however, because these lands are more strongly tied to a particular set of citizens and their political decisions and because they are less strongly justified by our natural duties. If some group of citizens were transferred involuntarily from one state to another, presumably nonessential public lands should be divided accordingly—but compensation might sometimes go in a different direction than we would expect. What will matter, in such circumstances, is the ratio between the population transferred and the public lands included along with them. If the territory involved has extensive public lands and few citizens, then the new state will be required to compensate the former one. If, on the other hand, the territory is heavily populated with few public lands, the new state will, it seems, be entitled to compensation from the old for the value of property otherwise lost to its citizens in transition.

12. A Rawlsian difference principle provides one method for thinking about the necessary trade-offs, although questions about the relevant time frame for the necessary comparisons would remain whatever standard we chose; see Buchanan (1991, 122–23).

13. There are reasons to believe that a Rousseauian account might also come down in favor of returning land to indigenous peoples rather than simply providing cash payments, since many commentators believe that this represents the best strategy for remediating indigenous poverty in any case. See Barsh (1982, 73–78); see also Canada (1996, vol. 5, chap. 3). For a contrary view, see Flanagan (2000, 174–91); see also Rosser (2005).

Chapter 5

1. Some elements of Kant's argument seem to suggest that he intends to base authority on consent rather than duties, since each individual recognizes the dangers of life without government. But statements like the following suggest otherwise: "Hence each may impel the other by force to leave this state [of nature] and enter into a rightful condition" (1996, 90). This suggests that individuals really have no choice in the matter, whatever their own inclinations may be.

2. If someone really took the strong position that each person's moral judgments were equally worthy of respect before authority was created, we would not even be able to provide a coherent

argument for why authority was justified. If everyone's views were of equal status, there would be no way of choosing between those of Kantians, monarchists, anarchists, or anyone else, and all we would be able to say was that disagreement exists.

3. Roger L. Sullivan (1996, xiv–xv) asserts that *The Metaphysics of Morals* is unique in making the argument from moral disagreement. I believe that Sullivan may be mistaken, although he is certainly far more versed in Kant's work than I am. On my reading, Kant gestures toward the argument from moral disagreement at several points when speaking about the state and the "original contract," and relies on something very like it in his recurrent denials that citizens have a right to overthrow even the most unjust of governments. His argument from human nature seems to be displayed much more prominently when discussing relations between states as a parallel to the condition of life without government. It may have been these differing contexts that allowed any tension to go unresolved. Again, however, I do not want to hinge anything of importance on the relationship between the two arguments; they seem to stand alone, and so can be evaluated on their own.

4. Even if we expect that most people will defend themselves from immediate threats no matter what the cost to others—so that moral exhortations to exercise more restraint can never have any effect and are therefore pointless—Kant's argument assumes no such immediacy, or even terribly high dangers. He seems to suggest rather that we always pose dangers to each other simply by our existence and character, rather than from anything we are actually doing.

5. One might suggest that my duty to preserve my own life requires me to live under state authority. Even if I have a duty to preserve my own life as Kant (e.g., 1964, 89) argued, however, natural liberty presumably allows me to risk my life in various ways. If I cannot choose to expose myself to life without a state, then presumably I cannot expose myself to various other forms of danger such as skydiving or kickboxing either, and my liberty is much less useful to me than it is often believed to be. At any rate, I do not find duties of self-preservation defensible or coherent, and so have left them aside here.

6. Without some further argument, we cannot plausibly suggest that mere social interdependence creates political duties, although one occasionally hears this claim made. Social interactions are not necessary to creating duties, which we can see clearly by considering duties against murder. Unless we make the trivial claim that meeting someone for the first time (say on a desert island) constitutes meaningful interaction, then the interaction-based view leads to the implausible conclusion that we can in good conscience murder any sufficiently complete stranger. Nor, as Nozick (1974, 183–89) notes, is interaction *simpliciter* sufficient to generate moral duties from scratch: if I trade something I own to you for something you own, no new moral forces are generated in the process of each doing what is permitted to us. This is not to say that interactions can never create special obligations between persons—some ways of interacting can indicate a desire to form such special relationships with other participants—but these do not result automatically. Social interaction makes rules of justice meaningful, but it tells us nothing by itself about their content. To determine content, we have to know first of all what freestanding duties individuals have, and then determine what additional obligations they might voluntarily have taken on.

7. If the magnitude and imminence of potential injuries matter, the strength of our duties may be partially additive as well, with our duty to accept risks increasing with the number of those threatened. Michael Walzer (1992, 253) suggests that individual rights may be overridden when the alternative is "of an unusual and horrifying kind." Similarly, individuals may have duties to accept severe dangers to themselves when the alternatives are sufficiently horrific. Our judgment here is particularly important for recognizing the limits of our duties in cases like military conscription. For a problematic formulation that may give insufficient consideration to the costs of the duties of specific soldiers, for example, see Buchanan (1999, 82–87).

8. Kant also thinks there are cases that do not involve attitudes of mind where coercion cannot be applied effectively and that therefore must remain outside the realm of right. Consider, for example, his argument against coercive punishment for shipwreck victims who kill others or

let them die to save their own lives: "For the punishment threatened by the law could not be greater than the loss of his own life. A penal law of this sort could not have the effect intended, since the threat of an ill that is still *uncertain* (death by a judicial verdict) cannot outweigh the fear of an ill that is *certain* (drowning)" (Kant 1996, 28; emphasis in original). Noting a slightly different version of this problem, Kant (27) bans adjudication for extracontractual considerations of equity, because attempts to enforce such a principle would undo the benefits of contract laws. I have left these issues aside here because they pose interpretative difficulties with no obvious benefits.

9. Some of Kant's own suggestions about coercibility and the damage caused by particular wrongs are perplexing, such as his claim that embezzlement should be relegated to civil courts, while instances of simple theft deserve criminal punishment "because they endanger the entire commonwealth and not just an individual person" (Kant 1996, 105).

10. Of course, the content of natural rights probably seems far clearer than it really should, because such rights are usually conceptualized through a broad set of Anglo-American legal standards. Even so, determining the exact content of our duties seems inherently more difficult, at least absent some demonstration of how this might be done.

Chapter 6

1. This does not mean that I must always obey the state, but that the commands of the state give me a powerful moral reason to do so that may sometimes be outweighed by other reasons. See, e.g., Simmons (1979, 29–30).

2. This statement is unfortunately ambiguous, leaving it unclear whether Simmons is acknowledging some limited version of a natural duty argument for state authority over most individuals (Simmons 1999, 768; cf. 1993, 242) or merely restating his claims about the necessity of consent (Simmons 1999, 767; cf. 1993, 265). On either reading, however, his basic point is evident: states cannot claim coercive rights over all within a territory simply because of residence.

3. My basic comparison of anarcho-capitalism and communitarian anarchism follows Christopher Morris (1998) in taking these as the two most likely alternatives to states as we know them.

4. Harry Beran (1987, 104) has argued for a consent-based theory of authority, but imagines that those who refuse to consent must migrate to a "dissenter's territory" where they can remain free of authority. If we reject the right of states to use coercion against noncitizens, it is difficult to see how this requirement can be justified.

5. There would be more potential for individuals on the territorial edges of a protection agency or consent-based state to choose the better of the two, but this type of competition is a severe reduction from that envisioned by anarcho-capitalists.

6. The status of duties to aid is particularly problematic in such communities because redistribution of wealth to assist others may be ultimately self-defeating. Since such societies are often desperately poor, many people would simply starve without redistribution of crops, game animals, and so on. In the absence of alternatives, traditional indigenous economies were highly dependent upon cooperation as a way of distributing luck and sharing risk. Yet as Morris (1998, 77) notes, this "enforced leveling" prevents the pooling of capital, along with the economic specialization and entrepreneurship upon which advanced economies depend (cf. Frantz 1999, 161–76; Hardin 2001). While individuals presumably have no duty to make themselves wealthy, they presumably cannot demand aid from others if the alternative would allow them to escape the circumstances making such aid necessary in the first place. This suggests that collective ownership may be plausible only if we can demonstrate that individuals have consented to it or that duties to aid require the maintenance of community for some other reason. The most promising justification for collective ownership may be religious—that duties to God or other nonhuman beings require land and other resources to be held in this way. I will try to say something about these claims in Chapter 8.

7. Despite the occasional myopia of urbanized and cosmopolitan academics, many nonindigenous communities with such extended face-to-face interactions continue to exist as well, and in these

instances most law and order continues to be maintained by such mechanisms. I must admit my own prejudices here—for reasons of personal history, I find the customs and expectations of urban life occasionally mystifying and those of small communities more conducive to a comfortable human life.

8. There may also be reasons for worries about the protection of property rights in such systems, but these concerns are complicated by considerations of cultural difference. See Chapter 8.
9. In strict logic, there is actually no linkage between refusing state protections and fulfilling our duties by alternative means—if we fulfill our duties at all, we seem to be in "good moral standing" and therefore entitled to full protection by the state in our territory, whether we offer it any direct support or not. But this seems so contrary to most people's intuitions that for expositional reasons I have left this point largely aside.
10. Recall Taylor's (1982) conclusion from a wide reading of anthropological evidence on indigenous communities: threats of retribution are often necessary to ensure compliance with moral principles (including aid to others) *despite* intensive socialization in such communities. If aid to others is unreliable even in small communities where moral suasion should be most effective, is it likely that individuals will behave substantially better in aiding those with whom they have had no face-to-face contact?
11. Nor can we claim that persons who fail to render aid merely engage in trivial forms of wrongdoing that do not merit coercion. Although it is difficult to determine exactly the limits of our duties compared to our rights, it seems obvious that these duties must have relatively equal strength for everyone, in the same way that rights provide relatively equal protections. Those who fail to perform their duties thus create a dilemma—either some people must go underprotected, or some individuals must go beyond the call of duty in rendering aid (cf. Mills 1995). Over the course of a lifetime, the effects of these failures to render aid, either on the unprotected or on those bearing unequal burdens, would seem substantial.
12. That is, unless our duties are partly additive and so sometimes require that we die to save many others from being killed. I have left this possibility aside so that the case for state authority does not seem to turn strongly on it.
13. While similar issues about high costs to oneself also apply to wrongful criminal convictions, these are inherent in all criminal justice and so have no novel implications for state policy.
14. What about the psychological costs of living under a regime that one dislikes? These might seem not to count if we are primarily concerned with costs as disruptions of our liberty, rather than of our happiness. But this may not be exactly right—some ways of losing one's liberty are generally seen as worse than others because of the psychological harms involved. Rape is often regarded as worse than kidnapping, for example, even if both go on for the same amount of time and neither causes permanent physical damage, because rape is experienced as a more profound violation of one's own integrity. Living under a state one dislikes is obviously not the same as rape, but it is for some people a heavy psychological cost nonetheless. Obviously, giving this sort of perceived harm a very heavy weight would return us to consent, with all its difficulties, but some intermediate position might be more plausible. For further discussion of this point, see Chapter 7.
15. Imagine, as an illustration, a state that directly mandates one day of labor from its citizens per week. (For whatever reason, no one has yet thought of professionalizing public services.) Across this country of several million, five people are murdered per week. A legislator argues that this murder rate is too high and proposes tripling the amount of labor required from each individual, to three days a week. The legislator projects that this will save one life per week. Is this too much? I think it very clearly is, although it is hard to say in principled terms how such lines should be drawn.
16. Where states seem to be suffering from a lack of expertise or resources, this would include providing these directly to them rather than, say, trying to redistribute borders to bring resources and expertise within their territorial boundaries. Aside from the difficulties of such border shifts, a strategy of direct assistance also fosters the right sorts of debates about the legitimacy of current

economic inequalities and the strength of our duties, since focusing on cross-border aid gives us something determinate to argue about—the current amount of assistance given per country per person, and what this does or fails to do (see, e.g., Pogge 1994).

17. A natural duty justification of authority also allows or encourages governments to create various regional subdivisions such as provinces or American states for primarily administrative purposes, but these raise no interesting issues for the current discussion.

Chapter 7

1. I have written about the question of strategy in the face of injustice elsewhere (Hendrix 2005b), and have acknowledged that strategic—and perhaps deceptive—actions may sometimes be necessary in pursuing justice. But these must nevertheless be used with care because they can easily do more harm than good. Justice can rarely be secured through such mechanisms over the long term, nor should we want it to be. See also Hendrix (2005a).
2. But we still might think that experts must necessary remain the better judges. After all, if one expert is a slightly better judge than one nonexpert, won't this expert also be more reliable than a thousand or a million nonexperts combined? Perhaps surprisingly, no—the combined judgments of many nonexpert can actually be far better than those of each individual taken alone. Bernard Grofman and Scott Feld (1988), drawing on the work of the marquis de Condorcet (1976, 48–50), have shown mathematically that democratic majorities are extremely likely to reach the objectively correct decision so long as the average voter is a good judge slightly more than half of the time. As average voters become increasingly good judges and as the number of those voting increases, the chances of a correct answer increase as well (Grofman and Feld 1988, 573n7). Grofman and Feld (1988, 571) note as an example that among 399 people who individually have a 55 percent chance of reaching the right answer, a majority among them has a 98 percent chance of being right. While I will not try to outline the mathematical arguments here, it seems agreed upon that these formulae really do produce the results claimed for them—so long as all of those involved are slightly better judges than worse, it is extremely likely for majorities to get objectively correct decisions. Good judgment, in this counterintuitive sense, really can be cumulative.

   But I do not want to overstate the force of this finding, since mathematical demonstrations are one thing, real political phenomena another. As Jeremy Waldron (Estlund et al. 1989, 1322–23) notes, the same forces that aggregate good judgment can have the opposite effect if the average person's judgment is slightly more often wrong than right—in that case, the cumulative judgment of a majority is almost guaranteed to be *wrong*. This danger of bad judgment seems particularly severe for specific policies, since specialized knowledge is often necessary in evaluating these (Estlund et al. 1989, 1323–25), and indeed Condorcet himself proposed that citizens should be limited to choosing representatives, since they lacked the knowledge to choose anything more detailed (Estlund et al. 1989, 1324–25).
3. A more substantial worry is that secessionists will often be prompted primarily by profit motives (cf. Ramet 1998). Such motives clearly can play an important role in poor states where natural resources confer great advantages to those who control them, but are also sometimes imputed to separatist movements within wealthy democratic states, such as Northern Italian secessionists (e.g., Buchanan 2004, 399n40). We could give this concern both a simple and subtle reading. In the simple version, secessionists will simply vote their material interest, while in the subtle version their interests will reshape their understanding of what justice is and of who belongs within their community. In either case there are legitimate reasons for concern.

   On the other hand, many existing states administer questionable policies of redistribution from weak groups to powerful (as the United States and Canada have traditionally done from resource-rich Indian reservations), and as Hurst Hannum (1990, 7–8) notes, there is no obvious pattern in extant secessionist movements suggesting that profit-seeking is essential to such movements—in fact, secessionists often pursue independence even when they would be considerably worse off. Moreover, a scramble for natural resources can rarely be as important within wealthy democratic states as it is within impoverished countries, because most of the wealth of the former comes from other sources, and these sources can be unpredictable in many ways. As the growth of the European Union demonstrates, contemporary economic success often lies in closer ties, not increased distance. So profit-seeking considerations may be very important within poor, otherwise unstable states, and I do not want to downplay that danger—but it seems much less of a danger where states are already governed by democratic principles, and these are the states that I am considering here.

4. Exactly how this spacing should be decided is an important question. Separating votes by five years, for example, would allow secessionist leaders to muster up two crests of political passion rather than one extended one, but would also allow for more extensive debate, so the exact trade-offs here remain undetermined.

5. It is worth considering briefly how such self-determination might work where populations have multiple and complex preferences. Within any particular territory, there will probably be those who would prefer to join another state if possible rather than seek independence. This larger set of options makes voting a somewhat trickier matter—if some of those within a territory want to pursue independence and others prefer to join a contiguous country, which option should be voted on first? Some of these problems might be reduced by allowing the division of preexisting political subunits, but clearly not all can be escaped in this way.

One option is simply to let political chance decide which of the potential options actually comes up for a vote (if any ever does). Generally, those whose option was not on the ballot might be expected to side with the status quo, in hopes of trying for their preferred option at a later time, so such divided preferences will usually result in no change. This seems like a reasonable outcome—if a majority of those involved cannot decide on what kind of change to pursue, it seems unlikely that the status quo is that bad or (alternatively) that the state created from change would be an improvement. The goal of procedural self-determination, after all, is to allow populations to escape states they dislike, not to ensure that every person gets exactly what he or she wants. Still, leaving this kind of decision up to whichever group acts first might create hard feelings among those whose first option was not considered, or might create a race among potential secessionists to bring their option to vote first. Of course, since acting prematurely could damage their chances forever, secessionist leaders would have to be cautious in any such race. But it is still worth thinking about what our further options here might be.

An alternative would be to allow people to express their judgments more precisely in the first round of voting. Thus, we might require, for example, that any group requesting a vote on independence include on the initial ballot whatever other political affiliations might be possible. Usually these will be very limited because few states are contiguous to any particular territory or willing to accept noncontiguous relationships, and few are eager to integrate new populations unless they already know those populations very well. But multiple options would still doubtless be possible in some cases, and where this does occur we might structure the first round of voting to use a more sophisticated technique like a Borda (1994) count. In this kind of count, voters rank their options in order of preference, with choices weighted by this ranking—on a ballot with three choices, for example, votes for a first preference would count as two points, second preferences as one, and third preferences as zero, with the choice receiving the most points "winning." This would then determine what option, if any, the status quo would compete against in a second referendum a few years later.

In practice, this kind of voting on multiple options would probably make many would-be secessionists less eager to put matters up for a vote, since they could not be sure that their preferred option would be the one up for decision in the second round. Moreover, such a voting situation, in which second-best preferences also matter, would spur those involved to provide reasons for having one ranking rather than another. While three-sided (or more) political debates might be perplexing at first, they would likely lead to some fruitful discussions about what makes a government worthy of allegiance. So while this abbreviated discussion is not sufficient to defuse all of the potential challenges associated with such complex preferences, it does seem likely that they can be dealt with through careful attention to the design of procedures.

6. This is always a problem for established federalist arrangements as well, of course—is it fair that American states all have the same representation in the Senate despite their varying size?—but constructing new balances in this way is never easy.

Chapter 8

1. I do not mean to suggest that states and their populations are freed from the responsibility to make political and cultural life as welcoming to different identities as possible, not only because this will allow more groups to feel tolerably satisfied with political life (cf. Ivison 2000; 2002, 14–26) but because it will make it easier for their concerns to receive a fair hearing among those within the majority group (cf. Miller 1995, 96–98). But if these identities are to be reflected in structures of governance over particular populations and geographical spaces, these structures are probably best shaped through the mechanisms outlined in the last chapter, to make sure that any changes are based as deeply as possible on extensive deliberation and the actual judgments of those involved, rather than just their putative leaders. Taken purely as a set of imagined connections, feelings of national attachment do make a difference for the character of particular political societies, but probably not in any direct way for the design of the mechanisms intended to shape the features of political boundaries.

2. Kymlicka (1995, 163–70) walks an ambiguous line in regard to groups that might not actually protect rights, suggesting that all groups *should* protect rights but that outside interference will usually do more harm than good. Since this factual claim may not be true, it is worthwhile to have a better sense of the degree to which the protection of rights as we know them really is mandatory.

3. Cook (1999, chaps. 5–6) argues that early anthropologists also were seeking to rebut earlier scholars who focused on ranking various groups as higher or lower on the scale of social evolution, which had unpleasant normative implications and seemed scientifically counterproductive.

4. I should also note the existence of a wide variety of issues that do not fall clearly into the categories of "neutral" and "deep" cultural difference. Consider something like family structure. This is not easily classed as the kind of "neutral" cultural difference I have outlined, because it can have important implications for the kinds of obligations and choices people are expected to have. It does not necessarily have any impact on rights, however, though it could if men claimed, for example, rights to beat or control their wives. Many of these questions, therefore, will fall into an intermediate zone. Consider questions like the following: Should one's obligations to family members extend only to the so-called nuclear family, or should they fully extend to aunts, uncles, cousins, or distant members of a clan? Should these obligations include expectations of sharing material goods broadly among all those involved, or should such sharing be regarded as outside these obligations' purview? Should people be encouraged to form new relationships with very diverse people who are not related to them, or should they focus on maintaining and deepening the relationships into which they have been born?

Deciding exactly where these kinds of issues impact rights in important ways can be complex. Even if such obligations will rarely be directly subject to enforcement through coercive means, they will probably have to be reflected in a variety of laws on inheritance, the placement of orphaned children, and so on. Because these kinds of disagreements are intermediate in this way, they can pull in ambiguous directions: they can provide potentially valuable alternate frameworks for conceptualizing how human life should be lived, but they can also entail some dangers for particular vulnerable members if they filter into law in excessive ways. Nonetheless, we can say that where these alternatives do not obviously endanger anyone, they seem worthy of protection and may also provide a valuable source of creative disagreement about what a morally good human life looks like. While there may be reasons for concern about some indigenous traditions in this regard, they are likely relatively limited and can generally be dealt with through procedural means.

5. One obvious concern is that allowing existing states to exercise anything like a veto on the institutional forms of groups seeking separation will simply result in illegitimate kinds of blocking behaviors, where states act in persistently bad faith even against groups with severe grievances. This concern, however, is less severe than it seems, because states will generally not have such pretexts against groups that are willing to adopt democratic mechanisms of their own. Moreover, these fears have to be balanced against the danger that some groups really would want to pursue extremely dangerous kinds of policies toward some of their most vulnerable members, and the more intermediate possibility that some groups (or their leaders) will have deeply mistaken ideas about the kinds of political systems that can be successful. So any option one chooses here, as in so much of political life, can create bad results in different kinds of circumstances. The question is how this balance can best be struck so that it allows groups to experiment with alternatives without leading to disasters.

WORKS CITED

Alfred, Taiaiake [Gerald R. Alfred]. 1995. *Heeding the Voices of Our Ancestors: Kahnawake Mohawk Politics and the Rise of Native Nationalism.* Don Mills, Ont.: Oxford University Press.
———. 1999. *Peace, Power, Righteousness: An Indigenous Manifesto.* Don Mills, Ont.: Oxford University Press.
———. 2005. *Wasáse: Indigenous Pathways to Action and Freedom.* Peterborough, Ont.: Broadview Press.
Anaya, S. James. 1996. *Indigenous Peoples in International Law.* New York: Oxford University Press.
Appiah, Kwame Anthony. 2005. *The Ethics of Identity.* Princeton: Princeton University Press.
Armitage, David. 2004. "John Locke, Carolina, and the *Two Treatises of Government.*" *Political Theory* 32:602–27.
Armstrong, H. W., and R. Read. 2000. "Comparing the Economic Performance of Dependent Territories and Sovereign Microstates." *Economic Development and Cultural Change* 48:285–306.
Arthur, John. 1987. "Resource Acquisition and Harm." *Canadian Journal of Philosophy* 17:337–48.
Baldwin, Thomas. 1992. "The Territorial State." In *Jurisprudence: Cambridge Essays,* edited by Hyman Gross and Ross Harrison. Oxford: Clarendon Press.
Barsh, Russell Lawrence. 1982. "Indian Land Claims Policy in the United States." *North Dakota Law Review* 58:7–82.
Barsh, Russell Lawrence, and James Youngblood Henderson. 1980. *The Road: Indian Tribes and Political Liberty.* Berkeley and Los Angeles: University of California Press.
Bederman, David J. 2001. *International Law Frameworks.* New York: Foundation Press.
Beitz, Charles R. 1980. "Tacit Consent and Property Rights." *Political Theory* 8:487–502.
Beran, Harry. 1984. "A Liberal Theory of Secession." *Political Studies* 32:21–31.
———. 1987. *The Consent Theory of Political Obligation.* New York: Croom Helm.
Boldt, Menno. 1993. *Surviving as Indians: The Challenge of Self-Government.* Toronto: University of Toronto Press.
Borda, Jean-Charles de. 1994. "A Paper on Elections by Ballot." In *Condorcet: Foundations of Social Choice and Political Theory,* translated and edited by Iain McLean and Fiona Hewitt. Brookfield, Vt.: Edward Elgar.
Borrows, John. 1999. "Landed Citizenship." In *Citizenship, Diversity, and Pluralism: Canadian and Comparative Perspectives,* edited by Alan C. Cairns, John C. Courtney, Peter MacKinnon, Hans J. Michelman, and David E. Smith. Montreal: Queen's–McGill University Press.
———. 2002. *Recovering Canada: The Resurgence of Indigenous Law.* Toronto: University of Toronto Press.

Brilmayer, Lea. 1989. "Consent, Contract, and Territory." *Minnesota Law Review* 74:1–35.
Brownlie, Ian. 1998. *The Rule of Law in International Affairs.* Boston: Martinus Nijhoff.
———. 2002. *Basic Documents in International Law.* 5th ed. New York: Oxford University Press.
Buchanan, Allen. 1991. *Secession: The Legitimacy of Political Divorce from Fort Sumter to Lithuania and Quebec.* Boulder: Westview Press.
———. 1997. "Theories of Secession." *Philosophy and Public Affairs* 26:31–61.
———. 1999. "The Internal Legitimacy of Humanitarian Intervention." *Journal of Political Philosophy* 7:71–87.
———. 2004. *Justice, Legitimacy, and Self-Determination: Moral Foundations for International Law.* New York: Oxford University Press.
Buchheit, Lee C. 1978. *Secession: The Legitimacy of Self-Determination.* New Haven: Yale University Press.
Cairns, Alan C. 2000. *Citizens Plus: Aboriginal Peoples and the Canadian State.* Vancouver: University of British Columbia Press.
Canada, Royal Commission on Aboriginal Peoples. 1996. *Report of the Royal Commission on Aboriginal Peoples.* 5 vols. Ottawa: Canada Communications Group.
Carens, Joseph H. 2000. *Culture, Citizenship, and Community: A Contextual Exploration of Justice as Evenhandedness.* New York: Oxford University Press.
Case Concerning the Frontier Dispute (Burkina Faso/Republic of Mali). 1986. ICJ Reports 554.
Cassese, Anthony. 1986. *International Law in a Divided World.* New York: Oxford University Press.
———. 1995. *Self-Determination of Peoples: A Legal Reappraisal.* New York: Oxford University Press.
Castellino, Joshua. 2000. *International Law and Self-Determination: The Interplay of the Politics of Territorial Possession with Formulations of Post-colonial "National" Identity.* Leiden: Martinus Nijhoff.
Chambers, Simone. 2002. "Constitutional Referendums and Democratic Deliberation." In *Referendum Democracy: Citizens, Elites, and Deliberation in Referendum Campaigns,* edited by Matthew Mendelsohn and Andrew Parkin. New York: Palgrave.
Chen, Lung-Chu. 2000. *An Introduction to Contemporary International Law: A Policy-Oriented Perspective.* New Haven: Yale University Press.
Chesterman, John, and Brian Galligan. 1997. *Citizens Without Rights: Aborigines and Australian Citizenship.* Melbourne: Cambridge University Press.
Christman, John. 1986. "Can Ownership Be Justified by Natural Rights?" *Philosophy and Public Affairs* 15:156–77.
Churchill, Ward. 1999. *Struggle for the Land: Native North American Resistance to Genocide, Ecocide, and Colonization.* Winnipeg: Arbeiter Ring.
Cohen, G. A. 1995. *Self-Ownership, Freedom, and Equality.* New York: Cambridge University Press.
Condorcet, Jean-Antoine-Nicolas de Caritat, marquis de. 1976. *Condorcet: Selected Writings.* Edited by Keith Michael Baker. Bobbs-Merrill: Indianapolis.
Cook, John W. 1999. *Morality and Cultural Differences.* New York: Oxford University Press.
Coombes, H. C. 1994. *Aboriginal Autonomy: Issues and Strategies.* New York: Cambridge University Press.

Copp, David. 1999. "The Idea of a Legitimate State." *Philosophy and Public Affairs* 28:3–45.
Dahl, Robert A. 1994. "A Democratic Dilemma: System Effectiveness versus Citizen Participation." *Political Science Quarterly* 109:23–34.
Deloria, Vine, Jr. 1969. *Custer Died for Your Sins: An Indian Manifesto.* New York: Macmillan Press.
———. 1974. *Behind the Trail of Broken Treaties: An Indian Declaration of Independence.* New York: Delta.
———. 2003. *God Is Red: A Native View of Religion.* 3rd ed. Golden, Colo.: Fulcrum.
———. 2004. "Philosophy and the Tribal Peoples." In *American Indian Thought,* edited by Anne Waters. Malden, Mass.: Blackwell.
Denis, Claude. 1997. *We Are Not You: First Nations and Canadian Modernity.* Peterborough, Ont.: Broadview Press.
Detter, Ingrid. 1994. *The International Legal Order.* Brookfield, Vt.: Dartmouth.
Duursma, Jorri. 1996. *Fragmentation and the International Relations of Micro-states.* New York: Cambridge University Press.
Dworkin, Ronald. 1981. "What Is Equality? Part 2: Equality of Resources." *Philosophy and Public Affairs* 10:283–345.
Elfstrom, Gerald. 1983. "On Dilemmas of Intervention." *Ethics* 93:709–25.
Estlund, David M., Jeremy Waldron, Bernard Grofman, and Scott L. Feld. 1989. "Democratic Theory and the Public Interest: Condorcet and Rousseau Revisited." *American Political Science Review* 83:1317–40.
Ferrara, Alessandro. 2001. "Of Boats and Principles: Reflections on Habermas's 'Constitutional Democracy.'" *Political Theory* 29:782–91.
Feser, Edward. 2005. "There Is No Such Thing as an Unjust Initial Acquisition." *Social Philosophy and Policy* 22:56–80.
Flanagan, Tom. 2000. *First Nations, Second Thoughts.* Montreal: Queen's–McGill University Press.
Franck, Thomas M. 1992. "The Emerging Right to Democratic Governance." *American Journal of International Law* 86:46–91.
Frantz, Klaus. 1999. *Indian Reservations in the United States.* Chicago: University of Chicago Press.
Friedman, David. 1989. *The Machinery of Freedom: Guide to a Radical Capitalism.* Chicago: Open Court.
Gale, George. 1973. "John Locke on Territoriality: An Unnoticed Aspect of the *Second Treatise.*" *Political Theory* 1:472–85.
Grofman, Bernard, and Scott L. Feld. 1988. "Rousseau's General Will: A Condorcetian Perspective." *American Political Science Review* 82:567–76.
Habermas, Jürgen. 1996. *Between Facts and Norms: Contributions to a Discourse Theory of Law and Democracy.* Translated by William Rehg. Cambridge, Mass.: MIT Press.
———. 2001. "Constitutional Democracy: A Paradoxical Union of Contradictory Principles?" *Political Theory* 29:766–81.
Halperin, Morton H., David J. Scheffer, and Patricia L. Small. 1992. *Self-Determination in the New World Order.* Washington, D.C.: Carnegie Endowment for International Peace.
Hannum, Hurst. 1990. *Autonomy, Sovereignty, and Self-Determination: The Accommodation of Conflicting Rights.* Philadelphia: University of Pennsylvania Press.
Hardin, Russell. 2001. "Group Boundaries, Individual Barriers." In *Boundaries and Justice: Diverse Ethical Perspectives,* edited by David Miller and Sohail H. Hashmi. Princeton: Princeton University Press.

Held, David. 1991. "Democracy, the Nation-State and the Global System." *Economy and Society* 20:138–72.

Hendrix, Burke A. 2001. "International Law as a Moral Theory of State Territory?" *Geopolitics* 6:141–62

———. 2005a. "Moral Minimalism in American Indian Land Claims." *American Indian Quarterly* 29:538–59.

———. 2005b. "Memory in Native American Land Claims." *Political Theory* 33:763–85.

———. 2007. "Moral Error, Power, and Insult." *Political Theory* 35:550–73.

Hester, Thurman Lee, Jr. 2001. *Political Principles and Indian Sovereignty*. New York: Routledge.

Honoré, Tony. 1987. *Making Law Bind: Essays Legal and Philosophical*. Oxford: Clarendon Press.

Howard, Bradley Reed. 2003. *Indigenous Peoples and the State: The Struggle for Native Rights*. DeKalb: Northern Illinois University Press.

Ivison, Duncan. 2000. "Political Community and Historical Injustice." *Australasian Journal of Philosophy* 78:360–73.

———. 2002. *Postcolonial Liberalism*. Cambridge: Cambridge University Press.

Kaikobad, Kaiyan Homi. 1996. "Self Determination, Territorial Disputes and International Law: An Analysis of UN and State Practice." *Geopolitics and International Boundaries* 1:15–54.

Kant, Immanuel. 1964. *Groundwork for the Metaphysic of Morals*. Translated by H. J. Paton. New York: Harper Torchbooks.

———. 1991. *Political Writings*. Translated by H. B. Nisbet. Edited by Hans Reiss. New York: Cambridge University Press.

———. 1996. *The Metaphysics of Morals*. Translated by Mary Gregor. New York: Cambridge University Press.

Keal, Paul. 2003. *European Conquest and the Rights of Indigenous Peoples: The Moral Backwardness of International Society*. Cambridge: Cambridge University Press.

Kershell, John E. 1992. "An Overview of the Concept of Smallness." In *Public Administration in Small and Island States*, edited by Randall Baker. Bloomfield, Conn.: Kumarian Press.

Kingsbury, Benedict. 1998. "'Indigenous Peoples' in International Law: A Constructivist Approach to the Asian Controversy." *American Journal of International Law* 92:414–57.

Kleinig, John. 1976. "Good Samaritanism." *Philosophy and Public Affairs* 5:382–407.

Klosko, George. 1992. *The Principle of Fairness and Political Obligation*. Lanham, Md.: Rowman and Littlefield.

Kofman, Daniel. 1998. "Rights of Secession." *Society* 35:30–37.

Kohen, Marcelo G. 2001. "International Law Is the Most Appropriate Moral Answer to Territorial Conflicts." *Geopolitics* 6:169–75.

Kolers, Avery. 2000. "The Lockean Efficiency Argument and Aboriginal Land Rights." *Australasian Journal of Philosophy* 78:391–405.

Kymlicka, Will. 1989. *Liberalism, Community, and Culture*. New York: Oxford University Press.

———. 1995. *Multicultural Citizenship*. New York: Oxford University Press.

———. 2001. *Politics in the Vernacular*. New York: Oxford University Press.

Laberge, Pierre. 1998. "Kant on Justice and the Law of Nations." In *International Society*, edited by David R. Mapel and Terry Nardin. Princeton: Princeton University Press.

Levy, Jacob T. 2000. *The Multiculturalism of Fear*. New York: Oxford University Press.
Lindley, M. F. 1926. *The Acquisition and Government of Backward Territory in International Law*. London: Ballantyne Press.
Locke, John. 1980. *Second Treatise of Government*, edited by C. B. MacPherson. Indianapolis: Hackett.
Lomasky, Loren. 1987. *Persons, Rights, and Moral Community*. New York: Oxford University Press.
Lyons, David. 1981. "The New Indian Claims and Original Rights to Land." In *Reading Nozick*, edited by Jeffrey Paul. Totowa, N.J.: Rowman and Littlefield.
Mack, Eric. 1980. "Bad Samaritanism and the Causation of Harm." *Philosophy and Public Affairs* 9:230–59.
Macklem, Patrick. 2001. *Indigenous Difference and the Constitution of Canada*. Toronto: University of Toronto Press.
Margalit, Avashai, and Joseph Raz. 1992. "National Self-Determination." *Journal of Philosophy* 87:439–61.
McCarthy, Thomas. 2004. "Coming to Terms with Our Past, Part II: On the Morality and Politics of Reparations for Slavery." *Political Theory* 32:750–72.
McIntyre, Alison. 1994. "Guilty Bystanders? On the Legitimacy of Duty to Rescue Statutes." *Philosophy and Public Affairs* 23:157–91.
McMahan, Jeff. 1994. "Self-Defense and the Problem of the Innocent Attacker." *Ethics* 104:252–90.
Mehta, Pratap Bhanu. 2000. "Cosmopolitanism and the Circle of Reason." *Political Theory* 28:619–39.
Miller, David. 1995. *On Nationality*. New York: Oxford University Press.
Miller, Fred D., Jr. 1982. "The Natural Right to Private Property." In *The Libertarian Reader*, edited by Tibor R. Machan. Totowa, N.J.: Rowman and Littlefield.
Mills, Claudia. 1995. "Goodness as a Weapon." *Journal of Philosophy* 92:485–99.
Mohanty, Satya P. 1997. *Literary Theory and the Claims of History: Postmodernism, Objectivity, Multicultural Politics*. Ithaca: Cornell University Press.
Moody-Adams, Michele. 1994. "Culture, Responsibility and Affected Ignorance." *Ethics* 104:291–309.
———. 1997. *Fieldwork in Familiar Places*. Cambridge, Mass.: Harvard University Press.
Morris, Christopher W. 1998. *An Essay on the Modern State*. New York: Cambridge University Press.
Murphy, Alexander B. 2001. "Territoriality, Morality, and International Law: A Response to Hendrix's 'Moral Theory of State Territory.'" *Geopolitics* 6:163–68.
Musgrave, Thomas D. 1997. *Self-Determination and National Minorities*. New York: Clarendon Press.
Newman, David. 1997. "Creating the Fences of Territorial Separation: The Discourses of Israeli-Palestinian Conflict Resolution." *Geopolitics and International Relations* 2:1–35.
Niezen, Ronald. 2003. *The Origins of Indigenism: Human Rights and the Politics of Identity*. Berkeley and Los Angeles: University of California Press.
Nozick, Robert. 1974. *Anarchy, State, and Utopia*. New York: Basic Books.
Okin, Susan Moller. 1999. "Is Multiculturalism Bad for Women?" In *Is Multiculturalism Bad for Women?* edited by Joshua Cohen, Matthew Howard, and Martha Nussbaum. Princeton: Princeton University Press.
O'Neill, Onora. 1994. "Justice and Boundaries." In *Political Restructuring in Europe: Ethical Perspectives*, edited by Chris Brown. New York: Routledge.

Orange, Claudia. 1987. *The Treaty of Waitangi*. Wellington, N.Z.: Bridget Williams Books.
Otsuka, Michael. 1998. "Self-Ownership and Equality: A Lockean Reconciliation." *Philosophy and Public Affairs* 27:65–92.
Phillips, Anne. 2005. "Dilemmas of Gender and Culture: The Judge, the Democrat, and the Political Activist." In *Minorities Within Minorities: Equality, Rights, and Diversity*, edited by Avigail Eisenberg and Jeff Spinner-Halev. New York: Cambridge University Press.
Philpott, Daniel. 1995. "In Defense of Self-Determination." *Ethics* 105:352–85.
Pippin, Robert. 1997. *Idealism as Modernism*. New York: Cambridge University Press.
Pirotta, Godfrey A., Roger Wettenhall, and Lino Briguglio. 2001. "Governance of Small Jurisdictions." *Public Organization Review* 1:149–66.
Pogge, Thomas W. 1992. "Cosmopolitanism and Sovereignty." *Ethics* 103:48–75.
———. 1994. "An Egalitarian Law of Peoples." *Philosophy and Public Affairs* 23:195–224.
Pollit, Katha. 1999. "Whose Culture?" In *Is Multiculturalism Bad for Women?* edited by Joshua Cohen, Matthew Howard, and Martha Nussbaum. Princeton: Princeton University Press.
Povinelli, Elizabeth. 2002. *The Cunning of Recognition*. Durham: Duke University Press.
Rabkin, Jeremy A. 2005. *Law Without Nations? Why Constitutional Government Requires Sovereign States*. Princeton: Princeton University Press.
Ramet, Sabrina. 1998. "Profit Motives in Secession." *Society* 35:26–29.
Ratner, Steven. 1996. "Drawing a Better Line: *Uti Possidetis* and the Borders of New States." *American Journal of International Law* 90:590–624.
Rawls, John. 1971. *A Theory of Justice*. Cambridge, Mass.: Harvard University Press.
Reference re Secession of Quebec. 1998. 2 S.C.R. 217.
Richter, Daniel K. 2001. *Facing East from Indian Country*. Cambridge, Mass.: Harvard University Press.
Rosser, Ezra. 2005. "This Land Is My Land, This Land Is Your Land: Markets and Institutions for Development on Native American Land." *Arizona Law Review* 47:245–312.
Roth, Brad R. 1998. *Governmental Illegitimacy in International Law*. Oxford: Clarendon Press.
Russell, Peter H. 2005. *Recognizing Aboriginal Title*. Toronto: University of Toronto Press.
Ryan, Cheyney C. 1983. "Self-Defense, Pacifism, and the Possibility of Killing." *Ethics* 92:508–24.
Sarkar, Husain. 1982. "The Lockean Proviso." *Canadian Journal of Philosophy* 12:47–59.
Shelby, Tommie. 2003. "Two Conceptions of Black Nationalism: Martin Delaney on the Meaning of Black Political Solidarity." *Political Theory* 31:664–92.
Simmons, A. John. 1979. *Moral Principles and Political Obligations*. Princeton: Princeton University Press.
———. 1992. *The Lockean Theory of Rights*. Princeton: Princeton University Press.
———. 1993. *On the Edge of Anarchy*. Princeton: Princeton University Press.
———. 1994. "Original Acquisition Justifications of Private Property." *Social Philosophy and Policy* 11:63–84.
———. 1999. "Justification and Legitimacy." *Ethics* 109:739–71.
———. 2001. *Justification and Legitimacy*. New York: Cambridge University Press.
Simpson, Audra. 2000. "Paths Toward a Mohawk Nation: Narratives of Citizenship and Nationhood in Kahnawake." In *Political Theory and the Rights of Indigenous Peoples*, edited by Duncan Ivison, Paul Patton, and Will Sanders. New York: Cambridge University Press.

Sparrow, Robert. 2000. "History and Collective Responsibility." *Australasian Journal of Philosophy* 78:346–59.
Steiner, Hillel. 1977. "The Natural Right to the Means of Production." *Philosophical Quarterly* 27:41–49.
———. 1994. *An Essay on Rights*. New York: Blackwell.
———. 1998. "Territorial Justice." In *Theories of Secession*, edited by Percy B. Lehning. New York: Routledge.
Stevens, Jacqueline. 1999. *Reproducing the State*. Princeton: Princeton University Press.
Sullivan, Roger L. 1996. Introduction to *The Metaphysics of Morals*, by Immanuel Kant, translated by Mary Gregor. New York: Cambridge University Press.
Swaine, Lucas. 2001. "How Ought Liberal Democracies to Treat Theocratic Communities?" *Ethics* 111:302–43.
———. 2006. *The Liberal Conscience*. New York: Columbia University Press.
Taylor, Michael. 1982. *Community, Anarchy, and Liberty*. New York: Cambridge University Press.
Teson, Fernando. 1998. "Kantian International Liberalism: A Reply to Pierre Laberge." In *International Society*, edited by David R. Mapel and Terry Nardin. Princeton: Princeton University Press.
Thompson, Janna. 2002. *Taking Responsibility for the Past: Reparation and Historical Injustice*. Malden, Mass.: Polity Press.
Tideman, T. Nicolaus. 1991. "Commons and Commonwealths: A New Framework for the Justification of Territorial Claims." In *Commons Without Tragedy*, edited by Robert V. Andelson. Savage, Md.: Barnes and Noble.
Tomuschat, Christian. 1993. "Self-Determination in a Post–Cold War World." In *Modern Law of Self-Determination*, edited by Christian Tomuschat. Boston: Martinus Nijhoff.
Tully, James. 1994. "Aboriginal Property and Western Theory: Recovering a Middle Ground." *Social Philosophy and Policy* 11:153–80.
———. 1995. *Strange Multiplicity*. New York: Cambridge University Press.
Turner, Dale. 2006. *This Is Not a Peace Pipe*. Toronto: University of Toronto Press.
Van Dervort, Thomas. 1998. *International Law and Organization: An Introduction*. Thousand Oaks, Calif.: Sage.
Von Glahn, Gerhard. 1996. *Law Among Nations*. 7th ed. Boston: Allyn and Bacon.
Wagner, R. Harrison. 1994. "Peace, War, and the Balance of Power." *American Political Science Review* 88:593–607.
Waldron, Jeremy. 1979. "Enough and as Good Left for Others." *Philosophical Quarterly* 29:310–28.
———. 1988. *The Right to Private Property*. Oxford: Clarendon Press.
———. 1992. "Superseding Historic Injustice." *Ethics* 103:4–28.
———. 1993. "Special Ties and Natural Duties." *Philosophy and Public Affairs* 22:3–30.
———. 1994. "The Advantages and Difficulties of the Humean Theory of Property." *Social Philosophy and Policy* 11:85–123.
———. 1995. "Minority Cultures and the Cosmopolitan Alternative." In *The Rights of Minority Cultures*, edited by Will Kymlicka. New York: Oxford University Press.
———. 2000. "What Is Cosmopolitan?" *Journal of Political Philosophy* 8:227–43.
———. 2003. "Indigeneity? First Peoples and Last Occupancy." *New Zealand Journal of Public and International Law* 1:55–82.
Walzer, Michael. 1970. *Obligations*. Cambridge: Harvard University Press.

———. 1981. "Philosophy and Democracy." *Political Theory* 9:379–99.
———. 1992. *Just and Unjust Wars*. 2nd ed. New York: Basic Books
———. 1994. *Thick and Thin: Moral Argument at Home and Abroad*. Notre Dame: University of Notre Dame Press.
———. 2000. "Governing the Globe." *Dissent* 47:44–52.
Ward, Alan. 1999. *An Unfinished History: Treaty Claims in New Zealand Today*. Wellington, N.Z.: Bridget Williams Books.
Webber, Jeremy. 2000. "Beyond Regret: Mabo's Implications for Australian Constitutionalism." In *Political Theory and the Rights of Indigenous Peoples*, edited by Duncan Ivison, Paul Patton, and Will Sanders. New York: Cambridge University Press.
Weinstock, Daniel. 2001. "Constitutionalizing the Right to Secede." *Journal of Political Philosophy* 9:182–203
Wellman, Christopher H. 1995. "A Defense of Secession and Political Self-Determination." *Philosophy and Public Affairs* 24:142–71.
———. 1996. "Liberalism, Samaritanism, and Political Legitimacy." *Philosophy and Public Affairs* 25:211–37.
Western Sahara. 1975. *ICJ Reports* 12.
Whelan, Fredrick G. 1983. "Prologue: Democratic Theory and the Boundary Problem." In *Liberal Democracy: Nomos XXV*, edited by J. Roland Pennock and John W. Chapman. New York: New York University Press.
Wilkins, David E. 2002. *American Indian Politics and the American Political System*. Lanham, Md.: Rowman and Littlefield.
Wilkins, David E., and K. Tsianina Lomawaima. 2001. *Uneven Ground: American Indian Sovereignty and Federal Law*. Norman: University of Oklahoma Press.
Williams, Robert A., Jr. 1990. *The American Indian in Western Legal Thought*. New York: Oxford University Press.
———. 1997. *Linking Arms Together: American Indian Visions of Law and Peace, 1600–1800*. New York: Oxford University Press.
Wolf, Clark. 1995. "Contemporary Property Rights, Lockean Provisos, and the Interests of Future Generations." *Ethics* 105:791–818.
Yack, Bernard. 2001. "Popular Sovereignty and Nationalism." *Political Theory* 29:517–36.

INDEX

Aboriginal land ownership (Australia), 191n.4
African Americans, impact of slavery on, 79–82
agreement, deliberative democracy and role of, 133–38
Alfred, Taiaiake, 2–3, 176–77, 179–80, 192n.1
American Indian Movement, 184
American Indians. *See also* indigenous peoples: challenges to state authority by, 1–4; identity, cultural difference, and change for, 167–73; repairing historical wrongs to, 78–82
anarcho-capitalism, state authority *vs.*, 104–8, 198nn.3, 5
anthropological research, cultural difference and moral argument in, 158–63, 202n.3
Armitage, David, 52, 193n.14
Arnhem Land, 191n.3
Assimilation, communitarian anarchism and, 111–13
asymmetries of power, international law and, 187–88
Australia, indigenous communities' autonomy in, 7, 111
authenticity, cultural difference and, 170–73
authority. *See* political authority; states, authority of baseline income, wealth distribution and, 194n.19

Beitz, Charles R., 62–63
Beran, Harry, 138–39, 198n.4
Borda counts, voting for separation using, 201n.5
Borrows, John, 37
boundaries: indigenous rights and, 118–22; recursive territorial boundaries, 139–41
Brownlie, Ian, 19, 32, 191n.2
Buchheit, Lee, 28

Calder decision, 7
Canada, indigenous sovereignty claims in, 7–9
charity, natural property rights and, 193n.13
Churchill, Ward, 15–17, 18–19, 30, 35, 38, 71–72
citizenship: ownership rights and, 64–65; protectorate status and, 148–51
coercion: anarcho-capitalism and potential for, 105–8, 198n.5; duties to aid and, 94–97, 114–18, 189nn.8, 9, 199nn.11, 12; indigenous cultures and absence of, 176–80; moral foundations of duty and, 97–98; natural duties and, 87–92
collective property rights: consent theory and, 74–75; contract theory and, 65–68, 71–72; duties to aid and, 199n.7; indigenous political authority and, 195n.6, 196n.10; public land acquisition and, 73–75
colonialism: contract theory and, 64–65; cultural difference and impact of, 157–58; impact on property rights of, 57–58; international law and, 15–16; Locke's views on, 52, 193n.14; self-determination and, 22–26; treaties of cession as tool of, 19–22, 191n.1
commercial property, historical ownership and concept of, 49–50
communitarian anarchism, 11–13; alternatives to, 174–80; just states concept *vs.*, 113–18; state authority *vs.*, 104, 108–13, 198n.3
community, indigenous peoples' commitment to, 175–80
Condorcet, Marquis de, 200n.2
conflict, natural property rights and avoidance of, 192n.7
Congressional plenary power, indigenous sovereignty claims and, 6–9
conquest, international law concerning, 19–22, 36–37

consensual politics: in indigenous cultures, 176–80; international law and, 187–88

"consent of the governed" concept, contemporary ownership choices and, 68–72, 195n.3

consent theory: anarcho-capitalism *vs.*, 104–8, 198n.4; collective property rights and, 74–75; fairness principles and, 195n.7; human nature and political authority, 87–92; indigenous rights and, 69–72, 176–80; Kant's view of, 85–87, 197n.1; political authority, 11–13, 198n.4; separation from state and, 130–38; state authority and, 68–72, 104–8, 198n.4

Constitution Act of 1982 (Canada), 7

contract theory: colonialism and, 64–65; contemporary ownership choices and, 68–72; duties and coercion and, 94–97, 198n.8; indigenous cultures and, 65–68; ownership rights and, 62–68, 195n.2; property rights and, 40–42

Cook, John, 158, 161, 202n.3

Coombs, H. C. ("Nugget"), 111

cosmopolitan democracy, self-determination and, 22–26

costs of natural duty, 126–29; psychological costs, 199n.14

criminal law: communitarian anarchism and, 111–13; duty to aid and, 96–97, 199n.13; indigenous rights and, 5, 119–22

cultural difference: alternatives to separation and preservation of, 174–80; commodification of, 170–73; communitarian anarchism and, 111, 199n.7; identity and, 167–73; moral disagreement and, 154–63, 202nn.1, 4; moral pluralism and, 34; political boundaries and, 120–22; procedural separation and role of, 166–67; reservations as protection of, 195n.6; self-determination and, 12–13, 27–30; separatist movements and protection of, 137–38

danger. *See also* security; violence: duties to aid and threat of, 93–94, 197n.7

Declaration on Friendly Relations, 20–22

decolonization: international law and, 15–22; post-World War II history of, 16; self-determination and, 21–22, 27–30

Deganawida, 65, 172

Delgamuukw decision, 7

deliberative democracy: procedural separation and, 163–67, 203n.5; separationist movements and, 12–13, 131–38

Deloria Jr., Vine, 110, 142, 147–48, 169–73, 177–78

democratic governance: contemporary ownership choices and, 68–72; enclave and size characteristics and, 143–44; indigenous people's autonomy and, 118–22; international law and, 186–88; limitations of, 113–18; rights and, 162–63; self-determination and separation and, 22–26, 129–38, 200n.2

Denis, Claude, 160–61

disadvantaged populations. *See also* minority rights: anarcho-capitalism *vs.* consent-based organizations and fate of, 107–8; procedural separation and role of, 165–67

duties of right: balancing of, 128–30; coercion and, 94–97; moral foundations for, 97–98

duties to aid: coercion and, 94–97, 115–18, 199nn.11, 12; just states concept and, 114–18; Kant's discussion of, 92–94; as natural duties, 91–93, 197n.6; protection of rights and, 120–22, 163, 199n.15; wealth distribution and, 199n.7

economic reciprocity, communitarian anarchism and control via, 120–13

electoral politics: self-determination and, 129–38; separation movements and role of, 134–38, 201n.4

eminent domain, state authority and public lands and, 196n.8

enclave characteristics, separation from state and impact of, 141–44

"enough and as good" principle: contract theory and, 66–68; fairness and, 195n.7; historical ownership limitations and, 78–82; labor and equality and, 52–58, 194n.17

entitlement theory: natural property rights and, 44–50, 81–82, 192n.7, 193n.10; promise-making and, 193n.8

environmental protection: importance in indigenous cultures of, 178–80; public land acquisition and property rights and, 73–75

equality issues, property rights and, 54–58, 194n.19

European Union (EU), 190, 200n.3

fairness, political obligations linked to, 195n.7

federalist structures, partial separation status and, 148–51, 202n.6

Feld, Scott, 200n.2

Feser, Edward, 194n.15

forcible secession, state creation and, 19–22

Friedman, David, 105–8

gender: cultural difference and, 159–63; procedural separation and role of, 165–67

geographical space: anarcho-capitalism and intermixing of, 106–8; historical ownership

INDEX 215

issues and, 31–33, 51–58; international law concerning, 17–22; political boundaries and characteristics of, 119–20; recursive territorial boundaries and, 139–41; state control of, 62–68; transferable property rights for, 33–34; trusteeship of, 75–77
globalization, transcendence of state authority and, 188–90
Good Samaritan laws, 96–97
goods distribution: contract theory and, 66–68; fairness principles and, 195n.7; labor and equality in, 55–58, 194n.17; slavery and inequality of, 79–82
Grofman, Bernard, 200n.2

Habermas, Jürgen, 131–32
Hannum, Hurst, 200n.3
historical ownership. See also property rights: contemporary conditions and, 80–82, 182–86; indigenous rights and, 23–27, 191n.4; international law and, 18–22; legal legitimacy of, 49–50; limitations of, 40–42, 78–82, 192n.2; modern context for, 50–58; moral relevance of, 11–13, 36–37, 48–50, 193nn.11, 12; natural property rights and, 44–50, 58–59; return to indigenous peoples of, 77–82; self-determination and, 23–27, 30–33
human rights: democratic governance and protection of, 34; international law and, 18–22; natural duty and, 87–92; natural property rights and, 42–50, 192n.5
Hume, David, property rights and philosophy of, 39–42, 49–50

identity, cultural difference and change and, 167–73
imminence of danger, duties to aid and, 93–94
independent status: enclave and size characteristics and, 141–44; indigenous peoples' right to, 2–3; just states concept and, 114–18
Indian Acts (Canada), 7
indigenous peoples: alternatives to separation for, 173–80; challenges to state authority by, 1–4, 69–72; communitarian anarchy and, 110–13; contract theory and rights of, 65–68; democratic governance and minority rights of, 68–72; historical ownership rights of, 30–33, 51–58; identity, cultural difference, and change for, 167–73; international law and, 15–16; natural duties and moral disagreement and, 84–87; natural property rights of, 43–50, 58–59; ownership rights of, 35–37; partial separation status for, 123, 147–51; philosophical traditions of, 6–9; political organizations of, 1–4, 62–68, 74–75, 195n.1, 196n.10; political rights of, 4–6, 11–13; repairing historical wrongs of, 78–82; saltwater test for colonial possessions and rights of, 20–21; self-determination and "peoples" concept, 27–30; separation and self-determination of, 20–26, 126–51; size and enclave characteristics and separation movements of, 141–44; state authority over, 118–22; state structures and social order for, 144–47
individual agency: duty to aid and, 93–94, 197n.7; in indigenous cultures, 176–80; natural property rights and, 44–50, 193n.8; state authority vs., 104
infinite divisibility, self-determination and, 28–30
inheritance rights: historical ownership and, 79–82; property ownership and, 55–58, 194n.18
intentionality, duty to aid and, 96–97
International Court of Justice, international law and, 17
international law: ambiguity of property rights in, 33–34, 191n.6; authority of states and, 10–13; indigenous rights and, 15–16, 186–88; principles of, 16–22; self-determination and, 22–26, 31
interpersonal relationships, indigenous cultures' emphasis on, 177–78
Iroquois Confederacy, 65

judgment: duties to aid and threat of role of, 197n.7; Kant on morality and, 85–87, 197nn.1, 2; self-determination and separation and, 22–26, 129–38, 200n.2
justice: absence in laws of, 80–82; duties and coercion and, 94–97; indigenous cultures' concept of, 178–80; property rights and concept of, 41–42, 192n.4; strategic actions in pursuit of, 200n.1
just states concept, communitarian anarchism and, 113–18

Kant, Immanuel, 11, 83–84, 197nn.1, 2; on coercion and duties, 94–97, 198nn.8, 9; duties to aid discussed by, 92–94; on human nature and natural duties, 87–92; natural duties and moral disagreement and, 84–87; on state authority, 102–3
Kashmir, political allegiance in, 5
Kleinig, John, 93–94

Kohen, Marcelo, 22, 26
Kymlicka, Will, 136, 149, 157–58, 202n.2

labor: natural property rights linked to, 51–58, 193n.14, 194n.15; slavery and, 79–82
land use, historical ownership and property rights issues and, 51–58
laws and legislation: Kant's discussion of, 85–87; right to enforcement of, 1–4, 100–104
liberalism, cultural difference and moral disagreement and, 160–63
liberty: communitarian anarchism and, 111–13; duties balanced with, 128–30; natural property rights and, 45–53; political boundaries as threat to, 119–22; self-defense and principles of, 89–92, 197n.5
Locke, John: on colonialism, 52, 193n.14; historical ownership limitations and proviso of, 78–82; property ownership proviso of, 51–58, 62–63, 66, 193n.13, 194nn.15, 16; public land acquisition and proviso of, 73–75; on state authority, 69, 106, 195n.3

Mabo decision, 7
magnitude of danger, duties to aid and, 93–94
market forces, 112–13; anarcho-capitalism and coercion with, 105–8; enclave and size characteristics and, 143–145; injustice in, 79–82; sale of public lands and, 73–75, 196n.9; separation movements motivated by, 200n.3
Marshall, John (Chief Justice), 195n.1
Marshall cases, indigenous sovereignty claims and, 6–9
material goods, natural property rights and, 45–50
military service: as consent to state authority, 69, 195n.5; duties to aid and, 117–18
minority rights. *See also* disadvantaged populations: cultural difference and, 157–58, 202n.2; democratic governance and protection of, 68–72; separationist movements and, 137–38
Moody-Adams, Michele, 159–60
moral disagreement: cultural difference and, 154–63, 202n.1; natural duty and, 84–87; political authority and, 88–92; procedural separation and, 163–67, 203n.5
moral duty (morality): communitarian anarchism and, 110–13; duties to aid as, 92–94; foundations of, 97–98; historical ownership and moral innocence, 47–50, 193n.11; individual rights and, 47–50, 193n.11; international law and, 16; Kant's concept of, 83–84; of natural property rights, 42–50, 192n.6; ownership and, 11–13, 71–72; property rights and, 39–42; public land administration and, 72–75; self-defense and, 89–92; to state authority, 100–4; traditions of, 158–63; trusteeship and, 75–77
moral pluralism, cultural difference and, 34
moral recusal, Cook's concept of, 161

nationalism: cultural difference and moral disagreement and, 154–58, 202n.1; identity, culture and change and, 167–73; self-determination and, 12–13, 29–30; separation theory and ideology of, 134–38, 184–86
natural duty theory. *See also* moral duty: coercion and, 117–18; duties to aid as, 92–94; human nature and, 87–92; indigenous rights and, 118–22; legal principles and, 198n.10; moral disagreement and, 84–87; ownership and, 11–13, 71–72; partial separation status and, 123, 183–86, 200n.17; political authority and, 114–18; public land administration and, 72–75; separation from state and, 126–29; to state authority, legitimacy of, 100–104; state authority as trusteeship and, 75–77
natural property rights: historical ownership and, 44–50, 58–59; legal legitimacy of, 49–50; moral justification of, 42–50, 192n.5, 193n.9; political authority and, 71–72; resource use and, 51–58; restoration of, to indigenous peoples, 78–82; social conventions concerning, 38–42; state authority and public lands and, 73–75, 196n.9
natural resources: historical ownership issues and, 53–58, 194n.16; public lands and distribution of, 76–77, 196n.11; separation movements and ownership of, 200n.3
neutral differences, social practices and, 155–58, 202n.4
Niezen, Ronald, 186
noncoercive political structure, indigenous peoples' commitment to, 175–80
normative tradition, cultural difference and, 160–63
Nozick, Robert, 44–47, 81–82, 105, 192n.13, 194n.19

O'Neill, Onora, 189–90
ostracism, communitarian anarchism and, 110–13
ownership. *See also* property rights: authority and, 10–13; communitarian anarchism and control via, 120–13; contemporary choices and role of, 68–72; definitions and cultural differences

concerning, 36–37; indigenous peoples rights concerning, 35–37; international law and historical ownership, 18–22; liberty and, 45–50; limits of, 35–59; Locke on limits of, 194nn.16, 18; self-determination and, 30–33; social contract and, 61–82; social conventions concerning, 38–42; state ownership concept, 76–77; by states, 63–68

partial separation status, creation of, 123, 147–51
peace, property rights and, 39–42
"peoples," self-determination and concept of, 26–30
personal retribution, communitarian anarchism and, 109–10, 199n.10
philosophical anarchism, Simmons's concept of, 101–4
Pippin, Robert, 90–91, 95
Pledge of Allegiance, 69, 195n.4
political authority. *See also* states, authority of: consent to, 11–13, 86–87, 104–8, 197nn.1, 2, 198n.4; cultural concepts of, 1–4; globalization and transcendence of, 188–90; in indigenous cultures, 70–75, 118–22, 195n.6, 196n.10; just states concept and, 113–18; Kant's justification of, 87–92; moral duty and, 71–73, 83–84; nation concepts and, 155–58, 202n.1; ownership and, 61–82; procedural separation and, 163–67, 203n.5; property ownership and, 11–13, 71–72; trusteeship and, 75–77
political outcomes: consent theory and, 69–72; historical ownership rights and, 32–33
population groups: equality in property rights and variations in, 55–58; international law and authority over, 17–22
poverty: liberty and role of, 46–50; Rousseauian concept of, 40–42; slavery and, 79–82
Povinelli, Elizabeth, 170–73
private property, natural property rights and, 192n.7
private protection systems, consent theory and, 104–8, 198nn.4, 5
probable consistency principle, cultural difference and moral argument and, 158–63
profit-seeking agencies, anarcho-capitalism and, 105–8
promise-making, natural rights and, 193n.8
property rights. *See also* historical ownership: authority and, 10–13; cultural differences in concept of, 37; Lockean proviso on, 50–58, 193–94nn.14, 15, 194n.18; political authority and, 62–68; self-determination and, 31–33;

183–86; social conventions concerning, 38–42; state authority and public lands and, 72–75; territorial integrity and, 19–22
protectorate status for indigenous peoples, 147–51
psychological costs of coercion, 126–29, 199n.14
public lands: boundary issues on, 76–77, 196n.11; historical ownership and concept of, 50; indigenous property rights and, 81–82, 196n.13; state authority and, 72–75, 196nn.8, 9

rational choice theory, communitarian anarchism and, 108–9
Ratner, Stephen, 25, 191n.3
Rawls, John, difference principle of, 196n.12
recursive territorial boundaries, separationism and, 138–41, 201n.5
referenda, as secessionist tool, 134–41, 201nn.4, 5
relationships, indigenous peoples' commitment to, 175–80
remedial-rights theory of separation, political boundaries and, 122
representative republics, self-determination in, 129–38
reservations, political authority in, 70–72, 195n.6, 196n.10
"residual sovereignty" principle, 19, 191n.2
resources, public lands and distribution of, 76–77, 196n.11
rights: anarcho-capitalism and protection of, 105–8; cultural differences and, 12–13, 157–58, 202n.2; deliberative democracy and role of, 132–38, 162–63; duties balanced with, 128–30; political authority and, 62–68, 195n.1; psychological violations of, 127–29; relationships vs., 175–80
Rousseau, Jean-Jacques: natural property rights concept and, 45–50, 193n.12; property rights and philosophy of, 39–42, 81–82, 192n.6, 196n.13
Royal Proclamation of 1763, 7

sacred lands, property rights and, 192n.3
saltwater test for colonial possessions, 20–22
security: consent theory and, 69–72, 104–8; moral duties and, 199n.9; property rights and, 39–42; state authority as tool for, 103–4
segregation, effects of, 79–82
self-defense: duties to aid and, 92–94; Kant on right to, 87–92, 197nn.4, 5
self-determination: colonialism and, 20–22; cosmopolitan democracy and, 22–26; democracy and judgment concerning, 130–38; enclave and size characteristics

and, 141–44; indigenous contemporary movement toward, 7, 12–13; international law and, 10, 17–22, 186–88; nationalism and, 12–13; ownership and, 30–33; partial separation status and, 147–51; "peoples" concept and, 26–30; political authority *vs.*, 78–82; recursive territorial boundaries and, 139–41, 201n.5; separation from state and, 26–30, 122–23, 125–51; state structure and social order and, 144–47

self-regulation, communitarian anarchism and, 111–13

separation from state: alternatives for indigenous peoples to, 173–80; balance of rights and duties and, 128–30, 183–86; democracy and judgment factors in, 129–38; enclave and size characteristics and, 141–44; indigenous rights and, 11–13; international law concerning, 16–22; moral disagreement and, 163–67; partial separation status, 123, 147–51; preferences as grounds for, 127–29; profit as motive for, 200n.3; recursive territorial boundaries and, 138–41; self-determination through, 26–30, 122–23, 125–51; social order and, 144–47; territorial integrity and, 20–22

shaming, communitarian anarchism and, 110–13
Simmons, A. John, 64, 100–4, 114–15, 198nn.1, 2
size characteristics: separation from state and impact of, 141–44; state structure and social order and, 144–47
slavery, effects of, 79–82
small population groups: separation from state and viability of, 141–44, 180; state structure and social order and, 144–47
social contracts: communitarian anarchism and, 110–13; duty to aid and, 92–94, 197n.6; moral duty to, 100–4; ownership and, 61–82
social practices: cultural difference and, 155–58; identity and changes in, 167–73; ownership connotations and, 38–42
South America, state sovereignty in, 21–22
sovereignty: absence in indigenous culture of, 176–80; historical ownership rights and, 31–33, 183–86; indigenous claims of, 6–9; international law's principles of, 18–22
spiritual beliefs, importance in indigenous cultures of, 178–80
states, authority of. *See also* separation from state: alternatives to, 11–13; challenges to, 1–4, 100–4; communitarian anarchism *vs.*, 104, 108–13, 198n.3; consent theory and, 68–72, 106–10; cultural difference and moral disagreement and, 154–58, 202n.1; enforcement of natural property rights and, 192n.5; historical context for, 4–6; human nature and consent to, 87–92; indigenous peoples rights and separation from, 36–37, 69–72; international law and, 17–22; justification *vs.* legitimacy of, 100–4; just states model, 113–18; Kant's view of, 84–87, 197nn.1, 2; Locke's contract theory and, 62–68, 195n.2; military service as consent to, 69, 195n.5; moral duty and, 11–13; natural duties and, 89–92; procedural separation and, 163–67, 203n.5; property ownership and, 10–13, 62–68; psychological costs of, 199n.63; public lands and, 72–75, 196n.9; separation from, 12–13; social order and, 144–47; transcendence of, 188–90; trusteeship and, 75–77

stolen property, moral innocence concerning, 47–50, 193n.11

strategic action, partial separation policies and, 185–86

Taiwan, independent status of, 5
taxation: duties and coercion in laws of, 96–97; public land acquisition through, 73–75, 196n.9
Taylor, Michael, 108–10, 112–13, 199n.10
terra nullius principle, international law and historical ownership, 18–22
territorial integrity: citizen rights and, 3–4, 17–22; consent to authority over, 104–8, 198nn.4, 5; enclave characteristics and, 141–44; globalization and transcendence of, 188–90; historical ownership and, 32–33, 51–58; international law principle of, 10–13; political authority and, 118–22; recursive boundaries and, 138–41; self-determination and, 22–26; state authority over, 76–77; state structure and social order and, 144–47; violence and, 25–26
Trail of Broken Treaties, 184–86
transferable property rights: "consent of the governed" concept and, 68–72, 195n.3; geographical space and, 33–34; indigenous cultures and, 65–68; natural property rights concept and, 46–50; public lands and, 73–77, 196nn.9, 11; social conventions concerning, 38–42; state authority and, 63–68
treaties of cession, international law and, 19–22, 191n.1
trusteeship, state authority and, 75–77
Tully, James, 7

unanimity, moral disagreement and, 164–67

United Nations declarations, international law and, 17, 19
urbanization, communitarian anarchy and, 199n.7
uti possidetis principle: decolonization and, 17–23, 191n.3; self-determination and, 23–30, 191n.3

Van Dervort, Thomas, 22
violence: anarcho-capitalism and threat of, 106–8; indigenous rights and protection from, 5, 119–22; political authority and prevention of, 87–92, 197n.5; psychological costs of, 184–85, 199n.14; *uti possidetis* principle and, 24–26
voluntary cession, international law and, 19–22
voting procedures: partial separation status issues, 149–51; self-determination and, 129–38; separation movements and role of, 134–38, 201nn.4, 5

Wagner, R. Harrison, 106–8
Wake Island, ownership debate over, 5
Waldron, Jeremy, 10–11, 38–43, 47–48, 58, 88, 193n.13, 194n.20, 200n.2
Walzer, Michael, 132
wealth: baseline income and creation of, 194n.19; duties to aid and distribution of, 198n.7; property rights and creation of, 45–50, 56–58, 194n.19; separation movements and redistribution of, 200n.3
Wik decision, 7
Williams, Robert, 7, 177

Yugoslavia: self-determination and violence in, 28–29; *uti possidetis* principle and violence in, 25–26

www.ingramcontent.com/pod-product-compliance
Lightning Source LLC
Chambersburg PA
CBHW021944290426
44108CB00012B/958